Play for Today

The evolution of television drama

IRENE SHUBIK

Manchester University Press
Manchester and New York

distributed exclusively in the USA by St. Martin's Press

First published 1975 by Davis-Poynter Limited

This edition published 2000 by
Manchester University Press
Oxford Road, Manchester M13 9NR, UK
and Room 400, 175 Fifth Avenue, New York, NY 10010, USA
www.manchesteruniversitypress.co.uk

Distributed exclusively in the USA by
St. Martin's Press, Inc., 175 Fifth Avenue, New York,
NY 10010, USA

Distributed exclusively in Canada by
UBC Press, University of British Columbia, 2029 West Mall,
Vancouver, BC, Canada V6T 1Z2

British Library Cataloguing-in-Publication Data
A catalogue record for this book is available from the British Library

Library of Congress Cataloging-in-Publication Data applied for

ISBN   0 7190 5686 1   *hardback*
       0 7190 5687 X   *paperback*

This edition first published 2000

07 06 05 04 03 02 01 00   10 9 8 7 6 5 4 3 2 1

Typeset in Sabon
by Best-set Typesetter Ltd., Hong Kong

Printed in Great Britain
by Biddles Ltd, Guildford and King's Lynn

Contents

List of illustrations

Preface (1975)

ABC Television, later transformed into Thames, must surely have the most pleasant and sylvan setting of any of the London-based television companies. The studios overlook the Thames at Teddington Lock. From the offices at the back, one can stare out at the passing river traffic. In summer it is almost impossible not to adopt a certain holiday attitude to work. At lunch time there are tow-paths for a stroll, grassy banks for a snooze and the lawn of the adjacent pub on which to have a drink.

It was in this Utopia that I made my start in television, a circumstance for which I will always be grateful. The date was 1960 and, in encouragement to all those young hopefuls who may at this moment be thinking of blowing out their brains or giving up their struggle to get into television, I can only say 'keep trying'. If ever anyone seemed destined not to become a television producer, I did.

The other circumstance for which I will always be grateful is that it was Sydney Newman who decided to give me the job. Sydney, a Canadian, once affectionately described (by Peter Luke) as 'a cross between Ghenghis Khan and a pussy-cat' and elsewhere depicted in the press as looking like a 'sawn-off Clarke Gable' and 'a Mexican peasant', was undoubtedly one of the most dynamic men who ever worked in English television. He had started out as a graphics artist, directed and produced documentaries for the National Film Board of Canada, become Head of Drama at the CBC and come to ABC from there to head the Drama department and produce 'Armchair Theatre'. His most notable characteristic was a Groucho-Marx-like sense of humour – sometimes cruel but always excessively funny – which was totally impossible to resist and proved on many occasions a perfect weapon for breaking up arguments, winning battles and bringing rebellious employees to heel.

My own background had been an academic one. I had a BA and a London MA degree, having wasted, as I then thought, the two best years of my life writing a thesis on 'The Use of English History in the Drama from 1599–1642'. After completing this epic work, I crawled out of the darkness of the British Museum Reading Room and the Public Record Office, well on the road to myopia and eccentricity, looked at the sunlight and decided that the world of scholarship – once so aptly described as the transferring of old bones from one cemetery to another – was not for me.

It was then that I, like many other arts graduates before and after me, began to bombard the BBC and all the publishing houses with applications for jobs. Not one of these met with any success, not even, as I recall, an interview.

I applied to be everything and anything; meanwhile making a meagre living as a professional historical researcher, becoming an expert on all sorts of subjects, like the history of the Virginia Company and the status of the Jews in the Ottoman Empire.

Finally, having at a peak of frustration written an impassioned letter to the Director General of the BBC, asking to be allowed to come and view the young Byrons and Shelleys who were getting the jobs for which I was not even deemed worthy of an interview, I decided to give up.

Luckily for me, my two brothers were both in America. I headed first for brother number one, who was teaching mathematical economics at Princeton. After my brother had been called before the Dean for keeping a woman in his bachelor quarters, and my search for a job in TV or publishing in New York had proved as unsuccessful as in London, I moved on to Chicago.

Here, my eldest brother – a brain-drained pathologist, who knew no one in show-biz – was living in a suburb called Wilmette. In the same suburb was a small film company. *Encyclopaedia Britannica* had been bought by the University of Chicago and Encyclopaedia Britannica Films was operating in Wilmette, producing educational films and documentaries for distribution in schools and colleges.

One day, I walked into their offices, bearing under my arm the bulky copy of my MA thesis which I had been toting around the United States as my one claim to fame. My father, a man I respected deeply, had always held the belief that education was the passport to everything good in this world: inner satisfaction, self-respect and good jobs. He was a Russian Jew who had never had the benefit of a university education himself and dated back to an era when to get into the 'gymnasium' and then university was the highest ambition one could possibly achieve. Somehow, although I had been given an entirely different background, his particular philosophy had so permeated me that I was naive enough to walk around with 'the ocular proof'.

Much to my astonishment, I got an interview on the spot with one of the directors at Britannica. He seemed as much amused as impressed by my credentials and commissioned me (for $100) to write a trial script for him. The subject was the structure of the mediaeval guilds. I put enough research into this particular script to have written another thesis. It paid off because Britannica liked the script, made it into a film and offered me a job as a staff writer. I had my first pay-cheque photostated and sent the copy home to my long-suffering parents as evidence that I'd made it at long last.

In some ways Britannica was the ideal, if amateur, starting place for anyone wanting to learn the film business. Being educational it was outside any union regulations. Consequently everyone did a little of everything. One picked up information about editing or shooting film either by osmosis or by practical, if primitive, application.

The following incident may illustrate the point. Just before I left Britannica, we went filming in Virginia. To celebrate the tricentenary of the founding of the colony, a reproduction had been built of the first settlement. Wattle and daub huts had been put up like those that Captain John Smith and his fellows had constructed and in which most of them had died of malaria or been massacred by the Indians. A replica of their ship had also been built and Britannica decided to make use of both reconstructions and also of a group of somewhat hammy actors who were performing a pageant on the subject for the benefit of the tourists at Williamsburg.

The founding of Virginia happened to be one of the subjects I had researched in the Record Office. I got very excited and wrote two scripts: one called *Jamestown* and the other based on an episode in Smith's journals where he described how a cabin boy (in my script called Tom Savage) was given by the settlers to the Indians as a hostage, how he grew up with the Indians and became an interpreter between the two groups.

This was the first script I had written in which I felt my full creative powers had at last come to fruition. However, the director (quite rightly) disagreed. He thought the script pedantic and not comprehensible to the school-kids in Idaho for whom it was aimed. I on the other hand felt that it would pass muster with both the Institute of Historical Research and Eisenstein. We came to blows both on the artistry of the work and the fact that he claimed the budget would not run to taking the writer on location. I spent sleepless nights imagining my *Tom Savage* being murdered in Jamestown while I was left behind in Wilmette to get on with next week's script on 'Your Body and How it Works', designed for eight-year-olds.

As it happened, I did get on location. It was all like a bad Hollywood movie. At the last minute, the make-up man who was scheduled to go on the filming fell ill. For the first time in my life, I told a really big lie. Writer's paranoia had demolished all rational thought processes. I claimed to have had considerable make-up training and experience in England. There was no one in Wilmette, Illinois, to disprove me. So desperate was I to defend my script from the director, I could think no further. Even more astonishingly, I was actually believed and not even asked to furnish proof of my skill before we left for location.

It was only after we had arrived at the Williamsburg Motel and I began to unpack the trunkload of beards and moustaches and spread out matching sets on one of the twin beds that the reality of the situation sank in.

I had never, not even in a school play, had any make-up experience. I did not have a clue as to how to stick beards on so that the surrounding canvas would not show . . . let alone how to transform actors from healthy young men into haggard, malaria-ridden aged ones . . . all of which was called for in ultra-pedantic detail in my script.

The German cameraman who had been an accomplice in my crime and encouraged me to come on location and defend my work came to my room, surveyed the hair-strewn bed and was overcome with hysteria. 'Now we bin shootink Santa Claus parade in Virginia,' he said comfortingly. 'Ya, die first settlers vas all Santa Clauses!'

To say I was panic-stricken would be a pale understatement. Had there not been, amongst the actors, an exceptionally charming man who looked after make-up for their theatrical performances, I would undoubtedly have been undone on the first day. I confessed fully to him; he taught me some primitive rudiments of make-up and we divided the whiskers between us. However, stills which I have kept from the production, which even now bring beads of sweat to my brow, indicate that Sir Henry Irving would not have looked amiss in the cast (even though *his* were real).

I vacillated, during the production, between sticking on crooked beards, eavesdropping on the director to make sure he wasn't conspiring with the actors to change my lines, seeing that the tribe of Indians we had hired for the occasion didn't get too beer-sodden to do their bit, holding reflectors, and other odd bits of manual labour. That particular production taught me more about writer's megalomania, about production values and cutting one's coat according to one's cloth than any I have worked on since. Luckily, I never got to see the final product. I am sure Britannica would have been fully justified in firing me, but in the event they never got the chance.

After the filming, I had some leave due and I had also been offered, and accepted, a contract for the forthcoming year to go to the National Film Board of Canada.

Now that I had 'made good' in America, I planned a triumphant three-week holiday in England. As things turned out I never went back to work in America; I came home to find both my parents seriously ill. Some time later, when my father had died and I had burned my bridges with both Britannica and the Film Board, I found myself back to square one in England. I wrote the odd commentary for documentaries, had a brief job in a cutting room, was assistant director on some commercials and once more wrote letters of application to the BBC. I also went the rounds of almost every writers' agent in town with my portfolio of Britannica scripts and with a new, improved version of *Tom Savage*, which I now had mapped out as a children's serial for television. One agent went so far as to send this script to Sydney Newman at ABC. In retrospect, he could not have sent it to a more unlikely customer; however it turned out to be a lucky chance for me that he did.

In the same agent's outer office, a few weeks later, I met Ted Kotcheff, who was then working as a director on 'Armchair Theatre' and whom I had known some years before. He promised to ask Sydney about my script. The following week I was summoned to see Sydney. He began by telling me in so many words what a 'load of crap' *Tom Savage* was and that ABC, in any case, wasn't really geared to spend the money on costume drama for a children's serial. To my complete surprise, he then went on to ask me if I wanted a job as a story editor. This was on a Friday; I started work the following Monday.

Later when I asked Sydney, who knew very little about me at the time, why he had offered me the job, he said, 'I thought you had an intelligent face.' Sydney was probably one of the last proponents of the old Hollywood 'Lana Turner was discovered in Schwab's drug-store' principle. He liked to think of himself as spotting talent where no one else suspected it existed, a good if risky characteristic in a producer. A couple of years later, Sydney agreed to let me prepare scripts for a brainchild of mine, the anthology science fiction series 'Out of this World'. Having given me the go-ahead, I believe he began to worry that I would come up with a collection of metaphysical works by authors like Karel Čapek, instead of 'a popular adventure TV series'.

In the lift and other casual rendezvous he had engaged in conversation with a serious young man from the accounts department who had admitted to being a science fiction aficionado from birth and to having amassed from childhood one of the most extensive libraries of pulp science fiction in existence. Sydney offered him a transfer on the spot to the drama department; this was how I acquired an assistant, known in the department as 'Shubik's bug-eyed monster' . . . a watchdog to ensure that I kept in touch with popular taste.

Sometimes Sydney's principle of discovery paid off; other times it didn't. In my case it was how I got into television.

Preface (2000)

Since the first edition of this book came out in 1975 the entire face of British television has changed radically thanks both to the incredibly rapid technical revolution brought about by the discovery of the microchip and to the gradual dumbing down of the public service tradition in broadcasting, not only at the BBC but at such commercial companies as Granada in their ever increasing pursuit of ratings and advertising revenues.

When I began in TV there was scarcely any competition for audiences; the choice was limited to only two channels, one BBC and one ITV. There were no videos, no satellite TV and no cable channels. In many ways we had a captive audience. Now, as I write, we are entering the age of digital TV and multitudinous choice and competition. When I began working in TV drama, everything was made in the studio with video cameras, there was no filming and very little tape editing, a few drama productions were still going out live; there was no colour either.

The debate now rages in the world of media studies (which again did not exist as an academic discipline at that time) as to whether or not the 1960s and 1970s were indeed a 'golden age' of television drama. As someone who was personally responsible for some of the output I prefer not to comment on this, as regards the quality of what went on the screen. However, I *can* say unequivocally that it was indeed a 'golden age' from the point of view of the programme makers. They were allowed a degree of responsibility and a freedom of choice in what programmes they could make that no longer exists on any channel. There were Heads of Drama but no teams of executive producers and co-producers with their fingers in the pie, as there so often are now. The training courses for technicians, make-up, costume, design, and directors ensured a standard of excellence that was taken for granted, certainly at the BBC, which has incomprehensibly done away with these excellent schemes. There was a feeling of security even among short-term contract people like myself which made for continuity and the chance to develop unique styles of production by working continuously with like-minded colleagues. There was no frenzied lobbying by multitudinous independent producers attempting to prove to the networks that they can bring in programmes more cheaply than other 'indie-prods' by cutting corners, especially where production values are concerned. It was also a 'golden age' for writers who wanted to express their individual ideas. Depite the fact that there were only two channels there was a much larger market for single plays than there is now. Lastly, there was still the semblance of a code of morality when it came to appropriating other people's ideas, and a duty to acknowledge letters and telephone calls.

I wrote the original of this book, largely at night, while on location, in a glorious year of filming in the West Country a series of six Thomas Hardy stories called *Wessex Tales*. When it came to research, I had the advantage of being able to consult my own production files and the extensive files on writers etc. then kept by the BBC script unit at Television Centre, where I was greatly helped by Betty Willingdale. Nowadays, under the 'producer's choice' scheme introduced by John Birt, I would have to travel to Reading and pay £50 a time to look up those same files, even my own. All comments about the demographic composition of audiences and their responses to various programmes are based on the reports of BBC audience research. Again in this field I was greatly helped by Mr Michael Behr.

With the wisdom of hindsight I think I started this book because I had already begun to sense impending radical changes in TV drama and thought it important to record my own first-hand experience of the period and the key people I worked with before they receded too far into distant memory. There was, of course, much excellent drama being produced at the time elsewhere, by such companies as Granada and ATV and by colleagues at the BBC, but I confined myself only to what I knew first-hand. In view of all the subsequent radical changes in TV drama, the book has assumed the aspect of a historical document, rather than a practical guide to how television and the people in it work today. In the light of that, the choice that faced me for this edition was whether to attempt to update it or to let it stand as an account of how it was then. Ultimately I decided the latter course was more valuable to the reader. I have also added new material in Part Two which describes my subsequent experiences in ITV and how *Rumpole of the Bailey* evolved from a single 'Play for Today' and how *The Jewel in the Crown* came on to the screen.

Sadly, as happens in history, a number of the key figures, alive when I originally wrote the book, are now dead; Sydney Newman, Peter Luke and, much before their time, the brilliant director Alan Clarke and the writers John Osborne and Rhys Adrian, as well as Tony Parker, Robert Muller, James Hanley and Alun Owen. I hope this new edition will contribute to their memory.

Part one

Chapter 1

Scripts, authors and script editing – background

When I started out as a 'trial' script editor on 'Armchair Theatre', I had to ask a question which people are now always asking me. Where do the plays come from? An elementary question, of course, but one to which very few people outside TV drama production know the answer. It is amazing how many people have the vague concept that somewhere a stock of scripts is at hand (as though Selfridge's had a script counter) and from this stock the producer picks and chooses. The fact that dramatists have to be found, created and commissioned, or that they have to learn their trade, like anyone else, is seldom considered.

How, then, does one go about finding them? First let me dispel a few widely held misbeliefs about television writing. Most common of all is the one which runs, 'If I had the time, I could do better than the rubbish you see on TV': the belief that almost anyone can write a TV play if they put their mind to it. The same is seldom said of plays in the theatre or of films, although at the moment, in my opinion (allowing for the fact that many writers write for all three media), the general standard of TV writing is superior to either of the other two. The immediate living-room availability of TV drama has bred the contempt of familiarity. The TV writers, having revealed themselves, warts and all, to an audience of millions and having often made personal appearances on the air, justifying or explaining their own work, begin to get treated as one of the family and no one is a prophet in their own living room.

Whether this increasing intimacy between writer and audience is a good or bad thing could be debated. Personally I think it far better for writers and their work to remain separate entities, aloof from each other, or anyone could find their play being judged by the way their hair was combed on *Late Night Line-Up*.[1] A little remoteness is, in my opinion, a very good thing. For the fact is that the ability to construct a dramatic plot, write unstilted dialogue and create believable characters on the screen is a rare gift. It is also a gift which needs a great deal of help and patience from the production unit who turn the written word into pictures and sounds, if it is to come across successfully.

Another commonly held belief is that there are hundreds of undiscovered geniuses 'wasting their sweetness on the desert air'; that a select clique of TV producers and script editors are busily trying to keep out new talent. The truth is diametrically opposite. They are trying desperately to *find* new talent to fill that endless air time stretching out before them. Almost every producer I know has the same recurring nightmare . . . the empty studio with no script to fill it. No other worry is so productive of ulcers as that of 'what script are we going to do next?' This is the most difficult part of any producer's job. (I speak here, of course, of single plays – not adaptations of existing material or series with running characters which have their own and separate problems.)

I began my first week on 'Armchair Theatre' by sitting down to read some of the plays which were in production or waiting to be produced. The first three scripts I read were *Where I Live* by Clive Exton, *A Night Out* by Harold Pinter and *After the Funeral* by Alun Owen . . . probably three of the best scripts I have ever read since working in TV; best from the point of view of construction, dialogue and reality of subject matter.

Clive Exton's play, which undoubtedly many people will remember (it was re-produced by the BBC in 1968) was about a family dispute as to who was going to look after the elderly widowed father – a subject which now has been done so many times it has become almost a cliché, but which remains valid and true in any time or place. Alun Owen's subject, post-funeral disputes in the family, has also been treated many times since. Peter Nichols's *Hearts and Flowers*, which I produced on 'Play for Today' in 1970, is one of many examples of this theme, as is Alan Plater's *Rest in Peace, Uncle Fred*.

---

[1] A popular review programme on BBC-2 which went out late at night in the late 1960s and 1970s.

This brings up another problem of production. The death of a parent is a strong experience in any writer's life and one which most would want to write about. I can remember Sydney Newman, at a script meeting, saying jokingly to Peter Luke, 'Don't bring me any more plays about sick old men,' and accusing the department of 'gerontophilia'. Sydney, as a producer, of course was right. He wanted as much variety as possible on the programme and a few plays starring 'blondes with big boobs' to temper the gloom of the 'sick old men'. The unfortunate fact is that, by now, most of the important shared subjects in life – like a death in the family – have been portrayed so frequently on TV that even an excellent play might be turned down simply on the grounds that it has all been said before. This was years ago and it is interesting to note *en passant* that Exton, Pinter and Owen had all been actors and that from their ranks, as in Shakespeare's day, have been recruited some of the best playwrights. Actors will never write unspeakable dialogue or require characters to make impossible moves. Their acting experience has given all of them certain tools to use when they sit down to write.

Granted that there are especially now, with the increase in air time (as opposed to in the beginning of TV drama) a host of writers clamouring to get in and a host of script editors and producers clamouring for scripts, how do the two come together? It is often quite a haphazard affair but I find it difficult to believe that any writer with a minimum of talent will remain undiscovered.

When I asked various well-established writers of my acquaintance how they came to have their first TV scripts produced, the answers varied considerably.

Rhys Adrian had begun by writing short stories, one of which won the *Observer* story competition – he then turned to radio plays, which were produced by Barbara Bray and came to the agent Peggy Ramsay, who introduced him to TV. David Mercer wrote a stage play, *Where the Difference Begins*, and showed it to his friend and landlord Rudolf Nassauer, who also took it to Peggy Ramsay. When she had failed to set it up as a stage play, she sent it to Don Taylor, then directing at the BBC, who was so keen on it that he managed to get it put on. Douglas Livingstone, while acting (among other parts, he played in the West End in Peter Schaffer's *Public Eye and Private Ear* for some time), had written several plays (all of which he now says were 'no good'). One was sent by an agent, Elspeth Cochrane, to Stella Richman, then producing at ATV. She didn't buy that one but commissioned another.

These are fairly typical case histories – the sources being fiction, radio, stage – the paths in via agents, directors and producers. Sometimes it happens even more haphazardly. Peter McDougall, whose first play *Just Your Luck* was done in 1972 on 'Play for Today', was painting Colin Welland's house and showed him a film script he had written. Colin Welland thought it good and introduced McDougall to 'Play for Today'.

Contrary to the belief of many rejected writers, it is accurate to say that all unsolicited scripts sent in to TV companies *do* get read. When I was doing a research job in the Public Record Office, going through much Home Office and Foreign Office correspondence, it never ceased to amaze me how many letters there were included in the neatly bound files, preserved for posterity, from people on the lunatic fringe or well and truly into outright lunacy. All were carefully answered and filed along with serious political correspondence. Though many people, I know, will not believe it, the same could basically be said of all written material submitted to television companies. It *does* all get treated seriously. Unsolicited material comes in from various sources: a great deal comes from agents and a steady flow from private individuals pours in, often addressed ambiguously to 'the producer of television' or 'the drama department'. My first elementary advice to anyone attempting to sell a script independently is that he should at least do some primitive research into markets and acquaint himself with the programmes on which he presumably hopes his material will appear. Sending scripts into limbo with no direct market in mind is both stupid and discourteous.

To purchase a copy of *Radio Times* and *TV Times* does not involve an outlay of money beyond the purse of even the most penurious writer. This will give them all the information they need – the length of the programmes required and the names of the people who produce and script-edit them. It will, of course, also give the name of the director, to whom writers often address themselves first in the belief that if they can interest the director in their work, he will provide their *entrée* into television. Although this approach can sometimes work, and nothing is more satisfactory or productive of good drama than a close affinity between director and writer, it is not really advisable, for practical reasons. Most directors are freelance, working for one company one month, another the next. Most don't have personal secretaries to keep track of the scripts that come in and the loss rate tends to be high. Sometimes a director may try to get himself work via a script he thinks will interest a producer. The producer will be asked to take him and the script as a package deal and though the producer might want the script, he might not want the director, so the script does not get done.

The most intelligent way to attempt to get in is therefore to spend some time viewing; decide which programme seems to bear most affinity with what you consider your style of writing and the length of your script. (To send thirty-minute plays to a producer of seventy-five-minute ones is a sheer waste of everyone's time.) Then have the common sense and courtesy to find out who produces or edits the programme and submit the material to him or her. Amazingly simple, one would think, but I, for instance, producing a programme which only does seventy-five-minute original contemporary drama, am forever receiving thirty-minute historical adaptations, documentary ideas, comedy series ideas etc. These are often accompanied by a letter saying 'I believe you produce television programmes. I never watch.'

If, on the other hand, a novice writer sends me a script of a thirty-minute historical drama and an accompanying letter saying, 'I know your programme only puts on contemporary seventy-five-minute plays but I would like your advice on whether this script works for television and whether I can write and where else I should send it, etc.,' I will always read the script and give the advice. And if the script shows that they can handle dialogue and dramatic situations I will ask them to come in and discuss whether they *do* have any ideas for writing a contemporary play. A number of commissions have come about this way. It will certainly always benefit the aspiring writer if he shows the people to whom he has submitted his work that he knows who they are and what sort of programmes they put on.

What happens to all the miscellaneous material that comes in addressed to no one in particular? At the BBC it goes to a central script unit which employs readers to report on it. Their reports give a synopsis of the plot, list the number of cast and sets and film locations involved and pass an opinion on the virtues or otherwise of the script. Unfortunately, few if any of the readers chosen by the script department have any practical knowledge of television production. The people who do have presumably don't want to become readers. Their assessments will therefore tend to be on the literary, rather than the practical, side. Even so it is unlikely, in fact almost impossible, that anything of real merit would pass through their hands without being recognized as such and recommended. At worst, readers' reports will tell the producer or editor whether the subject matter of the script is of any interest. It will certainly sort out for him the lunatic-fringe scripts and it will channel material to the right people – thirty-minute plays to the producer of 'Thirty Minute Theatre', longer plays to 'Play for Today' etc.

What does the producer or editor do then? It seldom happens that an unsolicited script sent in 'on spec' gets put on. Why? Because they are almost never suited to the medium. What such a script does show the producer is that the writer has something to say, and is capable of saying it in terms of dramatic incidents and in dialogue rather than narrative. It's up to the TV expert then to help acquaint the writer with the special requirements of TV as opposed to fiction, radio, the stage etc. What usually happens in this case is that the writer is commissioned to write another play on a subject that *is* of interest to the programme and in a way suited to the medium.

What does this mean exactly? In the days when I started on 'Armchair Theatre' it meant something very different from what it does now. In those days, all our plays were recorded on videotape and videotape editing was primitive if not unheard of. Some plays were still done 'live'. No exterior filming was done. Writers had then, by necessity, to observe the Aristotelian unities of time and place. If a character left a room you could not then immediately cut to him driving along in his car or see him twenty years later, old and grey. A filler scene had to be written for another character in order to give the first one time to change and appear on another set.

Perhaps one of the reasons why the first three scripts I have mentioned were so excellently constructed is that the writers were forced to restrict themselves in this way. TV plays were undoubtedly closer to the theatre than the cinema then, the word being as important as the image, or more so. Now TV is getting closer to the big screen. So the TV playwright of ten years ago had to be a better craftsman than he does now. The plotless 'slice of life' play could not really be made to work in a studio set-up without the surrounding documentary images of film.

What *were* the influences in those days? On 'Armchair Theatre' there was unquestionably a very strong American and Canadian influence. When Sydney Newman had left North America in 1958 to produce 'Armchair Theatre', drama on American TV was in its heyday with such programmes as 'Playhouse 90' and 'Play of the Week'. Writers like Tad Mosel, Paddy Chayefsky (of *Marty* fame), Rod Serling (*Requiem for a Heavyweight*) and Reginald Rose were writing about those very subjects that the kitchen-sink dramatists in England were about to tackle, though perhaps in a more senti-mental way – strikes, working-class underprivileged misfits, boxers, etc., all speaking the language of the 'working class' – the antithe-sis of drawing-room drama.

A survey of 'Armchair Theatre' in its early days shows a sur-prisingly high percentage of plays of American or Canadian origin. Take 1958, for instance. Among the transmissions were: *Tragedy in a Temporary Town* by Reginald Rose; *The Five Dollar Bill* by Tad Mosel; *Paid in Full* by Mordecai Richler; *Noon on Doomsday* by Rod Serling; *The Travelling Lady* by Horton Foote; *The Great-est Man in the World* by James Thurber (adapted by Reuben Ship, a Canadian); *Please Murder Me* by Gore Vidal, as well as two American classics: *The Emperor Jones* by Eugene O'Neill and *The Time of Your Life* by William Saroyan.

The following year was about the same statistically and then the number of imports began to decline as a school of native play-wrights was emerging or being discovered. 'Armchair Theatre' was, of course, at that time largely stocked with directors who were either of Canadian nationality like Ted Kotcheff and Alvin Rakoff or had worked in Canada like Charles Jarrott and David Greene, or in the United States like Alan Cooke, John Moxey and Philip Saville. With the opening of commercial TV, there was a shortage of trained directors; Canadians did not need work permits. There was not only a great deal of ready-made material to import from North America, there was also a group of trained people to sup-plement the English BBC-trained directors. (I do not talk here of the BBC drama output of the time, which will be dealt with in the next chapter, or of the other commercial companies, of which I have no personal experience.)

The fact was that 'Armchair Theatre' went on the air an average of forty-six weeks a year and that there was, as yet, no real British school of TV dramatists. Consequently there was a desperate short-age of material. Hence the borrowing from American and Cana-dian TV ... something I find ironically reversed now that the mainstay of 'class' drama in the United States and Canada seems to be BBC and some ITV imports. The wheel appears to have come full circle. There is no doubt in my mind, however, that much of the vitality of the new 'slice of life' drama in England was inspired by American films and television.

One of my jobs when I first started at ABC was to read the *New York Times* review section, hunting desperately for plays which seemed in any way suitable for purchase. I can remember one panic situation when we were so desperately short of material for 'Armchair Mystery Theatre' (the summer replacement for 'Armchair Theatre') that I sent a telegram to a New York agent for the immediate purchase (sight unseen) of a play which had just been transmitted on the 'United States Steel Hour' and had been well reviewed. When the script, entitled *Madeleine*, arrived, it was immediately flung into production with Adrienne Corri, Maurice Denham and Michael Gwynn playing 'American style' French characters. The script appeared to be the right length on arrival, but when I had finished trimming the surrounding advertising material, I found it to be about twelve minutes short: a nasty shock in view of the absence of the writer and the immediacy of the situation. On American TV there was a guest introducer telling the audience about the stars, future programmes and the merits of steel sink units. At the end of the play, he introduced the following week's guest stars. The play itself seemed to be the least important element: something to wrap around the sponsor's message. I remember writing the missing twelve minutes, in a manner reminiscent of *The Archers*. The heroine was a murderess who served people toadstools; I had her reading out recipes for mushroom soup from a cook-book.

While transatlantic plays and adapted stage plays and novels were forming the bulk of the output in 1958, Sydney was gradually putting into action his policy of finding new dramatists and doing more real-life, 'gutsy' English drama (in which, unconsciously perhaps, I believe he was very much influenced by the American TV programmes I have mentioned before) as opposed to the 'tea and crumpets' variety.

A play by Ray Rigby, who later wrote the movie *The Hill*, was probably the first controversial piece after Sydney's arrival in 1958. It was called *Boy with a Meat Axe* and I can do no better than quote Norman Hare in the *News Chronicle* of 22 November 1958 in his description of what has now become almost a cliché image of 'kitchen sink' drama and dramatists: 'This former laundry hand, vacuum-cleaner salesman, factory worker, soldier, mental hospital attendant and butler to a member of the Government had plenty of experience to call upon. A year ago he was scrubbing floors in a West End hair-dressing salon.

'But when he included a murder accusation, a young girl getting drunk, and a street fight in his play, as well as using a lavatory as one of the settings, he was likely to cause a few eyebrows to rise.'

It is almost like reading about the *Lady Chatterley* trial. How innocent it seems now! Ray Rigby was one of the first 'natural' writers I have encountered. By this, I mean writers who have a marvellous capacity for recording real dialogue and portraying real characters but a great deal less ability when it comes to constructing a plot and conforming with the disciplines of a production; such authors as Jeremy Sandford, Roy Minton and others, to whom I will return in a later chapter.

In 1959 Peter Luke, then chief script editor on 'Armchair Theatre' took Sydney along to the Lyric Theatre, Hammersmith, to see a stage play, *The Rough and Ready Lot* by a new writer, Alun Owen. Sydney liked the play, invited Alun to lunch with Peter, commissioned another play for the programme and cast Ted Kotcheff to direct it. Thus Sydney created a successful team – someone with valuable editorial judgement (Peter Luke), someone with good technical knowledge (Ted Kotcheff), and a new creative talent which needed initial help in learning about the medium (Alun Owen). This is the key to being a good producer – the ability to assess personalities and match talents successfully.

Clive Exton's play *Where I Live* was similarly acquired. It was given to Ted Kotcheff to read by the actress Anne Lynn, a mutual acquaintance of his and Exton's. He brought it to Sydney, who bought it and another long-standing director–writer team was formed.

So at that time, the sources which were being tapped for script material were existing North American plays, adaptations of existing stage plays and novels, new stage authors, radio authors (like Rhys Adrian), 'natural' discoveries like Ray Rigby, who drew from a wealth of 'off-beat' personal experience and observation and, occasionally, sophisticated literary authors like Angus Wilson.

Two plays by Angus Wilson, on which I acted as story editor, remain in my mind as outstandingly original and skilled pieces of work: *The Stranger* directed by Ted Kotcheff in 1960 and *The Inva-*

sion directed by Charles Jarrott. The latter was a highly amusing satirical piece about the battle going on between a snobbish established family and a *nouveau-riche* family who were trying to get accepted socially. Both were so wrapped up in their petty squabbles that they failed to notice a Martian invasion taking place around them.

I remember that, as Angus Wilson was out of the country when we were rehearsing *The Stranger*, I had to cut some of the script, which was over-length (in commercial television of course, as opposed to the BBC, a script *has* to conform exactly to a specific time-slot). Usually cutting a script is a fairly easy editorial job, but this one was so carefully constructed and each word of dialogue was so meaningful in terms of character revelation and satire that each deleted line was a genuine loss. Not until I worked with William Trevor some years later did I encounter once more literary craftsmanship of this order in television writing.

The question of script editors now arises. On series where there is a preconceived format which must be observed; where there are running characters every week who must be consistently written; where sometimes story-lines by one writer are given to another to develop, script editors are undoubtedly a necessity. But are they on single plays?

On 'Armchair Theatre' Sydney Newman obviously felt that two, three, even four heads were better than one in finding material and overseeing its preparation for production. The sheer number of transmissions per annum of the programme made it more or less physically impossible for one person to do the job alone. The story editors (for most of my time at ABC, Peter Luke and I were the only two on 'Armchair Theatre' but others briefly came and went) would go out scouting for material from sources already described; we would go to such theatres as Joan Littlewood's Theatre Royal, Stratford East (*Sparrer's Can't Sing*, for instance, was first purchased by me for 'Armchair Theatre' before being made into a film), the Royal Court one-shot Sunday night performances, the Dublin Theatre Festival, the Edinburgh Festival; we would approach journalists like Bob Muller, then drama critic of the *Daily Mail*, who wrote his first play for 'Armchair Theatre' and novelists (like Angus Wilson and Simon Raven), and we would talk over ideas for new plays with TV dramatists. Then, at a monthly script meeting with Sydney, we would discuss the properties we wanted to commission or purchase.

We would discuss them not only in terms of their own intrinsic or potential merit, but also in terms of the balance of the programme. Were there too many plays about 'sick old men' for one season? Were Peter and I, as Sydney so often accused us of being, too long-haired-intellectual for the audience (an ironic remark in retrospect both in terms of fashion of hair and the comparatively unintellectual nature of the programme). Were there enough plays of sheer entertainment value? Sydney was always very conscious of this aspect, which, taking an objective look at current TV drama, is something that has been very much lost sight of lately, even by most of the commercial companies, with the notable exception of Yorkshire. He wanted a good scattering of glamour and of thrillers amongst the contemporary realism.

Once we had agreed on the desirable projects to follow up, the story editors would go away and commission them and would not submit them to Sydney until rewrites had been done and the script was considered ready for production.

The other aspect of the scripts which was discussed was their suitability for the regular directors on the programme. This is the advantage of a small company over a large one – the regular working intimacy which grows up between all the people concerned in a production. Writers, quite naturally, assume that the only judgement that is exercised about their scripts is a qualitative one. In this they are often quite wrong. A script also has to be considered in terms of subject matter (and whether there are others around on similar subjects), sometimes in terms of suitability for stars or for a director.

When I first became a producer, I had great difficulty in establishing the precedent that I did not want the services of a story editor and that, even though it meant a great deal more work, I wanted to continue this function myself. Unlike Sydney, who was undoubtedly more interested in the vital active part of production than the literary origins, and who had a great talent for delegating to people whom he trusted, I could never bear the obstacle of a third person coming between myself and the author. To me, the most gratifying part of any production is the realization on the screen, months later, of a germinal conversation between myself and the writer. To be handed a ready-made script by a third party would rob the production of all this excitement. Occasionally I have had a young trainee foisted on me unwillingly and have found the only useful way to employ him is as a talent scout. To go out to the fringe theatres, to read the new novels and see the university drama productions. But I have never been able to entrust to anyone else the formative decisions about a script. This may indeed be a personal failing. Most producers do employ script editors. I myself would never have entered TV had the function not existed but, to my mind, the only way the producer is likely to get the sort of play he wants on the screen is if he is in close communication with the writer.

In March 1965 (when Sydney had been two years in the chair as Head of Drama at the BBC) Lord Ted Willis (who had had several plays, among them *Hot Summer Night* and *The Scent of Fear* produced by Sydney on 'Armchair Theatre'), at a Royal Society of Arts lecture, called for the wholesale sacking of story editors at the BBC. He went on to advocate a utopian set-up in which the BBC should scout the country for six first-class directors, put them in direct contact with writers and leave them alone. Sydney's reply to this (quoted by David Nathan in *The People* on 19 March 1965) was typical. 'What is Ted yacking about? What's this dream of finding six hot-shot directors and giving them their own slot? You can't win and hold audiences on a catch-as-can basis.' He also pointed out elsewhere that Lord Willis seemed to have forgotten 'what television was like in the days before the story editor, when the writer had to cosy up to a director who possibly lost it [the script] or forgot about it because he didn't have the courage to tell the author it was not good enough.'

As Sydney so aptly pointed out, a middleman is absolutely essential to maintain a continuum on a programme and to assume responsibility for all the script material. But should this function be performed by the story-editor or the producer?

Perhaps what I am calling into question here is not the function of editing but the quality of editors as a whole and the system of recruitment, which seems to be entirely haphazard. At various times, there have passed through my office young men straight from university with no practical knowledge whatsoever of television, assistant floor managers with a yen to more literary outlets, ex-actors, ex-rep. company directors, etc. Now there is nothing to say that any one of these might not have shown great potential as an editor but he needed at least two years of reporting on scripts, attending rehearsals and sitting in on sessions with writers before, in my opinion, he could responsibly be left to deal with a writer on his own. To face John Osborne, John Mortimer or any mature writer with a story editor who has done six months' training, knows nothing about production, etc., is sheer lunacy, yet this is the average training period deemed necessary.

A story editor of any real value should be mature enough to be taken seriously by the writers, have a thorough technical knowledge of TV production and good literary judgement and taste. Peter Luke had all these qualities. By the time I started dealing with authors on my own, I believe I also had them. When I began reading scripts my judgements were essentially literary not dramatic ones, a common fault with university-trained people who have no practical production experience. The script which reads most fluently is not always the one which plays well. If one has no practical theatre experience, one does not realize this.

By listening to Peter's discussions with writers (my quarters for some time were a corner of his office) I learned a great deal. By attending rehearsals all the time I learned more. Although I had considered the two years spent on my thesis a waste of time, I began to realize that it was invaluable to me in my job. In it I had taken various minor Elizabethan and Jacobean playwrights, examined the source material of their plays – the Chronicles, Homilies, etc. – and studied the plays in the light of how this material had been dramatized especially to illustrate contemporary problems. For two years I had been analysing how playwrights (the seventeenth-century equivalents of Jeremy Sandford, Tony Parker, etc.) turned historical material into dramatic form. I had also written scripts and knew the techniques of filming. The biggest problem to overcome was shyness. It takes courage to face an established author and criticize his work. It is a job which automatically makes many enemies.

One system which we used at ABC, and which I have always felt was invaluable, was that of keeping a 'master script'. Once a script goes into rehearsal it is basically in the hands of the director and the actors. Actors, of course, very often would like to rewrite some of their lines (often with good reason); it is not unknown that directors may think they can improve on the author's work. The result of an accumulation of lots of little changes can often be disastrous; the whole logic of the script or the rhythm of the author's style may be lost. It is up to the director who wants to make changes to ask the writer to do so, through the editor or producer.

At ABC a master script was kept in which the assistant floor manager, at the end of every day's rehearsal, presented the changes made to the story editor, who could thereby safeguard the writer's interests and keep an eye on the script as a whole. Responsibility to writers has since then increased a great deal and, in accordance with the Writers' Guild regulations, no one is allowed to rewrite without first asking the author to do so.

In January 1963 Sydney left ABC to become Head of Drama at the BBC. The *Daily Mail* heralded his transfer with the headline 'BBC signs ITV "dustbin" man'. It also described 'Armchair Theatre' as 'TV's most respected series, with audiences of over 16,000,000' (*Daily Mail*, 19 April 1962). The size of the audience, as Sydney was always modestly reminding us at script meetings, was undoubtedly helped greatly by the fact that the programme followed *Sunday Night at the London Palladium*. The *Mirror* at the same time put the audience figure at 21 million. Opinion as to the quality of the programme varied; as Marshall Pugh so aptly put it in the *Daily Mail*, 'to some he was the great impresario of commercial television, to others the purveyor of pretentious pigswill'. At ABC he had been responsible for two hours of drama a week, and a handful of directors and editors. At the BBC he was to be responsible for twelve hours a week and fifty-one staff directors. Michael Barry, the previous Head of Drama, had left the BBC for Irish Television in 1961 and the post had been vacant since his departure. Sydney himself was quoted as describing his new job as 'sprinkling humus on the manure of dramatic production. The drama department was too big. I want to see how we can break it down into much tighter groups . . . we have to be organized for increased productivity.'

Chapter 2

Background of drama at the BBC

Before discussing Sydney's advent at the BBC, it may be valuable to go into the background of what he found on arrival there.

Historically, television drama in England can be said to have started in December 1936 when BBC-TV started transmitting plays. A survey of the transmissions in 1937 reveals the astonishingly high figure of 123 – many, of course, were repeats and most were very short in length, from ten to thirty minutes. Most of these productions consisted of scenes from famous plays – Shakespeare, Chekhov, Thornton Wilder – directed by a group of young men who had been selected from other areas of drama, like Eric Crozier (from the Old Vic), George More O'Ferrall, Moultrie Kelsall, etc. But even in 1937 there were two pieces put out which were original commissions for the medium: *The Underground Murder Mystery* by I. Bissell Thomas (lasting ten minutes) and *Turn Round* by S. E. Reynolds (lasting thirty minutes). These were the first two pieces of original English TV drama.

In 1939 there were another two short original pieces, *Rehearsal for Drama* by Roy Carter and E. Wax (thirty-five minutes) and *Condemned to be Shot* by R. E. J. Brooke (twenty minutes). Because of the war, transmissions ceased until 7 June 1946. There was one original sixty-minute piece in that year, *The Murder Rap* by Gilbert Thomas (the remainder of the programmes consist of stage plays or adapted novels). There is nothing in 1947; one original piece lasting thirty minutes in 1948 – *The Unknown Lobster* by Denis Johnston – and nothing at all for the next three years; although there were as many as fifty ninety-minute plays transmitted in 1950, they were all watered-down stage plays.

1952 marks the arrival on the scene of certain names still well known and recognizable to the current TV audience. In that year appear the first Francis Durbridge serials: *The Broken Horseshoe* and *Operation Diplomat*; the directorial names for the year include Tony Richardson, Dennis Vance and Julian Aymes. The following year we hear for the first time of Donald Wilson and Nigel Kneale as original writers. Donald Wilson was, of course, probably to make his major mark when he came to produce *The Forsyte Saga* many years later, but Kneale established himself in 1953 as an original science fiction writer with *The Quatermass Experiment* – undoubtedly the most revolutionary original television drama event to that date.

The reason why certain names keep recurring from that year, Wilson, Kneale, Philip Mackie, John Elliot, and Anthony Stevens, among them, was that a policy had been adopted of putting certain promising writers on the staff, to form a sort of writers' workshop. The idea was that by adapting and story-editing other people's scripts, and working close to the productions, this nucleus of writers could best learn about the medium. Hierarchically, the structure of the department was Head of Drama (Michael Barry) and Head of Script Department (Donald Wilson), with a group of writers and directors working on all types of drama (plays, series and serials) under their supervision.

Nigel Kneale was the first writer to be put on this scheme, in 1951. He was of Manx origin, had done two years at the Royal Academy of Dramatic Art and acted at Stratford. His book of short stories *Tomato Cain*, published in 1949, won him two literary prizes (the Atlantic and Somerset Maugham Awards) and convinced the BBC drama department to give him a contract (at £5 a week), first to adapt one of his own stories and later (eventually at £15 a week) to become a staff writer and adapter. I mention these salary figures for the benefit of current young aspiring writers to demonstrate that many of the big names of television were only too glad to work for a pittance in order to gain practical knowledge of their craft.

Was this workshop idea a good one? Undoubtedly it was at the time and still could be, on a short-term basis. But writers like Kneale found themselves indentured for a long period, while their successful work, like *The Quatermass Experiment*, when sold to a film company belonged essentially to the BBC and not to them. A more satisfactory arrangement seemed to be the later one, used by both the ITV companies and the BBC, of giving writers contracts for x number of plays a year, thereby guaranteeing their services and giving them some financial security without loss of freedom. With the advent of commercial TV in 1955, of course, the companies were vying with each other for the exclusive rights to the handful of experienced and established writers.

Among the names which loomed large from 1954 onwards, but which seem to be all but forgotten today, is that of Iain McCormick, who died in 1965. The first major BBC play to be written specially for the medium was his eighty-nine-minute piece *Good Partners*, transmitted in June 1954 and directed by Al Rakoff. This was the first part of a quartet of plays called *The Promised Years* with varied wartime settings; Italy, the Berlin airlift, Korea, etc., were the themes, and the style was rather that of the English wartime movies. MacCormick, who was also trained as a director, wrote another major quartet of plays, *English Family Robinson*, which was transmitted in 1957 and he had six other separate plays produced between 1955 and 1957.

He was perhaps more financially-minded than most writers of the time. He saw television in terms of the film industry. At one point he formed a company, called International Playwrights Group Ltd, with the idea that his group of writers (the names, among them T. E. B. Clarke, Jack Davies, Jack Whittingham and Monja Daniechewsky, were mainly drawn from the film world) should guarantee to supply the BBC with 90–120 half-hour subjects annually; that the writers would be free to write for other media, like films, but that commercial TV would be thereby cut off from their services. Although this kind of writers' stable might well work for predetermined series, it could not guarantee good original work and the BBC rightly declined to contract blind for subjects not yet written.

MacCormick's last major project of his own was a cycle of plays about English settlers in Kenya, entitled *The Last Adventure*, which covered a period from the first outbreaks of Mau-Mau to the prophetic emergence of a fascistic all-African state (prophetic, anyway, in terms of Uganda if not of Kenya). Because of its very specific political allusions, it was never done. Perhaps, too, it was this very political topicality of McCormick's work which made it date so fast. In 1966 and 1969 his wife suggested to the BBC repeats of some of his award-winning plays and a production of *The Last Adventure* but all were found to have values and attitudes belonging to another era.

In my opinion, McCormick is a good illustration of the fact that the more topical and specific a TV play is, the more likely it is to date rapidly. John Hopkins's allegorical play *Fable* (transmitted in 1965), for instance, in which a black majority was seen behaving to a white minority as the South Africans did to the black Africans, during apartheid, will keep its relevance for years to come, while McCormick's more specific work was bound to date rapidly. He seems an illustration, too, of the fact that while formula-written serials and series can be produced in the atmosphere of a financial consortium, the individual play of merit can never be written in this 'battery' way, but must come directly from the writer's mind, heart and experience.

Much less dated are the first 'drama documentary' plays which Colin Morris was beginning to write at this time. Morris, before he was put on the BBC course in 1954, had been actor, theatrical producer and, when in the army, a military observer working with the Army Film Unit. He had also won the Atlantic Award for Literature and had the West End hits *Reluctant Heroes* and *Desert Rats* to his credit. While acting in *Reluctant Heroes* he had become a voluntary social worker, out of which experience grew his interest in the subjects he later dramatized.

The Unloved, transmitted in June 1955, was the first major play of this 'drama documentary' type. Directed by Gilchrist Calder, who became part of a permanent team with Morris, it was a carefully researched piece on a home for delinquent children, and a reading today shows the play to be still moving and valid; the dialogue, as a whole, shows that it was based on real-life observation and only becomes slightly stilted when the author is trying to preach a point. The play was followed by many others by the same team on such subjects as the plight of the unmarried mother, prostitution, strikes, handicapped children, etc. The technique of production, too, was innovatory in that actors were sometimes rehearsed and then set down in outside locations and filmed in true-life backgrounds against ordinary people. Certainly, these plays were the forerunners of *Cathy, Come Home* and the Tony Parker plays, and *Edna, the Inebriate Woman*, which I was later to produce.

Up to 1957 there very little evidence of Canadian or American influence in the BBC's transmissions. Two Canadian-written plays were produced: *Go Fall in Love* by Ted Allan in 1955 and *For the Defence* by Stanley Mann in 1956, and one American, *Three Empty Rooms* by Reginald Rose in 1955. In 1957, however, there was a massive import of Canadian produce in the form of a purchase of thirty-five CBC drama productions, thirty of which had been produced by Sydney Newman (nine directed by Ted Kotcheff and one by Charles Jarrott). It was not, however, policy, as at ABC, to re-produce many existing American and Canadian scripts.

At this time, too, the regions and radio were feeding new writers into television. In 1956, Willis Hall, for example, was highly recommended to Donald Wilson by Victor Menzies in the Birmingham radio drama department as a 'British Chayefsky'. Hall had begun writing when stationed in Malaya in the regular army; his first scripts were broadcast by Radio Malaya. Having written a large number of radio scripts, many produced by Peter Dews, he was asked to write for TV and began writing on such 'realistic' subjects as the police (*The Calverdon Road Job*), a football club committee (*Final at Furnell*) and young soldiers (*One Man Missing*). In 1958 he was commissioned to write a play for the Oxford University Theatre Group to be put on at the Edinburgh Festival, *The Disciplines of War*, which became the famous *The Long and the Short and the Tall*.

Other writers whose names are now well known were also having work done in the regions: *A Game for Eskimos* by Tom Clarke was a regional production in 1958, so was *Walk on the Grass* by Peter Nichols in 1959.

Between 1957 and 1962 plays were being written in the BBC drama department by such writers as Peter Shaffer (*Balance of Terror*, 1957), Jack Pulman (*All You Young Lovers*, 1959), Giles Cooper (*Where the Party Ended*, 1960), John Mortimer (*David & Broccoli*, 1960), John Osborne (*A Subject for Scandal and Concern*, 1960), David Turner (*The Train Set*, 1961), John Hopkins (*By Invitation Only*, 1961) and David Mercer (*A Climate of Fear* and *A Suitable Case for Treatment*, 1962).

At the time of Sydney Newman's arrival on 'Armchair Theatre' in 1958, therefore, there was a not inconsiderable number of interesting writers writing original work for the BBC, their work appearing on Tuesday nights on 'Television Playwright'. The fact was, however, that the drama department had grown too large for its simple hierarchical structure and that the somewhat haphazard nature of the play programming was not getting the right audiences or popularity.

In an interview in the *Daily Sketch* on 5 May 1969, Sydney retrospectively described the background to his invitation to become Head of the BBC drama department. The Director General, Sir Hugh Carlton Greene, on discussing the job with him, said, 'You've managed to collect writers like Harold Pinter, Alun Owen, Clive Exton and Bill Naughton for your "Armchair Theatre". They got their start on BBC radio. I want you to get them back – and find all the new ones you can.' Now this statement was not, of course, in anyway historically accurate, but the fact was that in the early 1960s it was 'Armchair Theatre' and not BBC drama which was attracting attention in the single play field.

On 11 October 1967, *The Times*, looking back on Sydney's arrival in the BBC five years before, said, 'When Newman came to the BBC five years ago, the single play was a sickly child, a pallid brother to the stage production. Today it has become, he says, "anti-theatre" and the Wednesday Play has built up a regular audience of ten to twelve million.'

In my opinion, it was Sydney's quality of 'showmanship' which was his most attractive feature to the BBC at that time. Also, as an outsider who had had nothing to do with the evolution of the BBC drama department until that point, he could assess its position more objectively than one who had grown up in it. First of all he realized that, with the vast increase in the number of programmes being produced and with the coming further increase when BBC 2 was to open, some sort of breaking down into units was essential. The department was therefore split into three sections: *Plays*, for all single productions; *Series*, for all productions with recurring characters (like *Finlay*, *Maigret* etc.) and *Serials*, with episodes continuing every week. Each department was assigned a Head.

With his American and Canadian background, Sydney was perhaps more aware of the audience than those at the BBC who had enjoyed a non-commercial monopoly for so long. First of all he realized that audiences operate very much on a Pavlov's dog principle. They will tune in to see those programmes they are conditioned to having seen and enjoyed. Series always have larger audiences than one-shot plays because audiences build up loyalty to characters or subjects they see week after week. A play spot should desirably, therefore, have some sort of specific character if it is to build up audience loyalty. This, perhaps was the problem with the transmission of plays on the BBC up to that point; although good plays were going out, audiences did not know what to expect: modern and classical were mixed and there was little evidence of a specific continuing taste or style behind the choice of material. Also there was little sense of occasion attached to these transmissions.

Sydney's idea was to divide the type of plays into groups. 'Festival', under Peter Luke, who went with him to the BBC as a producer, was to do the more classical pieces, ancient and modern: plays by Noel Coward, Cocteau, James Joyce, Ionesco, etc., were included in the first 1963–64 season. 'First Night', produced by John Elliot, was to concentrate on the new writers and was to go out on Sunday night in opposition to 'Armchair Theatre'. The first season included plays by Terence Frisby (later best known for *There's a Girl in my Soup*), Arnold Wesker and Alun Owen. Specific producers and editors would give the different slots their distinct character.

By now, many of the early writers like Donald Wilson, Colin Morris, etc., were concentrating their efforts in the series and serials departments which, as Sydney realized, were well ahead at the BBC. He wanted to give to the single plays the same 'team spirit' that operated in such series as *Z Cars* (one of the first realistic police series), by appointing producers to look for specific types of programmes and by giving these programmes generic titles and advertising them in such a way that audiences would know better what type of plays to expect. All his talk of 'spontaneous contemporaneity' was undoubtedly half tongue-in-cheek but it did have the effect of making certain programmes appear to be unified by an 'up-to-date' attitude. Although Sydney was not noted for modesty, he had admitted to the *Daily Telegraph* on 30 May 1960, when asked about the 100 plays he had produced on 'Armchair Theatre' since his arrival in England two years before, that only 15 per cent had been successes. But, at the same time, he had managed to create an illusion of success. 'I came to Britain at a crucial time in 1958,' he said to the *Daily Express* on 5 January 1963, 'when the seeds of *Look Back in Anger* were beginning to flower. I am proud that I played some part in the recognition that the working man was a fit subject for drama, and not just a comic foil in a play on middle-class manners.'

He talked of himself elsewhere as a 'creative midwife', not a 'frustrated director or a frustrated writer'. But perhaps most telling of all was his description of his policy as a producer in an article he wrote in *The Observer* on 22 April 1962. 'To me the most important moment in any play is the first minute. We try always to get plays really going with a bang in the most provocative possible way. John Grierson used to say "You want to start big and then build." It's not bad, that advice.' And this, in fact, was the advice, usually delivered in a serio-comic manner, which Sydney had been giving to all his directors and story editors at ABC. On American TV the idea of 'the teaser' – the pre-titles planting of something intriguing (like a man being shot, a body lying on the ground, etc.) was well recognized as an audience hook. Sydney never forgot this, or the advice of his mentor Grierson of the Film Board. He was not ashamed to advertise or use conscious devices to attract an audience. If you want to tell people something, first make sure you have engaged their interest.

Chapter 3

Preparing for Channel 2: learning to be a producer

The planned opening, in April 1964, of a second channel on the BBC presented the department heads, Sydney amongst them, with the problem of where to find more trained staff to supply the extra programme material required. A lot of internal promotions were, naturally, being made. A large batch of stripling directors was being hatched on the BBC training course; some came from repertory theatres, some (like Ken Loach) had been production assistants, some actors.

Amongst many people who were approached or applied to come to the BBC from commercial television, I was one. I was, in fact, approached by Sydney to come to the BBC in November 1963, as a story editor, to prepare a new drama series for BBC-2, called 'Story Parade' (a typical Sydney title), which was to consist of adaptations of modern novels . . . a sort of anthology of new fictional writing.

At first I was loath to leave the pleasant and familiar surroundings of ABC for the forbidding institutionalized-looking building of the Television Centre at White City. I also pondered the advisability of leaving a programme like 'Armchair Theatre', which had an enormous audience, to go to one which, at the start, would be viewed by a tiny minority. Sydney, however, with his usual psychological skill, set about convincing me of the challenge and excitement of working for a brand new channel with new people in new surroundings. Reluctantly, he agreed to a codicil that I wanted in my contract, saying that I would be considered for promotion to producer within nine months of coming to the BBC. I knew (as it turned out quite correctly) that he did not really consider me right for that job, but wanted me badly as a story editor.

The shock to the system of anyone who has been used to working in a small company is considerable when trying to get accustomed to a vast corporation. For weeks, I literally sat alone in an office, reading novel after novel, without talking to a soul. As yet, there was no producer appointed to the programme and Sydney had become totally inaccessible. Gone were the days of script conferences ending in a Chinese restaurant. It took weeks even to find the way to the BBC canteen. Moreover, as one of Sydney's disciples, one was aware of a certain, quite understandable, suspicion and resentment on the part of those who had been at the BBC for years. Eighteen months after I had joined the organization I was still a story editor, so I wrote Sydney a memo asking if I had to shoot my way into his office to get to see him and demanding to discuss the codicil in my contract. The result of that particular meeting I will return to: suffice it to say that a Kafka-like despair had descended upon me at this time, enclosed within the circular walls of a building where everyone seemed to have a collection of initials like H.P.D.Tel and no one had a recognizable face.

It was in this period, however, that I began to appreciate what the function of a producer should really be. I learned in a negative rather than a positive way, from seeing the wrong way to go about things. I began to discover that many aspects of production that I had taken for granted on 'Armchair Theatre' did not come automatically and were far from the norm.

At ABC, for a start, I had been used to working with a handful of truly individualistic directors whose technical knowledge had long since become second nature to them, directors like Charles Jarrott, Alan Cooke, Ted Kotcheff, Philip Saville and David Greene. I had also been used to the highly individual designers on the programme, like Assheton Gorton (who later designed the film *Blow Up*), Timothy O'Brien and Voytek. It never occurred to me that the standard of work put out by these people was in any way unusual. We also always worked with the same excellent camera crew. Everyone concerned with productions on a week-to-week basis knew the talents and temperaments of everyone else.

In an organization the size of the BBC such intimacy was, of course, impossible; moreover, I had come to work on a new programme where not only fledgling directors but also newly promoted designers, wardrobe and make-up people and newly made-up camera crews were to be broken in, along with a few more experienced people. In a sense, it was like going from university back to primary school. The producer who was finally appointed to 'Story Parade' was also a new producer. He had been a director for many years under the pre-Sydney Newman system in which producers basically did not exist. He was, in fact, a 'reluctant producer' who felt embarrassed by his function especially *vis-à-vis* the directors.

The function of the producer has, of course, always been the most ambiguous one in television. 'What,' people are always asking me, 'does a producer *do* exactly?' (And often, the tone of voice implies, 'Would not the orchestra play just as well without him?').

I can only answer for myself and from my own experience. First and foremost, as I have said before, I feel it is up to the producer himself to find the right scripts for his programme. Having done this, it is up to him to assemble the right group of creative and technical people, who will best bring the scripts to life, and to so orchestrate them that the end product will be what he and the author had in mind when the script was originally commissioned. How does he go about achieving this?

Anyone visiting an electronic television studio for the first time during a rehearsal or recording of a drama programme is immediately struck by the sheer number of people milling about the studio floor and by the great complexity of the machinery on hand. A total count of the number of those concerned with one seventy-five-minute 'Play for Today' studio production in 1973 would probably have reached at least seventy, behind the cameras alone – i.e. excluding the actors.

Here is a brief description of who these people might be and where the visitor would find them. Of the *writer, story editor* and *producer* we have already spoken. The most vital appointment the producer will have made is, of course, the *director*. He is often not on the studio floor, but sitting upstairs in the gallery with his camera script in front of him, communicating through their earphones with the cameramen and with his production assistant (or floor manager, as the job is often designated in commercial television), who are all on the studio floor.

Beside him in the gallery will be his *secretary*, who will be calling out to the cameramen the shots that are coming up in the script which each one is expected to take on his particular camera. On the other side of the director will be the *vision mixer*, who will physically mix the shots, cutting from one camera to another to produce the final sequence of pictures that will be transmitted.

Also to be found in the gallery, sitting next to the vision mixer, will be the 'Tom' or *Technical Manager No. 2*, who with the *Technical Manager No. 1* shares the responsibility for the technical side of the programme, the cameras and other equipment. He will also be in direct telephonic communication, during the recording of the production, with the *Videotape Recording Operators* who, behind the scenes, perhaps in another building, will, on his instructions, be recording the show in stops and starts.

There might also be, in the gallery, an *Inlay Operator* in control of special visual electronic effects. And, behind the scenes again, a *Tele-Cine Operator* who will feed into the studio any sections of the play that have already been recorded on film or extraneous film material (like stock from newsreels etc.) that are part of the show but are not being shot in the studio.

On either side of the central control gallery are two other galleries, one for lighting control, one for sound. In the former will be the TM1, or *Lighting Supervisor*, who has control of the vast panel of lights which hang from the studio ceiling in quantities that always amaze the visitor. Next to him are numerous *assistants* and below, on the floor, more practical *electricians*. Throughout the rehearsal he will be going round the studio lighting and re-lighting each shot.

In the sound gallery will be the *Sound Supervisor*, the *Grams Operator* and one or more *assistants*. Like the lighting supervisor, the man in control of sound will constantly go round the studio floor, shifting microphone or 'boom' positions as scenes are rehearsed. Under his supervision will be the *boom operators* who actually handle the sound on the floor.

The camera crew on the floor will often consist of six *cameramen*, as well as all the accompanying *grips* pushing the heavy cameras along 'dollies' for moving shots, shifting cables etc., as the cameras move from shot to shot.

All around the studio floor sets are being put up, dressed with props, floors are being painted, etc. The *designer* is, of course, in charge of this and with him one, or possibly two, *assistants*, aided by a *property buyer*, *property men*, *scenery builders* and *painters* and *movers*, practical *carpenters* and sometimes *plumbers*. Added to these may be some *special effects men* and eidophore or *Back Projection Operators* when a moving background or special lighting effect is required in a scene.

Assisting the floor manager will be the *assistant floor manager* and a *call boy*, who will be summoning and dismissing actors as required. Behind the scenes *wardrobe* and *make-up assistants* and *dressers* will be getting the *actors* and *crowd artists* (or extras) ready while the *make-up* and *costume supervisors* are usually up in the gallery looking at the effect of the make-up and costumes on the screen.

Behind the scenes and not visible at this time are many other people who are closely involved in the production. The *graphics designer* will have provided his captions and other work, the *composer* will have written his music and recorded it with the *musicians* and a separate set of *sound technicians*.

The filmed inserts which are being fed in by tele-cine will usually have been done three weeks before the production enters the studio, and the edited film will then be transferred to tape. Involved in the making of this section of the play will have been the *film cameraman*, his *assistants*, his *lighting men* and *grips*, a *film sound recordist* and his *assistant*. The film will have been developed in an outside laboratory where sometimes the cameraman or editor will go to supervise the *colour grader* to ensure that they get the effect they desire. The film will have been cut together by a *film editor* and his *assistant*.

This edited film transferred to tape, as well as all the material that has been recorded on tape in the studio, will then be handed over to the *Videotape Editor* who will put the entire show together. A further *sound dub* may be required to add music, special sound effects etc, and the play will, at last, be ready to go out on the air.

Behind all the people listed above are, of course, another group of administrative people: the *copyright department, the production unit manager*, who works out the initial budget; *service department heads* and *allocators, planners* and *studio managers; artist's bookers*. There are also all the unseen *engineers* responsible for the technical maintenance of the equipment, for examining the technical quality of the show before it goes out, and for transmitting it. But as these are not within the producer's direct province, although he will converse with some of them fairly often, one need not describe them further.

The rest of the people listed *are*, to a greater or lesser degree, within the producer's province. He realizes, as does the director, that the final quality of the production is only going to be as good as the collective talent of the people involved. It is up to him to acquaint himself with the work of as large a number of people as he can and then to beg, bargain and banter with the service departments to get those people he considers most desirable to work on his production. I speak here of such key people as designer, film cameraman, electronic camera-crew, lighting and sound supervisors, vision mixer, make-up and wardrobe, film and tape editors. No director, however brilliant, can produce good work without being backed by the talent of these people and without the administrative ability of a good production assistant to co-ordinate and choreograph all the work being carried out on the studio floor.

When a writer comes to see me to discuss a script idea, while he is talking, there will often be lists of people running through my mind. Even at this stage, the producer will be thinking of ideal casting, not only in terms of actors but also of director, designer, cameraman etc. The writer's idea is going to have to be turned into a series of images and sounds that most closely approximate what he intends. How is one going to achieve this?

Immediately he has a studio date and a script in hand (or even in mind), the producer will start working towards this end, trying to gather together all the best key people for that particular show. Here it is only his judgement that can guide him, his decision as to who is right or wrong, and also his psychological insight into which set of people are likely to be able to work together well and amicably.

I have, of course, been speaking idealistically. I have also been describing a studio production at the BBC (in 1973), where a vast pool of people exists to be drawn from. Inevitably, the producer will have to make compromises, inevitably there will be conflicts with other producers who want the same technicians and designers and with service departments who want to make their own recommendations. The battle, however, will have already been half won by the producer who has convinced people that he respects their talent and can offer them interesting programmes and stimulating directors to work with.

On 'Armchair Theatre', none of these problems of supply and demand had existed. Because of the smallness of the organization, the working teams were more or less constant and, as I remember, of high quality. On 'Story Parade' in 1964, one was running a nursery school from which there were bound to come some brilliant graduates and also some total failures. In this sort of atmosphere, the vitality, judgement and will of the producer are all-important; novices need leadership and stimulation. A reluctant, apologetic producer who is shy of asserting himself, or unable to make up his mind, can prove a disaster in such circumstances. By this, I mean the producer who accepts on his show unquestioningly all those people assigned to him by the service departments; a producer who is reluctant to 'interfere' too much with the director and ends up giving him no critical help whatsoever; a producer who cannot make up his own mind as to what is or isn't a good script and leaves it to a story editor to tell him. A producer who wants to avoid conflict at all costs can never be any good.

When the producer has got his script, lined up his key technical people and decided on a director, the production begins. It begins with meetings between producer and director and, very often, writer, about the meaning of the script and the characters, about the 'style' of the production and about casting. Once the play is cast, the producer comes to the first read-through, after which, quite often, certain cuts and changes in the script are necessary, and then he stays away for some time.

Planning meetings will have been going on with the people responsible for design, lighting, sound and cameras advising the director on the technical problems of shooting the play the way he wants it to look. The sets will then have to be built while the director and actors go away to an outside rehearsal room. Here the floor will have been taped to the exact dimensions of the, as yet unbuilt, sets in the studio. Duplicate props will be placed exactly where the real ones will be 'on the day'. The director and actors rehearse every move in a fantasy world where a taped line on the floor represents a studio flat and a smashed-up school desk may eventually be transformed into a piece of Chippendale.

It is in this fantasy world that the producer next sees the cast, at a first run-through of the play. It is up to him, on this occasion, by an effort of imagination backed by technical experience, to try to assess how the production is going to look shot by shot, against sets which, at the moment, are to be seen only as a model and a ground plan. It is up to him to try to judge the performances not by how they seem in this large room, but by how they will seem in close-up on camera. Is the pace right? Are the plot points clear? Has the author's intention been realized? These are all questions he asks himself.

In going with Sydney Newman to rehearsals, I had always taken for granted his dynamic personality and his keen instinct for what was dramatic in a production and what was boring and self-indulgent on the part of the director or actors. I had learned to look at an outside rehearsal not as a stage play, but through the eyes of the cameras. I had also taken for granted his outspoken, irreverent and often inconoclastic style of conversation with the directors. I assumed that most producers operated in this way; in this, of course, I was quite wrong.

On 'Story Parade', I worked with two different producers. The first, having been a director and being a shy and modest man, felt that almost everyone knew better than he did. He accepted all the scripts I commissioned without comment. His knowledge as a director was invaluable on the few occasions when novice directors literally could not plot their shots in the studio. But he seldom offered any critical judgement on performances or style, feeling that to do so would be an interference with the director's independence. Hence the productions were, as a whole, slack and without any distinctive flavour. The producer, in my opinion, must hold the arrogant belief that what he wants on the programme is right, and he must be prepared to fight to get it. Inevitably there will be conflicts with the director but, in my experience, mutual respect and good work usually come out of these conflicts.

When a producer goes to an outside rehearsal, he is not there to pat the actors and director on the back and tell them how talented they are. He is there to cast a completely objective eye on the production as a whole which, after several weeks' rehearsal, the director will not so easily be able to do. He is there to look for weaknesses and faults: a function that most directors appreciate, but which is not always designed to make the producer loved.

After three weeks of outside rehearsal (in the case of a seventy-five-minute 'Play for Today'), the play will move into the studio for three days of rehearsal with the sets and the cameras and, at the end of this period, the play will be recorded, usually in the evening of the third day (although the tendency to record in sections is increasing). For the first time the production will be seen in roughly the shape it is going to appear on the screen; the simple rehearsal script taken from the author will now have been broken down into a complex list of moves and shots, each one scripted for the five or six cameramen to use. Everyone on the studio floor will know, therefore, that when an actor says a certain line, Camera One will be showing a profile shot of him, and when he says another line Camera Six will be showing a three-shot of him and two other actors.

The producer is once more there in the role of critic. Time is running out, there can be no re-shooting of scenes the next day as in a film. This is the last chance, therefore, to get alterations made in the sets, costumes, make-up, in the shots, and performances. Such alterations are inevitably needed since, no matter how well planned a production is, things are bound to work out differently on camera than anticipated. The producer is there to confer with and help the director, to be responsible for emergency decisions with the technical managers, usually to do with completing the production in the allocated recording time. Throughout this operation he is somehow manoeuvring to make all the elements work together to produce the total effect he feels is right for the script.

He next confers with the director and editor on the editing together of the pieces of the show and, at last, it is ready to go out. The idea discussed with the writer months or even years before has now been transferred into pictures and sound.

Chapter 4

How to become a producer
by default

Channel 2 of the BBC started transmissions on 21 April 1964, an occasion that is well remembered from the power failure that preceded it and the joke that went around that Sir Lew Grade[1] had been seen leaving Battersea Power Station with a spanner.

'Story Parade' started three days later; the first drama programme designed especially for the second channel. The theory behind it seemed good, it was to be an anthology of modern fictional writing (as opposed to original dramatic writing).

Maurice Wiggin, reviewing the first programme in the *Sunday Times* (28 April 1964) wrote as follows: 'First comes "Story Parade", the dramatization of a novel a week. The supply of material should present no great difficulties and if they all come up anything like so entertaining as Max Frisch's *Condemned to Acquittal* this will become a hard date.'

It is always gratifying to get good reviews. This one, however, could not have been more ironic to me. Far from the 'supply of material' presenting no difficulties, it was almost impossible to get. This was still a relative golden age in the British film industry; consequently nearly every piece of fiction of any adaptability was under option to a film company, at a price well beyond our means. Authors like Max Frisch do not grow on trees and, as it turned out, his agent had made a slip-up in selling me the rights to this book, which was about to be made into a German film. Hence, we had to agree to destroy it immediately after transmission.

[1]Head of the commercial company ATV and a famous 'showman' who died in 1998.

Of those novels which were available, many were far too broad, in terms of locations and number of characters, ever to fit the physical and financial restrictions that were ours. Eventually, just over a year later, the programme was dropped for precisely these reasons. Among the properties left over was *The Raging Moon* by Peter Marshall about the romance of two young paraplegics. This I handed on to another programme where it was seen, and subsequently bought, for the film made by Bryan Forbes.

Of the twenty-four transmissions that did go out, including Muriel Spark's *The Bachelors*, which was probably a highlight, I have good reason to remember two: *The Unknown Citizen* by Tony Parker and *The Old Boys*[2] by William Trevor, two writers whom I met for the first time on this programme.

Tony Parker's book was brought to me by a writer friend of his, Philip Broadley, with whom I had worked at ABC. It was, of course, not fiction but a deeply moving account, based on interviews, of a recidivist, Charles Smith – an incurable petty criminal who had spent twenty-six of his fifty years in jail for the slenderest of crimes, simply because he was too inadequate to cope with the basic problems or relationships in life. It told how Carter, a compassionate businessman, had taken up Smith's case after reading of his re-arrest, while rifling mailbags at King's Cross station, on the very day of his release from jail. It explored Smith's background and the difficulties of attempting to rehabilitate someone so thoroughly institutionalized.

I bought the rights to the book and commissioned Philip Broadley to write the script. The book itself had upset me deeply; it was the first time I had ever thought about the problem of the rehabilitation of prisoners. The revelation that this man, of extremely low intelligence and with no friends, had been let out of prison with a sum of £1 2s 3½d and a railway warrant to the wrong town and had then been expected to re-enter society and make his way on his own, left me thunderstruck.

The director who was given the play was one of those young men, fresh from the training course, who would undoubtedly have risen to be a top-rank talent in a short time. His name was Bryan Stonehouse and immediately after the production was finished, at the suggestion of Victor Maddern, the actor who played Charlie Smith, he went off on a holiday to Majorca. There he was drowned.

---

[2] Davis-Poynter Playscript (1971).

For months, Victor Maddern tortured himself with the feeling that it was his fault. I, in turn, could not believe Bryan would not shortly return to do the next play we had discussed. I remembered that I had lent him a comb last time I saw him alive and have, since that day, always refused to lend one to anyone else.

William Trevor's book, *The Old Boys*, about a group of old men still fighting their school battles, struck me as one of the funniest and most original pieces of writing I had ever read. I bought the rights to it and commissioned Clive Exton to write the script. It went out in 1965 as the penultimate production of 'Story Parade', directed by Silvio Narizzano (who later directed the film *Georgie Girl*) and starring Roland Culver. Much later, in 1971, Trevor himself turned the book into a stage play which was put on at the Mermaid Theatre with Sir Michael Redgrave in the leading part of Jaraby. Such is the ephemeral nature of television that not one of the theatre critics seemed aware that the play had ever been televised.[3]

Also included in the programme was a science fiction story by Isaac Asimov, a detective story in which the detective was a robot – *The Caves of Steel*.

Science fiction of the 'adult', as opposed to the 'bug-eyed monster', kind had always been a pet subject of mine and while at ABC I had persuaded Sydney to let me get together an anthology series called 'Out of this World'. The series was produced by Leonard White and introduced by Boris Karloff and, when it went out in the summer of 1962, was counted a great success both by the ratings and the critics.

By far the greatest proportion of science fiction writing is, of course, semi-literate pulp fiction, but even amongst such stories there is sometimes a usable plot or idea to be found. At the other extreme, writers like Asimov, Arthur Clarke, Clifford Simak and Kurt Vonnegut undoubtedly provide some of the most original and philosophical ideas to be found in fiction writing today. Science fiction (for instance, the writings of Pohl and Kornbluth, authors of the *Space Merchants*) can also be an excellent satirical medium. To my mind, it is the nearest modern approach to the mediaeval romance, the fable and the work of such satirists as Swift. Much

---

[3]It is interesting to note that in this play, many years before Dennis Potter's *Blue Remembered Hills* we used the device of dressing the adult cast in school uniforms.

to my delight, after I had found the stories for the ABC series and started looking for adapters, I discovered that many first-rate writers like Clive Exton (and, as I discovered too late, David Mercer) were science fiction aficionados. It was, therefore, not difficult to find good adapters for the stories.

Two from this series stay particularly in my mind. *Target Generation* by Clifford Simak, adapted by Clive Exton and directed by Alan Cooke, about a closed community of people on a spaceship, 900 years out on a journey to another planet. So many generations had been born and died in the course of the journey that the goal of the mission had been forgotten and the bigoted community assumed theirs was the only way of life. The *Sunday Times* (Peter Laurie, 16 September 1962), reviewing this particular programme, reflected my own feelings about the story: 'This is what science fiction is good at: making us think about ourselves and our societies from the outside, making us realize that what we often assume is immutable is, in fact, only an adaptation to the very particular circumstances of our world. Soon, whether by technical development, or atomic war, or space travel, our civilization is going to be faced with new problems on a vast scale. Science fiction is one way of preparing to deal with them.'

Another point of view was expressed by John Russell Taylor, reviewing the series, in *The Times* on 4 August 1962: 'the role of science fiction today, despite an occasional excursion into comedy, usually seems to be vaguely analogous to that of the Gothic novel in the late eighteenth and early nineteenth centuries – to scare us out of our wits, and divert us thoroughly in the process'.

The other story I remember, *Pictures Don't Lie* by Katherine McLean, was about a radio operator who established contact with a spaceship, from another planet, heading towards Earth. On arrival, the spaceship could not be found. It, and its occupants, were microscopically small and were trampled underfoot by the desperate radio operator looking for them on the airfield. Both stories, of course, went out before the moon landings made space seem not so far away after all.

While 'Story Parade' was still on the air, Sydney and Michael Bakewell, who had left radio to become Head of Plays in television, asked me to find some more stories for a similar anthology science fiction series for the BBC. I had to find thirteen stories. (In the end, as it turned out, I was to produce twenty-six and line up another thirteen.)

I had discovered from 'Out of this World' that the best stories were those which were least ambitious in terms of costumes and machinery and concentrated on one simple 'allegorical' or satirical idea. I had also been astonished to find just how gullible an audience can be. For instance, one story, *Medicine Show*, had dealt with some men from outer space, who had superior medical knowledge, coming to earth and exchanging their medical powers for seeds. A host of letters poured in after the programme, asking for the addresses of the medicine men and whether they practised all types of medicine or only certain specialities. It is always difficult when producing non-realistic drama of any sort on television – fable, fantasy, allegory or satire – to get across to a certain section of the audience that it is not as real as the news they have just seen.

The great majority of leading science fiction writers, like Simak, Asimov, Bradbury etc., are American. It was proving difficult to sort out the copyright on a lot of the stories and it was finally decided that I should go to New York and deal with the agents and writers directly and look for more stories while I was there. At this point, I had a historic (for me) interview with Sydney. I had written him a memo reminding him of the fact that nine months had come and gone and nothing had been said about my being considered as a producer. I had asked if it was necessary for me to shoot my way past his secretary to get to see him and I had generally implied that I had been brought to the BBC on false pretences. Counting himself safe on the eve of my departure for America, Sydney granted me an audience.

In ABC days, he had always been known to develop laryngitis and to go home to build model atomic submarines and aeroplanes when he didn't want to discuss something unpleasant. On this occasion, he began by telling me what a hard day he had had, what a hard time Philip Saville, who had just left his office, flushed and perspiring, was giving him and how he hoped I wasn't going to add to his troubles. When, choked with the memory of my Kafka-like year and a half of frustration and isolation, I reminded him of the codicil in my contract, he blandly informed me that he really didn't think I had it in me to be a producer. He then advised me to go off to America and enjoy myself and rang his secretary to ask for Andrew Osborn, the Head of Series, his voice growing more laryngitic and his aspect more pathetic as he did so.

One of Sydney's recurrent ways of treating his protegées was to remind them, like a wounded parent, of their base ingratitude. One (possibly apocryphal) story was that on such an occasion with Ted Kotcheff, the following dialogue had taken place:

Sydney. 'You ungrateful guy. I brought you up from the gutter.'
Ted. 'From the gutter to you is *up?*'

With me his approach was usually to tell me that he (unlike 'dissatisfied me') had leapt at the offer of a job for seventeen dollars a week at the Canadian Film Board, although he was already a trained commercial artist. On another occasion, at ABC, he had cried out in pain to me, 'I'm so Goddamned sick of being father figure to a bunch of neurotics.'

I now have a deep-seated superstition about transatlantic trips. Every time I have taken one, things have changed radically in my life. I had only been in New York a few days when a telegram was delivered to me at the hotel. It was to tell me that Andrew Osborn wanted me to transfer from Plays to Series to edit and be *assistant producer* on thirteen stories by Georges Simenon. Andrew Osborn had been Sydney's next visitor after my interview and it was obvious that Sydney had made this suggestion to him while discussing the question of who should do this series, a follow-up to *Maigret*.

I had, meanwhile, become absorbed in meeting all the science fiction agents and writers I could find in New York. I had arranged to buy some more stories from Asimov, one of the most interesting and amusing men I have ever met. I had been offered a trip to meet a 'male witch' by John W. Campbell who published *Analog* and whose offices reminded me of nothing so much as those of Danny Kaye in *The Secret Life of Walter Mitty*; one way and another the earnest realities of Television Centre seemed far away.

Before I had had a chance to ponder the change of course from outer space to provincial France, a second telegram arrived. It was from Michael Bakewell. On no account did he want me to leave his department; he wanted me not only to story-edit the science fiction series but to produce it – a schizophrenic situation indeed, especially as I had seriously thought of trying to remain in the United States and picking up the traces from old Encyclopaedia Britannica days.

Being a fatalist, I decided there was nothing I could do at 3,000 miles' range. On my return it had all been decided for me. I was to produce the science fiction series and, as it turned out, also the Simenon stories, which were later taken over by Plays.

It was on these two programmes, 'Out of the Unknown' and 'Thirteen Against Fate', that I cut my teeth as a producer, but as they are outside the province of this book, I shall take a leap forward in time to the days of 'Wednesday Play'.

Chapter 5

The birth of 'Wednesday Play'

'Wednesday Play', under that title, was officially born in 1964. As described in Chapter 3, Sydney Newman, on his arrival at the BBC, had decided to channel single plays into two different programmes. 'First Night' and 'Festival'. The successors of these two programmes were 'Wednesday Play', on Channel 1, later called 'Play for Today' when transmission night was changed to Thursday, and 'Theatre 625' on Channel 2.

'First Night', which showed the work of many authors later found on 'Wednesday Play', came in for all the accusations later levelled at that programme. The *Evening Standard*, on 29 July 1964, for instance, accused it of having the tendency 'too often to mistake sleaziness for sensitivity'; 'Festival', on the other hand, with its diet of Cocteau, Beckett, Ionesco and Durrenmatt, was thought to be too esoteric, even for a minority audience. Sydney Newman, by changing the name of 'First Night', obviously hoped to give it a new image. His election promise for it in the press (*Daily Telegraph*, 11 December 1964) was that in the new series there would be less of the 'kitchen sink', more strong storylines, and less sex. James MacTaggart, a director who had been producing 'Teletales', an 'experimental' programme of adaptations done in a more narrative style than usual, was to become the new producer. The style of 'Teletales' was to carry over very much into MacTaggart's season of 'Wednesday Play'.

The following list of all the programmes in both 'Wednesday Play' and 'Play for Today', from October 1964 to December 1972, will give the reader an idea of the changes of producer and of who the writers and directors associated with the programme have been.

Plays marked + were specially written for television.

TRANSMISSION DATE	TITLE	AUTHOR	PRODUCER	DIRECTOR
28.10.64	A CRACK IN THE ICE	Nikolai Leskov/ Ronald Eyre	Peter Luke	Ronald Eyre
4.11.64	IN CAMERA	Jean-Paul Sartre/ Stuart Gilbert	Peter Luke	Philip Saville
18.11.64	THE BIG BREAKER +	Alun Richards	Peter Luke	Charles Jarrott
25.11.64	MR DOUGLAS +	John Prebble	Peter Luke	Gilchrist Calder
2.12.64	MALATESTA	Henry de Montherlant/ Jonathan Griffin	Peter Luke	Christopher Morahan
9.12.64	THE JULY PLOT	Roger Manvell/ Heinrich Fraenkel	Peter Luke	Rudolph Cartier
6.1.65	TAP ON THE SHOULDER +	James O'Connor	James MacTaggart	Kenneth Loach
13.1.65	SIR JOCELYN, THE MINISTER WOULD LIKE A WORD +	Simon Raven	James MacTaggart	Stuart Burge
20.1.65	THE NAVIGATORS +	Julia Jones	James MacTaggart	Vivian Matalon
27.1.65	FABLE +	John Hopkins	James MacTaggart	Christopher Morahan
3.2.65	DAN, DAN, THE CHARITY MAN +	Hugh Whitemore	James MacTaggart	Don Taylor
10.2.65	ASHES TO ASHES +	Marc Brandel	James MacTaggart	Alan Cooke
17.2.65	WEAR A VERY BIG HAT +	Eric Coltart	James MacTaggart	Kenneth Loach

TRANSMISSION DATE	TITLE	AUTHOR	PRODUCER	DIRECTOR
24.2.65	THE CONFIDENCE COURSE +	Dennis Potter	James MacTaggart	Gilchrist Calder
3.3.65	CAMPAIGN FOR ONE +	Marielaine Douglas/ Anthony Church	James MacTaggart	Moira Armstrong
10.3.65	HORROR OF DARKNESS +	John Hopkins	James MacTaggart	Anthony Page
17.3.65	A LITTLE TEMPTATION +	Thomas Clarke	James MacTaggart	Peter Duguid
24.3.65	MOVING ON +	Bill Meilen	James MacTaggart	Brian Parker
31.3.65	CAT'S CRADLE +	Hugo Charteris	James MacTaggart	Henric Hirsch
7.4.65	THREE CLEAR SUNDAYS +	James O'Connor	James MacTaggart	Kenneth Loach
14.4.65	THE INTERIOR DECORATOR +	Jack Russell	James MacTaggart	James Ferman
21.4.65	AUTO-STOP +	Alan Seymour	James MacTaggart	Brian Parker
28.4.65	THE GOOD SHOEMAKER AND THE POOR FISH PEDDLER	Jean Benedetti	James MacTaggart	John Gorrie
5.5.65	CEMENTED WITH LOVE +	Sam Thompson	Peter Luke	M. Leeston-Smith
12.5.65	A KNIGHT IN TARNISHED ARMOUR +	Alan Sharp	James MacTaggart	John Gorrie
26.5.65	FOR THE WEST +	Michael Hastings	James MacTaggart	Toby Robertson
2.6.65	AND DID THOSE FEET? +	David Mercer	James MacTaggart	Don Taylor
9.6.65	THE MAN WITHOUT PAPERS +	Troy Kennedy Martin	James MacTaggart	Peter Duguid

TRANSMISSION DATE	TITLE	AUTHOR	PRODUCER	DIRECTOR
13.10.65	ALICE +	Dennis Potter	James MacTaggart	Gareth Davies
20.10.65	THE GIRL WHO LOVED ROBOTS +	Peter Everett	James MacTaggart	Brian Parker
27.10.65	A DESIGNING WOMAN +	Julia Jones	James MacTaggart	Kenneth Loach
3.11.65	UP THE JUNCTION +	Nell Dunn	James MacTaggart	Kenneth Loach
10.11.65	THE TRIAL AND TORTURE OF SIR JOHN RAMPAYNE +	Alan Seymour	James MacTaggart	Peter Duguid
17.11.65	THE END OF ARTHUR'S MARRIAGE +	Christopher Logue	James MacTaggart	Kenneth Loach
24.11.65	TOMORROW, JUST YOU WAIT +	Fred Watson	James MacTaggart	James Ferman
1.12.65	THE BOND +	Dawn Pavitt/ Terry Wale	James MacTaggart	Mary Ridge
8.12.65	STAND UP, NIGEL BARTON +	Dennis Potter	James MacTaggart	Gareth Davies
15.12.65	VOTE, VOTE, VOTE FOR NIGEL BARTON +	Dennis Potter	James MacTaggart	Gareth Davies
22.12.65	THE COMING OUT PARTY +	James O'Connor	James MacTaggart	Kenneth Loach
5.1.66	THE BONEYARD +	Clive Exton	Peter Luke	James MacTaggart
12.1.66	A MAN ON HER BACK	William Sansom/ Peter Luke	Peter Luke	Waris Hussein

TRANSMISSION DATE	TITLE	AUTHOR	PRODUCER	DIRECTOR
19.1.66	RODNEY, OUR INTREPID HERO +	Brian Finch/	Peter Luke	Michael Simpson
26.1.66	CALF LOVE	Vernon Bartlett/ Philip Purser	Peter Luke	Gilchrist Calder
2.2.66	SILENT SONG	Frank O'Connor/ Hugh Leonard	Peter Luke	Charles Jarrot
9.2.66	WHO'S A GOOD BOY THEN, I AM +	Richard Harris	Peter Luke	James Ferman
16.2.66	A GAME LIKE – ONLY A GAME +	John Hopkins	Peter Luke	Christopher Morahan
23.2.66	WHY AREN'T YOU FAMOUS +	Ernie Gebler	Peter Luke	Peter Sasdy
2.3.66	MACREADY'S GALA +	Hugh Whitemore	Peter Luke	Waris Hussein
9.3.66	A WALK IN THE SEA +	James Hanley	Peter Luke	Geoffrey Nethercott
16.3.66	BOY IN THE SMOKE +	Patrick Galvin	Peter Luke	William Slater
23.3.66	BARLOWE OF THE CAR PARK +	Paul Ableman	Peter Luke	Gareth Davies
30.3.66	THE PORTSMOUTH DEFENCE +	Nemone Lethbridge	Peter Luke	James MacTaggart
6.4.66	PITY ABOUT THE ABBEY +	John Betjeman/ Stewart Farrar	Peter Luke	Ian Curteis
13.4.66	THE BIG MAN COUGHED AND DIED +	Brian Wright	Peter Luke	Peter Duguid

46

TRANSMISSION DATE	TITLE	AUTHOR	PRODUCER	DIRECTOR
20.4.66	THE SNOW BALL	Brigid Brophy/ Ursula Gray	Peter Luke	Charles Jarrott
27.4.66	A CHEERY SOUL +	Patrick White/ J. Anthony	Peter Luke	Gilchrist Calder
4.5.66	THE CONNOISSEUR +	Hugo Charteris	Peter Luke	Waris Hussein
11.5.66	THE RETREAT +	Hugh Leonard	Peter Luke	Charles Jarrott
18.5.66	APE AND ESSENCE	Aldous Huxley/ John Finch	Peter Luke	David Benedictus
25.5.66	TODDLER ON THE RUN	Shena Mackay	Peter Luke	James MacTaggart
1.6.66	THE EXECUTIONER	Robert Muller/ Isaac Don Levene	Peter Luke	Michael Hayes
8.6.66	WAY OFF BEAT +	David Turner	James MacTaggart	Toby Robertson
15.6.66	A SOIREE AT BOSSOM'S HOTEL +	Simon Raven	Peter Luke	Gilchrist Calder
22.6.66	COCK, HEN AND COURTING PIT +	David Halliwell	Peter Luke	Charles Jarrott
12.10.66	THE FRIGHTENERS +	Daniel Farson	Peter Luke	Gilchrist Calder
19.10.66	A PIECE OF RESISTANCE +	Terence Dudley	Cedric Messina	Geoffrey Nethercott
2.11.66	WHERE THE BUFFALO ROAM +	Dennis Potter	Lionel Harris	Gareth Davies
9.11.66	THE HEAD WAITER +	John Mortimer	Lionel Harris	Rex Tucker
16.11.66	CATHY, COME HOME +	Jeremy Sandford	Tony Garnett	Kenneth Loach
23.11.66	THE PRIVATE TUTOR +	Christopher Williams	Lionel Harris	Alan Gibson

TRANSMISSION DATE	TITLE	AUTHOR	PRODUCER	DIRECTOR
30.11.66	A PYRE FOR PRIVATE JAMES +	Simon Raven	Lionel Harris	Gilchrist Calder
14.12.66	THE LITTLE MASTER MIND +	Nemone Lethbridge	Tony Garnett	James MacTaggart
21.12.66	THE MAYFLY AND THE FROG +	Jack Russell	Lionel Harris	Robin Midgley
4.1.67	PERSON TO PERSON +	Joan Henry	Lionel Harris	Raymond Menmuir
25.1.67	EVERYONE'S RICH EXCEPT US +	Thomas Clarke	Lionel Harris	Brian Parker
1.2.67	THE LUMP +	Jim Allen	Tony Garnett	Jack Gold
8.2.67	WHO'S GOING TO TAKE ME ON? +	Andrew Davies	Lionel Harris	John Glenister
15.2.67	DEATH OF A TEDDY BEAR +	Simon Gray	Lionel Harris	Waris Hussein
1.3.67	IN TWO MINDS +	David Mercer	Tony Garnett	Kenneth Loach
8.3.67	ANOTHER DAY, ANOTHER DOLLAR +	Michael Standing	Lionel Harris	Raymond Menmuir
15.3.67	PUBLIC ENQUIRY +	Raymond Williams	Lionel Harris	Gareth Davies
22.3.67	A CRUCIAL WEEK IN THE LIFE OF A GROCER'S ASSISTANT +	Thomas Murphy	Lionel Harris	James MacTaggart

TRANSMISSION DATE	TITLE	AUTHOR	PRODUCER	DIRECTOR
29.3.67	A BREACH IN THE WALL +	Ray Lawler	Lionel Harris	Gilchrist Calder
5.4.67	THE VOICES IN THE PARK +	Leon Griffiths	Tony Garnett	John MacKenzie
12.4.67	DISMISSAL LEADING TO LUSTFULNESS +	Thomas Whyte	Lionel Harris	Rex Tucker
19.4.67	A BRILLIANT FUTURE BEHIND HIM +	Thomas Clarke	Lionel Harris	Robert Fleming
3.5.67	MESSAGE FOR POSTERITY +	Dennis Potter	Lionel Harris	Gareth Davies
10.5.67	A WAY WITH THE LADIES	Celia Dale/ Simon Gray	Lionel Harris	John Glenister
17.5.67	THE PLAYGROUND +	Hunter Davies	Lionel Harris	John Robbins
24.5.67	DRUMS ALONG THE AVON +	Charles Wood	Tony Garnett	James MacTaggart
11.10.67	SLEEPING DOG +	Simon Gray	Graeme MacDonald	Waris Hussein
18.10.67	WANTED: SINGLE GENTLEMAN . . . +	James Broom Lynne	Irene Shubik	John Gorrie
25.10.67	A BLACK CANDLE FOR MRS GOGARTY +	Edward Boyd	Pharic MacLaren	Pharic MacLaren
8.11.67	THE DEVIL A MONK WOULD BE	Peter Luke/ Alphonse Daudet	Lionel Harris	Waris Hussein
15.11.67	FALL OF THE GOAT +	Fay Weldon	Graeme McDonald	Gilchrist Calder

TRANSMISSION DATE	TITLE	AUTHOR	PRODUCER	DIRECTOR
22.11.67	THE PROFILE OF A GENTLEMAN +	Jimmy O'Connor	Graeme McDonald	John MacKenzie
29.11.67	DIAL RUDOLPH VALENTINO ONE ONE +	Ewart Alexander	Graeme McDonald	Gareth Davies
6.12.67	KIPPERS AND CURTAINS +	Vickery Turner	Lionel Harris	Alan Gibson
13.12.67	DEATH OF A PRIVATE	Robert Muller/ Georg Büchner	Irene Shubik	James Ferman
20.12.67	AN OFFICER OF THE COURT +	Nemone Lethbridge	Tony Garnett	James MacTaggart
27.12.67	THE FAT OF THE LAND +	Jack Russell	Graeme McDonald	Toby Robertson
3.1.68	TOGGLE +	Ian Roberts	Graeme McDonald	Waris Hussein
10.1.68	HOUSE OF CHARACTER +	David Rudkin	Irene Shubik	Alan Cooke
17.1.68	JAMIE, ON A FLYING VISIT +	Michael Frayn	Graeme McDonald	Claude Whatham
24.1.68	MONSIEUR BARNETT	Jean Anouilh/ Lucienne Hill	Lionel Harris	Donald McWhinnie
31.1.68	THE DRUMMER AND THE BLOKE +	Rhys Adrian	Irene Shubik	Herbert Wise
7.2.68	REBEL IN THE GRAVE +	Marc Brandel	Lionel Harris	Raymond Menmuir
21.2.68	COINCIDENCE +	Piers Paul Read	Graeme McDonald	Moira Armstrong
3.4.68	LIGHT BLUE +	Gerald Vaughan-Hughes	Graeme McDonald	Alan Cooke

TRANSMISSION DATE	TITLE	AUTHOR	PRODUCER	DIRECTOR
10.4.68	LET'S MURDER VIVALDI +	David Mercer	Graeme McDonald	Alan Bridges
17.4.68	THE GOLDEN VISION +	Neville Smith/Gordon Honeycombe	Tony Garnett	Kenneth Loach
1.5.68	THE MAN BEHIND YOU +	Jeremy Scott	Irene Shubik	Moira Armstrong
8.5.68	INFIDELITY TOOK PLACE +	John Mortimer	Irene Shubik	Michael Hayes
21.8.68	MRS LAWRENCE WILL LOOK AFTER IT +	Tony Parker	Irene Shubik	John MacKenzie
28.8.68	SPOILED +	Simon Gray	Graeme McDonald	Waris Hussein
4.9.68	THE GORGE +	Peter Nichols	Tony Garnett	Christopher Morahan
11.9.68	A NIGHT WITH MRS DA TANKA +	William Trevor	Irene Shubik	John Gorrie
18.9.68	CHARLIE +	Alun Owen	Irene Shubik	Michael Hayes
25.9.68	ANYONE FOR TENNIS? +	J. B. Priestley	Graeme McDonald	Claude Whatham
2.10.68	MOONEY AND HIS CARAVANS	Peter Terson	Irene Shubik	James Ferman
9.10.68	THE LOWER LARGO SEQUENCE +	Edward Boyd	Pharic MacLaren	Pharic MacLaren
16.10.68	HELLO, GOOD EVENING AND WELCOME +	Hugh Whitemore	Graeme McDonald	Claude Whatham
30.10.68	A BIT OF CRUCIFIXION, FATHER +	Julia Jones	Graeme McDonald	Geoffrey Nethercott

TRANSMISSION DATE	TITLE	AUTHOR	PRODUCER	DIRECTOR
6.11.68	NOTHING WILL BE THE SAME AGAIN +	James Hanley	Irene Shubik	Peter Hammond
20.11.68	A BEAST WITH TWO BACKS +	Dennis Potter	Graeme McDonald	Lionel Harris
27.11.68	ON THE EVE OF PUBLICATION +	David Mercer	Graeme McDonald	Alan Bridges
4.12.68	SWORD OF HONOUR Part 1: 'Men at Arms'	Evelyn Waugh/ Giles Cooper	Michael Bakewell	Donald McWhinnie
11.12.68	SWORD OF HONOUR Part 2: 'Officers and Gentlemen'	Evelyn Waugh/ Giles Cooper	Michael Bakewell	Donald McWhinnie
18.12.68	SWORD OF HONOUR Part 3: 'Unconditional Surrender'	Evelyn Waugh Giles Cooper	Michael Bakewell	Donald McWhinnie
8.1.69	THE FABULOUS FRUMP +	James Gibbins	Irene Shubik	Peter Hammond
15.1.69	SMOKESCREEN +	Fay Weldon	Graeme McDonald	Donald McWhinnie
22.1.69	DR AITKINSON's DAUGHTER +	Hugo Charteris	Graeme McDonald	Gilchrist Calder
29.1.69	THE APPRENTICES	Peter Terson	Graeme McDonald	James Ferman
12.2.69	BIRTHDAY +	Michael Frayn	Graeme McDonald	Claude Whatham
19.2.69	THE BIG FLAME +	Jim Allen	Tony Garnett	Ken Loach
26.2.69	A SERPENT IN PUTNEY +	Fred Watson	Graeme McDonald	Geoffrey Nethercott

51

TRANSMISSION DATE	TITLE	AUTHOR	PRODUCER	DIRECTOR
5.3.69	BAM! POW! ZAPP! +	Nigel Kneale	Graeme McDonald	William Slater
1.4.69	SLING YOUR HOOK +	Roy Minton	Irene Shubik	Michael Tuchner
9.4.69	A CHILD AND A HALF +	Owen Holder	Graeme McDonald	Alan Bridges
16.4.69	SON OF MAN +	Dennis Potter	Graeme McDonald	Gareth Davies
23.4.69	THE EXILES +	Errol John	Irene Shubik	Herbert Wise
30.4.69	BLODWEN, HOME FROM RACHEL'S MARRIAGE +	David Rudkin	Irene Shubik	Alan Cooke
6.8.69	THE PARACHUTE +	David Mercer	Tony Garnett	Anthony Page
24.9.69	PITCHI POI +	Francois Billetdoux/ Peter Meyer	Michael Bakewell	Roderick Graham
1.10.69	THE LAST TRAIN THROUGH THE HARECASTLE TUNNEL +	Peter Terson	Irene Shubik	Alan Clarke
8.10.69	PATTERSON O.K. +	Ray Jenkins	Pharic MacLaren	Pharic MacLaren
15.10.69	THE MARK II WIFE +	William Trevor	Irene Shubik	Philip Saville
22.10.69	CLOSE THE COALHOUSE DOOR	Sid Chaplin/ Alan Plater	Graeme McDonald	Bill Hays
29.10.69	THE SAD DECLINE OF ARTHUR MAYBURY +	John Gorrie	Irene Shubik	John Gorrie
5.11.69	ALL OUT FOR KANGAROO VALLEY +	Noel Robinson	Irene Shubik	Bill Bain

TRANSMISSION DATE	TITLE	AUTHOR	PRODUCER	DIRECTOR
12.11.69	HAPPY +	Alan Gosling	Irene Shubik	Marc Miller
17.11.69	THERE IS ALSO TOMORROW +	Hugo Charteris	Graeme McDonald	John MacKenzie
26.11.69	DOUBLE BILL + 'The Compartment' 'Playmates'	Johnny Speight	Graeme McDonald	John McGrath
3.12.69	THE BLOOD OF THE LAMB +	Leon Whiteson	Graeme McDonald	Alan Bridges
10.12.69	THE VORTEX	Noel Coward	Graeme McDonald	Philip Dudley
17.12.69	IT WASN'T ME +	James Hanley	Irene Shubik	James Ferman
7.1.70	SEASON OF THE WITCH +	Desmond McCarthy/ Johnny Byrne	Anne Head	Desmond McCarthy
14.1.70	MILLE MIGLIA +	Athol Fugard	Ronald Travers	Robin Midgley
21.1.70	THE HUNTING OF LIONEL CRANE +	Roy Minton	Irene Shubik	Michael Tuchner
28.1.70	REST IN PEACE, UNCLE FRED +	Alan Plater	Graeme McDonald	Michael Hayes
4.2.70	MAD JACK +	Tom Clarke	Graeme McDonald	Jack Gold
11.2.70	NATHAN AND TABILETH +	Barry Bermange	Gerald Savory	David Koning
18.2.70	THE ITALIAN TABLE +	William Trevor	Irene Shubik	Herbert Wise
25.2.70	THE BOY WHO WANTED PEACE	George Friel	Pharic MacLaren	Pharic MacLaren

TRANSMISSION DATE	TITLE	AUTHOR	PRODUCER	DIRECTOR
4.3.70	THE CELLAR AND THE ALMOND TREE +	David Mercer	Graeme McDonald	Alan Bridges
11.3.70	THE YEAR OF THE SEX OLYMPICS +	Nigel Kneale	Ronald Travers	Michael Elliott
18.3.70	NO TRAMS TO LIME STREET	Alun Owen/ Marty Wilde/ Ronnie Scott	Harry Moore	Piers Haggard
25.3.70	TO SEE HOW FAR IT IS Part 1: 'Murphy's Law'	Alan Plater	Michael Bakewell	Roderick Graham
1.4.70	TO SEE HOW FAR IT IS Part 2: 'The Curse of the Donkins'	Alan Plater	Michael Bakewell	Gilchrist Calder
8.4.70	TO SEE HOW FAR IT IS Part 3: 'To See How Far It Is'	Alan Plater	Michael Bakewell	Naomi Capon
15.4.70	WINE OF INDIA +	Nigel Kneale	Graeme McDonald	Gilchrist Calder
22.4.70	SOVEREIGN'S COMPANY +	Don Shaw	Irene Shubik	Alan Clarke
29.4.70	PARTY GAMES +	Hugh Whitemore	Michael Bakewell	Roderick Graham
13.5.70	EMMA'S TIME +	David Mercer	Graeme McDonald	Alan Bridges
20.5.70	CHARIOT OF FIRE +	Tony Parker	Irene Shubik	James Ferman
29.5.70	JOAN +	Alun Owen	Ronald Travers	Alan Clarke

TRANSMISSION DATE	TITLE	AUTHOR	PRODUCER	DIRECTOR
15.10.70	THE LONG DISTANCE PIANO PLAYER +	Alan Sharp	Irene Shubik	Philip Saville
22.10.70	THE RIGHT PROSPECTUS +	John Osborne	Irene Shubik	Alan Cooke
29.10.70	THE LARGEST THEATRE IN THE WORLD – THE LIE +	Ingmar Bergman/ Paul Britten Austin	Graeme McDonald	Alan Bridges
5.11.70	ANGELS ARE SO FEW +	Dennis Potter	Graeme McDonald	Gareth Davies
12.11.70	THE WRITE-OFF	George Salverson	Robert Allan	Rudi Dorin
19.11.70	I CAN'T SEE MY LITTLE WILLIE +	Douglas Livingstone	Irene Shubik	Alan Clarke
26.11.70	A DISTANT THUNDER +	Maurice Edelman	Irene Shubik	James Ferman
3.12.70	HEARTS AND FLOWERS +	Peter Nichols	Irene Shubik	Christopher Morahan
10.12.70	ROBIN REDBREAST +	John Bowen	Graeme McDonald	James MacTaggart
17.12.70	THE HALLELUJAH HANDSHAKE +	Colin Welland	Graeme McDonald	Alan Clarke
7.1.71	ALMA MATER +	David Hodson	Irene Shubik/ Ann Kirch	James Ferman
14.1.71	CIRCLE LINE +	W. Stephen Gilbert	Graeme McDonald	Claude Whatham
21.1.71	HELL'S ANGEL +	David Agnew	Graeme McDonald	Alan Cooke
28.1.71	THE PIANO +	Julia Jones	Graeme McDonald	James Cellan Jones

55

TRANSMISSION DATE	TITLE	AUTHOR	PRODUCER	DIRECTOR
4.2.71	BILLY'S LAST STAND +	Barry Hines	Graeme McDonald	John Glenister
11.2.71	THE LARGEST THEATRE IN THE WORLD – THE RAINBIRDS +	Clive Exton	Irene Shubik	Philip Saville
18.2.71	REDDICK	Munroe Scott	Robert Allen	Mervyn Rosenzveig
25.3.71	SCENES FROM FAMILY LIFE	Barry Bermange	Ronald Travers	Naomi Capon
1.4.71	WIND VERSUS POLYGAMY	Obi Egbuna	Michael Bakewell	Naomi Capon
29.4.71	THE FOXTROT +	Rhys Adrian	Irene Shubik	Philip Saville
6.5.71	WHEN THE BOUGH BREAKS +	Tony Parker	Irene Shubik	James Ferman
13.5.71	ORKNEY – THREE STORIES 1: 'A Time to Keep' 2: 'The Whaler's Return' 3: 'Celia'	George MacKay Brown/ John McGrath	Graeme McDonald	James MacTaggart
20.5.71	THE RANK AND FILE +	Jim Allen	Graeme McDonald	Kenneth Loach
27.5.71	THE MAN IN THE SIDECAR +	Simon Gray	Graeme McDonald	James MacTaggart
3.6.71	EVERYBODY SAY CHEESE +	Douglas Livingstone	Irene Shubik	Alan Clarke
14.10.71	TRAITOR +	Dennis Potter	Graeme McDonald	Alan Bridges

TRANSMISSION DATE	TITLE	AUTHOR	PRODUCER	DIRECTOR
21.10.71	EDNA, THE INEBRIATE WOMAN +	Jeremy Sandford	Irene Shubik	Ted Kotcheff
28.10.71	EVELYN +	Rhys Adrian	Graeme McDonald	Piers Haggard
4.11.71	O FAT WHITE WOMAN +	William Trevor	Irene Shubik	Philip Saville
11.11.71	THANK YOU VERY MUCH +	N. F. Simpson	Graeme McDonald	Claude Whatham
18.11.71	MICHAEL REGAN +	Robert Holles	Irene Shubik	John Gorrie
25.11.71	SKIN DEEP +	Michael O'Neill/ Jeremy Seabrook	Graeme McDonald	Michael Lindsay-Hogg
2.12.71	PAL +	Alun Owen	Irene Shubik	Silvio Narizzano
9.12.71	THE PIGEON FANCIER +	Peter Hankin	Irene Shubik	James Ferman
6.1.72	HOME NET/CBC	David Storey	Lindsay Anderson	
13.1.72	STILL WATERS +	Julia Jones	Graeme McDonald	James MacTaggart
20.1.72	STOCKER'S COPPER +	Tom Clarke	Graeme McDonald	Jack Gold
27.1.72	THE HOUSE ON HIGHBURY HILL +	Piers Paul Read	Graeme McDonald	John Glenister
3.2.72	IN THE BEAUTIFUL CARIBBEAN +	Barry Reckord	Irene Shubik	Philip Saville

TRANSMISSION DATE	TITLE	AUTHOR	PRODUCER	DIRECTOR
10.2.72	ACKERMAN, DOUGALL AND HARKER +	Don Shaw	Irene Shubik	Ted Kotcheff
17.2.72	THE VILLA MAROC +	Willis Hall	Irene Shubik	Herbert Wise
24.2.72	COWS +	Howard Barker	Graeme McDonald	John Gorrie
1.6.72	THE FISHING PARTY +	Peter Terson	David Rose	Michael Simpson
9.10.72	THE REPORTERS +	Arthur Hopcraft	Graeme McDonald	Michael Apted
16.10.72	A LIFE IS FOR EVER +	Tony Parker	Irene Shubik	Alan Clarke
23.10.72	CARSON COUNTRY +	Dominic Behan	Graeme McDonald	Piers Haggard
30.10.72	MAN FRIDAY +	Adrian Mitchell	Graeme McDonald	James MacTaggart
6.11.72	TRIPLE EXPOSURE +	David Halliwell	Irene Shubik	Alan Cooke
13.11.72	BETTER THAN THE MOVIES +	John Elliot	Graeme McDonald	Roy Battersby
20.11.72	THE GENERAL'S DAY +	William Trevor	Irene Shubik	John Gorrie
27.11.72	THE BANKRUPT +	David Mercer	Graeme McDonald	Christopher Morahan
4.12.72	JUST YOUR LUCK +	Peter McDougall	Graeme McDonald	Mike Newell
11.12.72	THE BOUNCING BOY +	John McGrath	Graeme McDonald	Maurice Hatton

The list starts with some orphaned productions left over from Peter Luke's 'Festival', which was killed off, along with 'First Night', which show clearly Peter Luke's literary tastes. It then starts, in January 1965, with the MacTaggart season. Sydney Newman's desired 'Gutsy, spontaneous contemporaneity' is immediately in evidence, in a play by James O'Connor, who was notorious for having once been convicted as a murderer. Many other writers on the list are names used on 'First Night'.

Certainly the image of the programme was changing only to become more extreme in all the areas for which 'First Night' had been attacked. For example, *For the West*, by Michael Hastings, a play about the Belgian Congo massacres, was so bloody in its presentation that it aroused enormous protest.

In an interview in *The Stage* on 16 May 1968, Sydney said retrospectively of the production, 'I was very upset . . . I thought that was a disgrace. It didn't help our understanding of the black movement for liberation. . . . In addition, the play involved an act of gross cruelty to a child, and I don't think anyone becomes emotionally or morally richer by seeing that sort of thing.' In a sense, the 'Wednesday Play', with productions like this, was attempting a tabloid approach to the audience and succeeding in selling itself on sex, violence and the sensational. Probably the best remembered play of the season was *Up the Junction* with its abortion scene; now the programme was attaining an image of presenting 'social conscience' and 'working-class' (an alternative name for 'kitchen sink') drama.

In 1966 the programme was back in the hands of Peter Luke. If anyone wonders what a producer has to do with a programme let him compare the Luke productions with the MacTaggart ones. Peter Luke frankly avowed that he did not consider television drama a suitable platform for politics; his approach, after the 'raw' season which preceded him, was that of a 'scholar and a gentleman'. The names of some of his contributors – Frank O'Connor, James Hanley, John Betjeman, Patrick White, Huxley, Simon Raven, are all ones associated more with publishers' lists than front page stories of murder trials, abortion and massacre. The audience gets what the producer's taste selects from what the writers offer or are encouraged to write.

After this season, Peter Luke retired to Spain and to the outstanding success of his stage play *Hadrian VII*, describing his departure from television in an article in *The Listener*, on 12

September 1968, entitled 'Peter Luke used to be a television producer. Then he escaped'.

James MacTaggart also escaped – back to directing. The turnover of producers on such programmes is rapid, for the strains, especially of finding enough workable scripts, are enormous. I was to remember, once on the programme, how James MacTaggart, a very strong and stocky Scot, described to me the feeling of waking up in the middle of the night covered in sweat, with fists clenched, wondering where he would get a script to put into production next week; a feeling I was to come to know well.

The next names on the list are those of Lionel Harris and Tony Garnett and, again, if anyone wonders what a producer has to do with a programme let him compare the choices of these two.

Lionel Harris is a director who has worked much in the theatre and was especially associated with the impresario 'Binkie' Beaumont'. John Mortimer, Simon Gray and Ray Lawler (author of *Summer of the Seventeenth Doll*) were, therefore, natural choices for him.

Tony Garnett, with whom he was sharing the programme, had been story-editing on the MacTaggart season of 'Wednesday Play', had strongly avowed political views and a strongly avowed social conscience. *Cathy, Come Home* about the homeless, *In Two Minds* about mental illness, were, therefore, natural choices of subject for him, while a more 'entertainment'-orientated producer might have shunned them as too 'downbeat'.

Garnett had managed to get himself into that most enviable position of any producer; that of doing only a very few productions a year which were to be blockbusters in that they could be made entirely on film. To be relieved of the pressure of constantly finding an enormous amount of new material is the greatest luxury anyone on television can have and the condition most conducive to good work. For the social conscience, 'drama-documentary' type of play, obviously a realistic film background is an essential element. Garnett had managed to achieve both these conditions for himself with outstanding results. *Cathy, Come Home*, which had originally been brought to the BBC three years before by Ted Kotcheff, was turned down by Sydney Newman as too downbeat and too costly; by the time it was re-offered by Garnett and Loach, the climate and the availability of film had changed and, with it, the writing and presentation style of much of television drama.

Between the time when I had begun editing 'Armchair Theatre' and the time when I was to come to 'Wednesday Play' in 1967, enormous changes had occurred both technically and in the style of writing for television. As described in Chapter 2, tape-editing on 'Armchair Theatre' was, to begin with, unheard of and used sparingly, even as it improved technically. Plays, therefore, had to be fairly well made; they had to be recorded strictly in sequence, strictly within a very limited recording time, and often 'filler' scenes had to be written to enable actors to get from one set to another or to change clothes. The writer, therefore, had to be a very careful craftsman.

By 1967, tape editing had reached a stage of such sophistication that it was quite possible to record sequences out of order, as one would in a film, and cut them together, as one would in a film. It had also become customary at the BBC to use a certain percentage of outdoor location filming on most plays and to edit this into the studio production. The writer's restrictions had, therefore, been greatly diminished; he could take his characters into realistic, outdoor locations (as opposed to studio-built exteriors) and project them backwards and forwards in time. The necessity of observing the unities, and for writing filler scenes, was gone. The 'well-made' play had begun to take on a somewhat old-fashioned look, as it had in the theatre.

Cock, Hen and Courting Pit, the David Halliwell play, produced by Peter Luke and directed by Charles Jarrott in 1966, was largely made on film, only about a quarter taking place in the studio. *Cathy, Come Home* was shot entirely on film, except for a short (seven to eight minute) sequence which had to be shot electronically in order to satisfy an agreement with Equity, the actor's union, that a certain proportion (originally 10 per cent) of any drama programme must be made in an electronic studio. By the time *In Two Minds* was made, an agreement had been reached between the BBC and Equity which allowed a programme to be made entirely on film. The drama department could now virtually make mini-films.

It was the prospect of being able to branch out into film which was to me the greatest inducement for producing 'Wednesday Play'. At the time when I was asked to do so, I had just finished producing 'Thirteen Against Fate' (thirteen stories by Simenon) and two series of 'Out of the Unknown' and was enjoying a holiday before launching into a third series of the latter. I was once more in New York when a phone call came through from Sydney Newman asking me if I'd come back right away. 'I'm giving you the biggest break you've ever had,' he said. 'Don't be ungrateful, come back.'

Like their predecessors, both Lionel Harris and Tony Garnett had decided that 'enough was enough'. Lionel Harris had gone back to directing and Tony Garnett, on the strength of his television film experience, had gone off to break into the world of feature films with Ken Loach. Sydney was obviously desperate. His plan was that I should co-produce the programme with Graeme McDonald, who had come from Granada TV to the BBC to produce 'Thirty Minute Theatre'.

My first reaction was to tell Sydney that I did not want the job. For one thing, I was being asked to take over at such short notice that I would obviously not have enough time to accrue a stock of scripts. Terrible memories of panic days on 'Armchair Theatre' floated back to me: the sheer sweat of finding, cajoling and preparing enough scripts for a season. I had gone on holiday to New York in the secure knowledge that all thirteen scripts were ready and waiting for the third series of 'Out of the Unknown', which I was due to produce. My stomach was already contracting into spasms.

There were a good many other considerations as well. I had now produced three series, two of 'Out of the Unknown' and one of 'Thirteen Against Fate'. 'Out of the Unknown' had been my own brainchild and had proved a fascinating technical exercise. 'Thirteen Against Fate' had been the most gratifying work I had done in television; I felt a special affinity for the thirteen Simenon novels and had tried to work out stylistically how to transpose them to the screen. They had been a great critical success and, more important to me, had succeeded, in my own terms, in transferring Simenon's style, mood and philosophy from the written page to the screen.

Now one was being asked to leave one's own creations and step into dead men's shoes. Moreover, 'Wednesday Play', as a programme, had somehow got itself into an absolutely schizoid position. On the one hand, as originally intended by Sydney, it was to have a mass audience appeal. At the same time the critics were evaluating it on criteria more suited to Sunday nights at the Royal Court Theatre; in their eyes, if it did not present every week a daring play by a new author with a 'message', it had failed. On the other hand, the audience, if they did get such a play, howled that they wanted a good old-fashioned story with a beginning, middle and end in which people didn't live in permanent squalor, swearing at each other and fornicating. Such was the schizoid criticism which was to persist and which had sent much stronger producers than myself running as fast as their legs would carry them. In the aftermath of *Cathy, Come Home*, almost every play that was not centred on a social problem was greeted with the question 'Where have the great days of social conscience gone?' and every play which was in that genre was compared unfavourably with it.

For the producer with an ego (and all naturally have considerable ones), the single play slot is the most disheartening of niches. If a play succeeds, it is the writer and director and cast who are praised. If a play fails, the producer is usually blamed for his choice, or blamed by the writer for allowing the director to murder the play, or vice versa. He is also blamed from above for those 'overspends' which often make the production visually worth watching, while the director receives acclaim from the critics for the beauty of the piece.

Was I, therefore, to leave my brainchildren and bury myself in the anonymity of a shared programme whose pattern was predetermined by those who went before and whose objectives were not necessarily mine and which was a sitting duck for the critics? I thought not. Sydney, however, reviling me for my ingratitude, dangled another carrot. The film effort, which Tony Garnett had managed to obtain, was still to be had. There was the chance to make some productions entirely on film. This was something I had not done until now. I decided to come back.

Chapter 6

Producing 'Wednesday Play' and 'Play for Today'

On pp. 65–7 there is a list of the forty-eight plays which I personally produced in the five years between autumn 1967 and February 1973 on 'Wednesday Play' and 'Play for Today'. As the previous list will show, many other plays went out on the programme, chiefly under the producership of Graeme McDonald, but the second list contains only those plays whose personal histories are well known to me. It is them alone which I am proposing to discuss. How did they come to be chosen or commissioned? Who were the authors? What were the particular production problems? What were the reactions from critics and audience? What, if any, are the lessons to be learned from them about television drama?

The apprehension which I felt on being asked to take over the programme at short notice gave way to total panic on my return to England; where was I going to find enough scripts to get on the air in time? I found, to my consternation, that I was to be cut off from commissioning a large number of authors with whom I had previously worked and others whom I would certainly have approached to write scripts. The reason for this 'excommunication' was that Graeme McDonald, my co-producer, had inherited all the existing scripts and the 'stable' of authors used in the previous era of Lionel Harris, along with Lionel Harris's story editor, Kenith Trodd. It was agreed that both producers could not approach the same writer to work on the same programme; I was, therefore, prevented from working with such authors as David Mercer, Denis Potter and Hugh Whitemore and denied access to any scripts in existence.

WEDNESDAY PLAYS – PRODUCED BY IRENE SHUBIK

TRANSMISSION DATE	TITLE	AUTHOR	DIRECTOR	VIEWING FIGURE
18.10.67	WANTED, SINGLE GENTLEMAN	James Broom Lynne	John Gorrie	6,000,000
13.12.67	DEATH OF A PRIVATE	Robert Muller/ Georg Büchner	James Ferman	6,000,000
10.1.68	HOUSE OF CHARACTER	David Rudkin	Alan Cooke	6,000,000
31.1.68	THE DRUMMER AND THE BLOKE	Rhys Adrian	Herbert Wise	5,000,000
1.5.68	THE MAN BEHIND YOU	Jeremy Scott	Moira Armstrong	6,000,000
8.5.68	INFIDELITY TOOK PLACE	John Mortimer	Michael Hayes	8,000,000
21.8.68	MRS LAWRENCE WILL LOOK AFTER IT (all film)	Tony Parker	John MacKenzie	9,700,000
11.9.68	A NIGHT WITH MRS DA TANKA	William Trevor	John Gorrie	8,000,000
18.9.68	CHARLIE	Alun Owen	Michael Hayes	5,000,000
2.10.68	MOONEY AND HIS CARAVANS	Peter Terson	James Ferman	9,100,000
6.11.68	NOTHING WILL BE THE SAME AGAIN	James Hanley	Peter Hammond	6,000,000
8.1.69	THE FABULOUS FRUMP	James Gibbins	Peter Hammond	6,550,000[1]
2.4.69	SLING YOUR HOOK (all film)	Roy Minton	Michael Tuchner	8,500,000
23.4.69	THE EXILES (all film)	Errol John	Herbert Wise	5,500,000
30.4.69	BLODWEN, HOME FROM RACHEL'S MARRIAGE (all film)	David Rudkin	Alan Cooke	6,550,000

[1]After this date, viewing figures were based on a new and more accurate population survey.

TRANSMISSION DATE	TITLE	AUTHOR	DIRECTOR	VIEWING FIGURE
1.10.69	THE LAST TRAIN THROUGH THE HARECASTLE TUNNEL	Peter Terson	Alan Clarke	5,850,000
15.10.69	THE MARK II WIFE	William Trevor	Philip Saville	6,000,000
29.10.69	THE SAD DECLINE OF ARTHUR MAYBURY	John Gorrie	John Gorrie	5,050,000
5.11.69	ALL OUT FOR KANGAROO VALLEY	Noel Robinson	Bill Bain	5,500,000
12.11.69	HAPPY	Alan Gosling	Marc Miller	6,550,000
17.12.69	IT WASN'T ME	James Hanley	James Ferman	4,500,000
21.1.70	THE HUNTING OF LIONEL CRANE (all film)	Roy Minton	Michael Tuchner	7,900,000
18.2.70	THE ITALIAN TABLE	William Trevor	Herbert Wise	6,500,000
22.4.70	SOVEREIGN'S COMPANY (all film)	Don Shaw	Alan Clarke	4,450,000
20.5.70	CHARIOT OF FIRE	Tony Parker	James Ferman	4,500,000
	PLAYS FOR TODAY – PRODUCED BY IRENE SHUBIK			
15.10.70	THE LONG DISTANCE PIANO PLAYER	Alan Sharp	Philip Saville	5,459,000
22.10.70	THE RIGHT PROSPECTUS (all film)	John Osborne	Alan Cooke	6,000,000
19.11.70	I CAN'T SEE MY LITTLE WILLIE	Doug Livingstone	Alan Clarke	6,000,000
26.11.70	A DISTANT THUNDER	Maurice Edelman	James Ferman	5,950,000
3.12.70	HEARTS AND FLOWERS	Peter Nichols	Chris Morahan	8,150,000
7.1.71	ALMA MATER	David Hodson	James Ferman	6,600,000

TRANSMISSION DATE	TITLE	AUTHOR	DIRECTOR	VIEWING FIGURE
11.2.71	THE LARGEST THEATRE IN THE WORLD – THE RAINBIRDS (all film)	Clive Exton	Philip Saville	4,450,000
29.4.71	THE FOXTROT	Rhys Adrian	Philip Saville	6,900,000
6.5.71	WHEN THE BOUGH BREAKS	Tony Parker	James Ferman	7,550,000
3.6.71	EVERYBODY SAY CHEESE	Doug Livingstone	Alan Clarke	3,250,000
21.10.71	EDNA, THE INEBRIATE WOMAN (all film)	Jeremy Sandford	Ted Kotcheff	9,250,000
4.11.71	O FAT WHITE WOMAN	William Trevor	Philip Saville	4,250,000
18.11.71	MICHAEL REGAN (all film)	Robert Holles	John Gorrie	4,800,000
2.12.71	PAL	Alun Owen	Silvio Narizzano	4,100,000
9.12.71	THE PIGEON FANCIER	Peter Hankin	James Ferman	5,000,000
3.2.72	IN THE BEAUTIFUL CARIBBEAN	Barry Reckord	Philip Saville	3,800,000
10.2.72	ACKERMAN, DOUGALL AND HARKER (all film)	Don Shaw	Ted Kotcheff	3,750,000
17.2.72	THE VILLA MAROC	Willis Hall	Herbert Wise	5,950,000
16.10.72	A LIFE IS FOR EVER	Tony Parker	Alan Clarke	6,000,000
6.11.72	TRIPLE EXPOSURE	David Halliwell	Alan Cooke	2,600,000
20.11.72	THE GENERAL'S DAY	William Trevor	John Gorrie	5,300,000
5.2.73	A SONG AT TWILIGHT	Willis Hall	Herbert Wise	5,350,000
5.3.73	ACCESS TO THE CHILDREN	William Trevor	Philip Saville	6,550,000

I was also asked to fill the first three studio dates, which were only a couple of months off, while the usual planning and rehearsal period for a seventy-five-minute play is six to seven weeks. This meant an emergency situation so far as scripts were concerned, leaving virtually no time for a specially commissioned play to be written or new writers to be discovered.

What does one do in such a situation? First of all, I began to phone round all the writers' agents in town and to approach all the writers with whom I had previous contact asking for any existing material for instant production. The first four plays on the list reflect this state of panic; of the four transmitted between October 1967 and January 1968 only one, Rhys Adrian's *The Drummer and the Bloke*, was written on commission. I had no time to think of finding startling new masterpieces; if I could find workable plays, that would be enough. Let us examine the history of the first three productions.

James Broome Lynne was an author already known to me from 'Armchair Theatre' days. A talented artist, he had worked as a graphics designer, advertising executive and, mainly, as a book jacket designer. He began writing in 1959 after winning the *Observer* Christmas competition and has by now written a number of novels. My first contact with him was several years before, when I went to see his play *The Trigon* at the Arts Theatre. The play had struck me then as ideally suited to television, especially the all-studio television being produced on 'Armchair Theatre'. It was extremely well constructed and tightly contained within one basic set. The relationships were close and claustrophobic. Two weak men share a flat and an amiable relationship, on an infantile level, with a girl. The three innocents are destroyed when a third man comes, as a lodger, to the flat, acting as a catalyst in a cynical and sinister way.

At that point I had tried to purchase the play for 'Armchair Theatre' but as there were hopes of a West End production the television rights were not available. Instead, I commissioned a new script from the author, which was produced on 'Armchair Theatre', directed by Philip Saville, starring Alec Clunes and entitled *Living Image*.

Now, in my desperate search, I remembered my attempt to buy *The Trigon*, and that no West End production had ever ensued. With hope in my heart, I phoned Broom Lynne's agent and a few days later had purchased the play with the understanding that it would have to be slightly re-written for television. This was done by Broom Lynne with the help of the director John Gorrie and myself. The play was renamed *Wanted, Single Gentleman* and began with a very small amount of filming, showing the new tenant (Peter Jeffrey) arriving. The rest of the play took place in one large studio set and, in terms of economy, this was an ideal television production. The rest of the cast were Eileen Atkins, John Stratton and Alan Rowe, all of whose performances were much praised both by the critics and on the audience research reports.

Was this a good play to start out with on a season of contemporary original television drama? Obviously not, if that was how the programme was being advertised. There was no escaping the fact that it was an old stage play. Several of the critics picked up this point. Both Sydney Newman and Gerald Savory (Head of Plays) had made the usual promises to the press that the programme would be full of 'gutsy contemporaneity'. So while, as a whole, the critics praised the play, they, at the same time, began to blame it for what it was not; what it had never set out to be.

Michael Billington, in *The Times*, began as follows: ' "Unashamedly controversial" was how last week's *Radio Times* described the bulk of the offerings in BBC's "Wednesday Play" series.' Going on to praise the play and especially the acting performances, Mr Billington ended, 'My only reservation is that if the "Wednesday Play" is so concerned to be provocative and controversial this was an erratic choice. Could not the BBC have persuaded Mr Broom Lynne to give us a new play?' Obviously none of the critics has ever been in the position of waking up in the middle of the night with clenched fists, wondering what play is going into the studio next.

The second play on the list, *Death of a Private*, by Robert Muller was also an existing script when I bought it. Robert Muller, before he began writing for television full-time, was probably best known as drama critic on the *Daily Mail*. As early as November 1952 he had been sending submissions to the BBC. At that date, Frank Marcus, the playwright, sent in to the BBC a play by Muller from the International Theatre Group. It was entitled *The Ceremony of Innocence* and dealt with the newspaper world. At the time, Muller was working in Paris as a journalist and novelist. The play was turned down, as was another, entitled *Rue de Seine*, submitted the following year.

1 Dudley Sutton in *Death of a Private*.

But on 'Armchair Theatre' Muller had better luck. While I was there four of his plays were produced: *Afternoon of a Nymph*, starring Ian Hendry and Janet Munro, describing the career of a young girl trying to get on in the theatre; *Thank You and Good Night*, about the meeting of a cultured girl and a pop singer on a train; *Paradise Suite*, about a movie star, starring Carole Baker; and *The*

Night Conspirators about Hitler, which was also put on as a stage play at Brighton. Muller drew most of his subject matter from his knowledge of 'show-biz' gained as a critic and from his own German background.

Not only had I worked with him on 'Armchair Theatre' but had bought his autobiographical novel about his childhood in Nazi Germany, *The World that Summer*, for 'Story Parade'. I now asked him for a play and he told me of the existence of *Death of a Private*, a modern version of Georg Büchner's classic play *Woyzeck*.

Woyzeck was, in a sense, the first kitchen-sink play: the first play in which the little man was the hero. It concerned a simple private soldier driven to murder by the various pressures of society and, finally, by the unfaithfulness of his mistress. Robert Muller's version of the story had originally been commissioned in 1964 for 'Festival', a programme which had now been killed off; the script had been sitting around since that date.

From the production point of view, *Death of a Private* was an enormous challenge, as Muller had written it almost as a folk opera. In the original, Woyzeck's rival-in-love had been an aggressive drum-major. In the television version he was turned into a pop singer, whom the soldier's mistress followed like a swooning fan. For this part the director, James Ferman,[1] had found a singer called Charles Stewart and a group called 'The Paper Blitz Tissue' for whom we commissioned Ron Grainer to write the songs. Having a live pop group in the studio in the middle of the dramatic action involved us of course in vastly expensive and complicated sound problems, while the attempt to counterpoint the real action with the fevered viewpoint of the hero by trick lighting effects and fast vision mixing appeared to confuse a large, more conservative section of the public.

So complicated did the production prove that editing on the programme (recorded eleven weeks before) was finished only two hours before transmission. At seven o'clock on transmission night I was lying in bed with flu when I received a phone call to say that the programme controller had been called from his dinner to be asked what he would substitute to transmit if the tele-cine people had not received the programme in time. Unlike *Wanted, Single Gentleman*, this production proved so wildly expensive that I was immediately forced to search for a simple two-handed play to

[1]Who later became the film censor.

recoup my finances. Robbing Peter to pay Paul is the eternal pattern of the television producer's life.

What was the response to this second production? Nancy Banks-Smith, then critic for *The Sun*, exclaimed: 'You can tell when the "Wednesday Play" is back into its accustomed gallop by the thundering headache you get.' So, according to this critic, *Private* was a 'Wednesday Play' indeed and, as such, she hated it; while the play before, though liked, should not have been on 'Wednesday Play' because it wasn't one!

The Times, at the same time, however, spoke of *Death of a Private* as going 'some way towards restoring the prestige of the series. It was by no means a success but at least it was operating on a high and ambitious level.'

Stanley Reynolds in *The Guardian* came closest to guessing the truth. 'Surely,' he said, 'the BBC's "Wednesday Play" is for beating the bourgeoisie around the head and shoulders and Theatre 625 is for doing adaptations from the classics.' It was, indeed, a play intended for the latter programme. The point I am trying to make is simple. The critics had been preconditioned to expect one thing and received another. *Wanted, Single Gentleman* on 'Armchair Theatre' and *Death of a Private* on 'Festival' would have received entirely different responses and reviews. Even my previous productions were ingeniously cited to explain the off-beat character of *Private*: 'What happens when Miss Irene Shubik, overall producer of that fantastic BBC-2 Science Fiction series "Out of the Unknown", is handed a very updated adaptation of a German play written 130-odd years ago?' asked Ron Boyle in the *Daily Express*, answering his own query with, 'Obvious – a TV freak-out.'

The third play on the list, *House of Character*, comes into a different category. It was newly written, unproduced and (many would have thought) almost unproduceable, for reasons that will be explained. Very occasionally a writer emerges whose personal vision of life and mode of expression are so outstandingly original that it may shock or frighten an audience. The bulk of television writing is inevitably dramatized journalism. By this I mean that the characters and situations are portrayed in a readily recognizable 'everyday' way and the level of observation of them and their lives is that of good journalism. The writers whose observation plumbs below this level, even down to the level of the subconscious, are very few, and often disturbing to a mass audience. Such authors, for example, as David Mercer, Clive Exton and David Rudkin stand out for this special vision. Had any of these three authors written *Cathy, Come Home* or *Edna, the Inebriate Woman*, for instance, their portrayal of the inner mental torture of Cathy and Edna might well have made audiences so uncomfortable as to have forced them to turn off. There is a certain level past which many people do not wish to be disturbed. David Rudkin's work is, to my mind, a classic illustration of this fact.

His unique talent first came to light with the production of his stage play *Afore Night Come*, the theme of which was the ritual murder of a tramp in an orchard by primitive agricultural workers: a dark, brooding work reminiscent of Thomas Hardy, one of Rudkin's most admired authors. Rudkin (perhaps tongue-in-cheek) said he looked on this play as documentary, based on his own experiences working as a fruit picker. Those who saw it thought differently. Herbert Kretzmer described Rudkin in the *Daily Express* as 'a playwright of strange powers, with a capacity to illuminate the dark crannies of the soul' (26 June 1964), while elsewhere the play was described as symbolist, ritualistic and 'British drama's first fully-fledged contribution to the theatre of cruelty' (*The Times*, 26 June 1964). Obviously, Rudkin's vision of life was outstandingly original, inevitably influenced by the fact that he grew up in a very puritanical Evangelical Christian background, his father having started as a revivalist pastor and became a member of the Church of Christ.

At the time when *Afore Night Come* was first put on at the Arts Theatre, on 7 June 1962 (it was later produced at the Aldwych in 1964 as part of the Royal Shakespeare Company's experimental season there), Rudkin was twenty-five and teaching classics and music at a school in Birmingham. In all his work, Rudkin's musical training is immediately recognizable in the deliberately patterned, almost poetic, speech of his characters, while his training as a classical scholar leads to meticulous attention to detail in his scripts, where every nuance of setting and character is underlined.

Of his approach to his characters, Rudkin said tellingly, in an interview with Harold Bolter in the *Birmingham Post* (30 July 1963), 'I am interested in people when they are at the point of greatest stress; when they are ready to break down. Then they are no longer conditioned by society. They behave according to the subconscious impulses.' In this he resembles such playwrights as Strindberg and such film-makers as Ingmar Bergman and Antonioni.

I was introduced to David Rudkin by Michael Imison, a director who was temporarily assisting me with the story editing on 'Wednesday Play'. I had always wanted to commission a play from him, but on 'Armchair Theatre' the limited facilities, as well as the 'popular entertainment' requirements, made this impossible.

Rudkin came with two ideas, one of which already existed in draft script form. The play, originally called *Malvern Flats*, was sparked off by his recent experience of moving into a new flat with his newly married wife and the script contained a good deal of satirical comment on the discrepancy between the estate agent's description and the actuality. It began with the taking of an inventory of items in the flat. There, the documentary resemblance ended as the new tenant Bisthorpe began to discover that he was not in a new flat at all, but a madhouse. The complexities of the script, of Bisthorpe's nightmare vision of the house and its strange occupants, were such that I realized there were few directors with sufficient technical skill to handle it in the studio. I therefore offered Rudkin a fee for the first draft on the understanding that re-writes would be done when the right director could be found.

The right director would be someone who was skilled at special effects and complex editing, and who could use the facilities of the electronic studio to their maximum effect. I showed the script to Alan Cooke, who had proved on two of the 'Out of the Unknown' series (*Andover and the Android* and *Tunnel under the World*) that he had all these skills. In both those productions, we had used an enormous number of special effects both practical and electronic: automatic drinks trollies which came up and asked guests what they wanted to drink, robots, inlay showing the characters in the play as miniatures on a table top being used in an advertising experiment. Cooke enjoyed the challenge of those sorts of problems and agreed to do the script. In October 1967 we went into production with Alfie Lynch playing Bisthorpe.

The prop list included such items as an electric fire which had to spit and splutter, a light bulb which had to explode, a ceiling fitting which had to come away with hunks of plaster, an exploding, flaring matchbox. There were other things that had to be done on the set: a staircase had to give way and a special floor with a hole in it had to be constructed through which one of the figures haunting Bisthorpe (a lithe negro) could thrust his hands. Included in the filming problems (the filming was done at Grims Dyke Manor and Ham House in thick fog) were some Alsatians supplied by

Zoorama which were meant to be black and 'bark, jump, snarl, slaver, scratch at the gate, race across the lawn etc.' bang on cue. The extras list included a mob of ancient crones who, at one point, charge across the lawn heading for Bisthorpe's flat, while the grand climax came in the studio a month later with an entire kitchen being smashed up by four quarrelling men in pinstripe suits (the governors of the asylum). Television writing had come a long way since the undemanding days of 'Armchair Theatre'.

It was estimated, on the audience research reports for this play, that 11.8 per cent of the UK population saw it, as opposed to 6.9 per cent who were watching BBC-2 and 18 per cent watching ITV. The reaction index (denoting audience appreciation), which is based on questionnaires completed by a sample audience of 193, was 32, the lowest for the series to that date (it had ranged from 34 to 74). According to the report, 'favourable impressions were far outweighed by adverse opinions, with dislike increasing to furious condemnation among the unenthusiastic majority'. Only a few reporting viewers, in fact, seemed unreservedly appreciative. Here are some sample comments on the report: 'Immense impact; to begin with, and at times hysterically funny. At all times one was completely committed. A play I shall remember for a long, long time.' (Widow)

'Absorbing, a good play; clever, baffling, a play to make you think.' (Designer)

On the one side, a sample member of the audience said, 'The whole thing made me shudder, yet I could not possibly have switched off; the play conveyed a madness which was frightening,' on the other, protesters declared that it was 'a horribly frightening experience' and 'could undo the good work of years' by giving 'the wrong impression of a mental home'. A remarkably simple-minded attitude, taken up by Peter Black in his review in the *Daily Mail*, as though the piece had been intended as a documentary on mental health, instead of a flight of imagination.

While the production *per se* was highly praised, a number of critics confessed to not wanting to be disturbed in this way. At the same time as his brilliance was acknowledged, Rudkin was taken to task for daring to portray the interior world of madness. In his own personal life, the play also had a resounding effect. The landlord who had let him a flat with the missing floorboard, broken bathroom window pane, fierce dogs and faulty light bulbs shown in the play evicted him. In a letter telling me this news, Rudkin wrote and thanked me for putting the play on and hoped I did not regret it. Far from this, I personally felt that this and his next play, which was produced in the following year, *Blodwen, Home from Rachel's Marriage*, were among the most fascinating scripts I had ever read and the most worthwhile productions.

Blodwen was the second idea with which Rudkin had come and I had commissioned it to be specially written for the programme. It was commissioned in May 1967, went into rehearsal, again with Alan Cooke directing, in August 1968, was filmed entirely on location in Wales and London in August and September, and transmitted the following April. This, in fact, is a fairly normal life cycle for a commissioned play, which will explain my initial panic at taking on a programme like 'Wednesday Play' at such short notice.

In *Blodwen* Rudkin obviously drew a great deal from his puritanical religious background. The play had a fascinating structure; in the first half, the Wilderness family are shown driving home from a cousin's wedding in Ireland. The family consists of father – a famous controversial Welsh religionist – a fiercely protective mother, a detached, ironical art teacher son and Blodwen, repressed and tending to religious mania. As they drive, each recalls his own version of the cousin's wedding, their various humiliations at it and, among other things, a hilarious place-card swapping sequence in which everyone wants to be at top table and ends in a wild Irish brawl.

In the second half, back in Wales, Blodwen is kidnapped by students on their Rag Day to be their 'festival queen' – a ritual counterpointing the wedding. This rude contact with reality heightens the strained relationships of the family even more. The play has an almost musical construction and, in it, we used a number of the same cast from the first half for the second, each being a reflection of the other. The production problems were almost as complex as in *House of Character*, but working on film one has a great deal more flexibility in editing to make things work.

What was the response? *Blodwen* appealed greatly to the type of critic to whom an Ingmar Bergman film would appeal. Its most enthusiastic reviewer was John Russell Taylor, *The Times* film critic, who said in *Plays and Players* (July 1969), 'The latest season of BBC-1 Wednesday plays went out in a blaze of glory with David Rudkin's *Blodwen, Home from Rachel's Marriage*.' Russell Taylor recognized and was fascinated by Rudkin's private world, in which 'Dark forces walk among men, sometimes possibly primeval presences'. The *New Statesman* (9 May 1969) said: 'Rudkin's haunted vision of life has always appealed strongly to me, and his stylized dialogue (based firmly, though, on the rhythms of ordinary speech) has never showed to better advantage than in this piece.'

Audience response was not as violent as to *House of Character*, but most people on the questionnaire found the meaning of the play difficult to discern, though many found it 'memorable' viewing. Undoubtedly, the normal composition of audience for this sort of work would be that found in one of the more 'avant garde' theatres or in an 'Art House' cinema. Were these two plays, therefore, the right sort of programmes to put on for a mass audience? When one considers that *House of Character* was estimated to have 6 million viewers and *Blodwen* 6.5 million, and that to a minority at least of these they constituted an unusual 'viewing' experience, which they would probably never have had elsewhere, the experiment seems, to me, very worth while.

Harold Pinter once estimated that it would take a thirty-year run of *The Caretaker* at the Duchess Theatre to get the same audience (6,368,000) as he got for his 'Armchair Theatre' play *A Night Out*, (*Daily Telegraph*, 30 May 1960). If television does not broaden the audience's viewing experience, what other medium can?

Chapter 7

The documentary approach

No world could be further removed from the private, interior mental landscape of Rudkin's plays than that of Tony Parker. Parker has been described by Anthony Storr in the *Sunday Times* (15 February 1970) as 'Britain's most expert interviewer, mouthpiece of the inarticulate and counsel for the defence of those whom society has shunned or abandoned'. A totally self-effacing writer, his world is one of pure external observation – journalism of the highest kind. An analysis of his plays produced on 'Wednesday Play' shows an interesting contrast to the works already discussed, both in their genesis and in their reception by audiences and critics.

Parker had started out as a businessman (who also wrote poetry), working as a publisher's representative. Then, in 1953, the Craig–Bentley case happened. Two boys were charged with the murder of a policeman; the younger, who had fired the shot, was too young to be executed; the older, Bentley, was just old enough and was hanged. So deeply disturbed was Parker by this that he wrote to the Howard League for Penal Reform asking what an ordinary person could do to change the penal system. Their only suggestion was that he should become a prison visitor, which he did. Later, learning that prison visitors must not associate with prisoners once they have been discharged (a time when they probably need most help), Parker became a voluntary associate – a person who offers friendship and practical help to discharged prisoners.

Parker not only began to 'associate' with prisoners, he began to write books about them. All his books have been built up from painstakingly accurate research and hours of interviews with actual prisoners, many of whom he has known for years before the actual interviews are recorded. So great a respect has the Home

Office for his books that he was granted by them the unique privilege of living for three months in Grendon Prison to record conversations with anyone, staff or prisoners, with whom he wanted to talk, without censorship – an experience recorded in his book *The Frying Pan*.

I first met Tony Parker when I bought his book *The Unknown Citizen* for 'Story Parade' (as described in Chapter 5). I had commissioned the adaptation of the book from Philip Broadley, a friend of Parker's. Broadley had hinted to me that Parker might be interested in trying to write a play himself. When I started producing 'Wednesday Play', it occurred to me that the time was ripe to approach him. Whether he would be capable of writing in dramatic form or not one could only ascertain by taking the risk. Certainly the material he had at his fingertips would be eminently suitable for television. It was a risk worth taking. One knows and expects on such a programme that there will have to be a certain failure rate with scripts. In Parker's case, it was a risk which more than paid off.

By the time he came to see me in April 1967, Parker had five books to his credit: *The Courage of his Convictions* (1962), a study of a professional criminal; *The Unknown Citizen* (1963); *The Plough Boy* (1964), based on the Clapham Common gang murder case; *Five Women* (1965), a portrait of five women criminals; *A Man of Good Abilities* (1966), the fascinating life story of an elderly compulsive embezzler. All the books had, of course, been built up from hours of taped interviews which Parker ingeniously edited, filling in the background and circumstances of his encounters with the subjects.

When he came to see me, we discussed various ideas. None of his existing books seemed immediately suitable for television adaptation but another original idea we discussed seemed very much so. This was the idea of exposing the world of the illicit baby-minder. In a synopsis, Parker described the theme of the proposed play thus. 'This play would highlight this contemporary social situation in which there is totally inadequate provision for unmarried mothers to maintain their children unless they have supportive families or choose to live in the very few mother-and-baby hostels available. Out of initial desire not to give away children for adoption this is what happens.' What happens is that they take the children to private non-approved child minders, often with dire results. At the point when I commissioned the play, in May 1967, all one knew was the general subject. Parker was going to research it and turn it into dramatic shape, with my help.

Originally I had to commission the script to be done electronically in the studio, as the film effort I had been promised was not yet forthcoming; but when the first version came in, I knew that the only way this play could ever be effective was to put it on to film, for reasons which will be explained.

The shape of *Mrs Lawrence Will Look After It*, as the script came to be called (the first draft was delivered three months after it was commissioned), became, in a sense, the shape of a detective story. Mrs Lawrence, an elderly women, collapses in the street and is taken to hospital where she is heard to moan about her 'children'. A police officer is sent to her home and there he finds fourteen tiny children, some of them babies, left on their own. The problem now becomes one for the Children's Department who have to look after the children while finding out to whom they belong. As each parent is tracked down a different case history is told. In the end, Mrs Lawrence (played by Constance Chapman) comes home from hospital and, despite all warnings that she is liable to prosecution, starts her illicit baby home once more.

It was apparent to me that the story would lose half its impact if the characters were turned into talking heads against studio sets. Only by showing the real circumstances in which the parents lived could one portray their true plight. Moreover, with the fourteen children one had an insoluble problem as far as the studio was concerned; they would have to be recorded on film. The only way to get good performances out of such young children is to shoot endless takes and edit them; nor, at that time, were such young children allowed in an electronic studio.

So my plea that this project, which I was certain would have a great impact, could not be done without film, went in to the Head of Plays' department. Eventually, I wrote to Tony Parker telling him that we could do the play on film and that now he would have to take all the interviews with the parents which he had carefully confined to studio sets and put them back into their natural environments.

The script went through numerous other major rewrites. A reporter figure whom Tony had invented to string the whole thing together came and went, was turned from a married man who was neglecting his family into a bachelor. The social workers, who came to take over the house and look after the children until their parents were found, also went through several permutations. I felt that while all the parents' interviews had a ring of total authenticity, being based on real people, the invented characters had less of the breath of real life. It has since been a standing joke between Parker and myself that every time he gives one of the characters in his plays (usually a social worker) a private life, I take it out again. In this case, it seemed to me to have no relevance to the story at all.

Having got permission to do the entire script on film, I invited John MacKenzie to direct it. I felt that John, who had got his training in 'documentary-type' directing while acting as Ken Loach's production assistant, would be good for this subject. We were then lucky enough to get Brian Tufano, a cameraman who was especially skilled at 'hand-held' work, to shoot the piece.

We started filming on 11 March 1968 (almost a year after the synopsis had been agreed) in various sordid locations around North London. Our main location was a tiny house in Cricklewood from which passers-by could hear all day long the collective cries of fourteen small children. Upstairs were crammed fourteen mothers and chaperones, peeping out occasionally to ensure the children's welfare, while downstairs, as in the famous cabin scene in *A Night at the Opera*, the entire crew were squeezed together in one tiny room in which a line of howling babies were laid out on the couch. My favourite moment of filming was the rebellion of one small boy, the eldest of the children. In the scene where the policeman first comes to the house and breaks in, the small boy emerges and the policeman asks his name. After about the third take the boy stamped his foot and shouted, 'I've already told you three times and I'm not telling you again.'

The play was transmitted on 21 August 1969 as the opening play of the new season. The critics greeted it like a long lost friend. Here was a proper 'Wednesday Play'. This was another *Cathy, Come Home*,' said Martin Jackson in the *Express* (23 August 1968). 'The Wednesday Play is back and bang on target.' At least four reviewers mentioned *Cathy* although, in fact, Parker's entire meticulous approach and reasoned attitude were totally unlike Sandford's impressionism. However, the play received the highest audience figures of the season (9,700,000) and unqualified praise. It dealt with an easily recognizable problem in easily recognizable terms, a problem with which almost everyone could identify. This was obviously the type of journalistic play which could have widespread appeal and demanded no more emotional or imaginative effort from the audience than did a newspaper article.

The next subject which Tony and I discussed was perhaps less easy to identify with. The beginnings of *Chariot of Fire* were fairly far removed from the end product. In March 1968 we agreed upon a commission called *The Associates*. This was based upon Tony's own first-hand knowledge of voluntary prison 'after care' workers. The play was to be about four of these workers: a young married woman with her own family; an unstable, rather cranky man; an elderly single woman; and a placid, unshakable middle-aged man. These were all actual types whom Tony had personally encountered. The idea was to explore the different motives of people volunteering for this work; the attitude of the prison authorities to them and their relationships with four prisoners: an elderly con man, a violent criminal, an unemployable inadequate, and a sex offender (all subjects of Tony's different books).

In November, Tony turned up with his research on all these characters but without a script. It struck me then that it would be immensely difficult to develop so many characters and engage an audience's sympathy for all of them in the space of one script. We therefore agreed to select one 'associate' and one prisoner and concentrate on them.

For most people the term 'sex offender' conjures up an immediate image of a maniac rapist. Tony, however, had just finished the research for a new book, *The Twisting Lane* (published in 1969), which consisted of interviews with eight sex offenders and revealed most of the subjects to be more pathetic than frightening. One of them (in the play he was to become Stanley Wood) was an innocuous little man in his fifties who, in all other respects, could be considered a model citizen. Wood had spent twenty years of his life in prison for sexual offences against small boys. These offences, in fact, were not actual assault (Wood was totally impotent) but mere fondling. Good psychiatric treatment might have helped him, but none was available in the prison system.

We decided that the play should concentrate on the story of Wood and his 'associate', a housewife, for his case was, in many respects, the most pathetic illustration of an inadequacy in the existing system. He was also a stock figure of derision and prejudice and to illuminate his real character seemed worth while. The storyline showed Wood in prison, the associate's attempts to help his rehabilitation and get him psychiatric help, and her eventual failure to prevent his return to prison.

Originally, I had intended the script to be shot entirely on film. It now appeared, however, that there was not sufficient film allocation or money to do so that year, while for the following year I had two scripts (*Edna, the Inebriate Woman* and *The Right Prospectus*) which I was anxious to produce and which could not possibly be done other than on film. I decided to save the film effort for these two scripts and I had once more to ask Tony to rethink the script, this time in terms of turning film into studio. This particular subject, anyway, seemed to be well suited to such a change.

What exactly do I mean by this? In *Mrs Lawrence* it was absolutely essential to establish, in as realistic a way as possible, the miserable backgrounds of most of the parents involved and the sordid and dangerous conditions of Mrs Lawrence's 'baby farm'. In *Chariot of Fire*, however, it was the interior character of Stanley Wood which counted, as he revealed it to his associate Shelley Mitchell. This intense study of character through long revelatory conversation pieces was well suited to the electronic camera. This is not to say we did not use film at all. We used it to establish the isolation of Stanley's life at his remote cottage and to show how his involvement with the children came about; we also used it to show fleetingly the lot of the sex offender in prison. Thanks to Tony's influence with the Home Office, we were allowed to film briefly from the roof of Pentonville Prison and showed the prisoner's exercise yard where Stanley, as a sex offender, was shunned by the others and exercised alone for his own protection, and we showed his release from prison. Apart from these scenes, most of the pieces was confined to the studio.

Although I had originally thought of a documentary-type director, now that we had changed to the studio I asked James Ferman, who I knew was excellent at getting to the heart of artists' performances in studio conditions, to direct the play. We decided to cast Rosemary Leach as the associate and Jimmy Gardner, a very frail actor, with the face of a mime, and more usually associated with comic parts, to play Stanley. The play went out in May 1970, two years and two months after it was originally commissioned, and was again extremely well received by critics and audiences, many of whom remarked that the play drew attention to a subject that was hardly ever openly discussed and aroused a compassion they had not expected to feel and an awareness of the inadequacies of the prison and social services in dealing with this type of case.

Parker's next play was very much in the same vein. This was *When the Bough Breaks*, which dealt with the subject of baby battering. The play was commissioned in August 1969, delivered in March the following year, recorded a year later and transmitted almost immediately after that, in May 1971. Like *Mrs Lawrence*, it had a vaguely detective-story structure. A baby is brought to hospital by its mother and, on being X-rayed, is found to have multiple fractures. The NSPCC then sends a social worker to find out which parent is responsible. The father, a giant layabout, seems the obvious choice, but it turns out to be the pretty, fragile mother who is the 'batterer'.

Again, the play was done chiefly in the studio, with a small amount of filming to establish the couple's background on a sleazy caravan site. Again, James Ferman directed it and we cast a young singer and dancer, Cheryl Kennedy, as the girl, a risk which proved worth taking. In most documentary subjects, the use of unusual or offbeat or unexpected casting goes a long way towards establishing realism.

This play was more obviously didactic than the previous one, in that Tony wanted to include a number of discussions at the NSPCC (and, again, wanted to include a personal life for the social workers which I immediately cut out). The most difficult feat in a documentary drama is to convey statistics, possible remedies etc. connected with a social problem without becoming dramatically stilted. Although *When the Bough Breaks* succeeded admirably on a human level, I felt we had never overcome this particular problem and that no amount of humanizing the social workers disguised the fact that they were mouthpieces for the author. There always comes a dilemma in this type of drama documentary as to whether to go for the drama or for the facts. One cannot always succeed on both levels.

The last of Parker's plays on the list, *A Life is Forever*, was two years in the writing. Our original discussion about depicting the plight of the 'lifer' began in May 1970; the script was commissioned in July that year and Tony went off to research it at the same time as researching a book on the subject. The final script was accepted in May 1972, the play going into rehearsal immediately. It was transmitted the following October.

In the writing of *A Life is Forever*, which showed the deterioration of Johnson, who was serving a thirty-year sentence for murdering a policeman, and the futility of such long, non-productive sentences, Parker had, to my mind, shown a great step forward as a playwright in his own right rather than a documentary journalist. The invented dialogue was far more natural than in any of the previous plays and the situations seemed to arise more naturally from character, as opposed to being contrived by the author for expository or didactic reasons. I introduced Tony to the director Alan Clarke at an early stage, when the first draft was delivered, so that Alan had the chance to gain all the knowledge of prison he could from Parker.

Two policy decisions had to be made early on about this production. For a start, we realized that it would be impossible to get permission to film inside a prison. Our feeling was, therefore, that we should use no film at all . . . a mixture of film and studio might make the studio part look 'phoney'. The designer, Richard Henry, consequently built his prison entirely in the studio, basing it on reference pictures, a viewing of a documentary on prisons and Tony Parker's advice. Sound also made a great contribution, the sound man, Chick Anthony, attempting to emulate the hollow, clanking sounds of prison. It is a measure of their success that the Home Office phoned up the day after transmission to find out how we had managed to get into a prison to film without their permission. Later they asked to borrow the film as training material for the prison service.

The other decision was to cast an unknown actor as the 'lifer', as we all felt that a well known star would lessen the audience's belief in the prisoner's plight. For this part the director Alan Clarke found a saxophonist, Maurice O'Connell, who had only been acting for a year. The rest of the cast were chosen on a similar basis and amongst them was a young rep. actor called Tony Meyer who played a snaky little 'queer' who had murdered his father. His advances to the central character, Johnson, who immediately repelled him, were so convincing that I congratulated Tony on writing the first convincing homosexual scene I had seen on television. His answer was to point out that the only time I had approved his depiction of a sex life for his characters it had to be a homosexual sex life.

The play was generally praised for the realistic picture it gave of the deterioration of a man in prison who knows that he has nothing to live for; for conveying the totally non-productive nature of the prison system as it exists, with no useful work or training programme offered for rehabilitation. Like all Parker's plays it had a large audience viewing figure and generally appreciative reviews. Like all his plays, rather than being blatantly propagandist, it showed all sides of the story and left the audience to think and draw their own conclusions.

Statistically, therefore, Parker's plays are proof that audiences like and want plays on realistic and identifiable subjects, treated in realistic terms. In Rudkin's play *House of Character* a man was locked within his own madness; in Tony Parker's play the steel bars were more easily recogizable.

Chapter 8

Observers and creators: democracy versus autocracy?

Half-way between the two extremes of total journalism and total creation which the last two chapters have sought to illustrate lie the majority of television writers. They are half observers, half creators. It is the uniqueness of each one's particular view of the world around him which fascinates. The variation in writers' working techniques is also astonishingly wide as will be demonstrated.

John Osborne, in an interview with Kenneth Tynan (*The Observer*, 30 June 1969), made some interesting comments on his own attitude to the various media. Tynan was suggesting to him that nowadays, if a play did not work for the stage, a writer might well sell it to television or a film company where, with visual effects, music etc., it could be made to work. Osborne's reply was as follows: 'Yes, and that subscribes to the democratization of art, where a lot of people get together on something and make it work. One should only do things that stand by themselves.' Tynan then remarked that the fact that Osborne never revised, after he had finished a play, was obviously his way of opposing 'democratization'.

About working in films, Osborne went on to remark: 'I'm very uneasy about the idea of working with a director because it absolutely goes against my function in the theatre. One is in a master–servant relationship with a director and it's not one that I relish. I've always resisted the idea of being a hireling.' Television is, therefore, a difficult medium for a writer like Osborne to accept. It is in the nature of the beast that the writer's ideas will have to filter through far more levels of interpretation than on the stage.

Peter Terson, on the other hand, is on record as subscribing to the opposite view from Osborne. 'Terson is unique among our dramatists in that he does not believe he functions at all efficiently in isolation, writing a finished text in his study, which will then be produced essentially as it stands, with only minor modifications suggested in rehearsal ... nearly all his plays, even when completely written out in what appears to be a final form before rehearsals begin, have been extensively reworked with the production group, Terson regarding what he has written alone as merely the starting point.' (From an article by John Russell Taylor in *Plays and Players*, September 1970.)

Brian Dean, in an article in the *Daily Mail* (29 July 1968), described how, three weeks before *Zigger-Zagger* was due to open in London, Terson had not finished the script. 'I developed this way of working when I was resident playwright at the Victoria Theatre in Stoke,' said Terson. 'I get the first draft done and then reshape it as we go along.'

On the medium of television, in which a vast body of technical and production people must be involved to produce any end product, a certain amount of 'democratization' is almost inevitable. For some authors like Terson, Minton and Sandford, who are strong on dialogue and weak on structure, it is often only strong editorial or directorial help that can make their work come together on the screen. In all cases, it is up to the producer to attempt to transpose the author's intention to the screen as faithfully as possible. His initial means of doing so, once he has acted as editor, to get the script into its best possible shape, is to find the director whom he believes will be most closely in empathy with that particular script or whose strengths (technical or *vis-à-vis* actors) will bring most to it. The next step is to cast, with the director and possibly writer, those actors whom he feels will most surely realize the character as visualized by the writer. Then it is a matter of finding the right designer, cameraman etc. to realize the intention visually. Then it is up to the producer to play the role of critic all the way through the formative stages of rehearsal or filming, keeping the author's intention in mind.

If this process works successfully, a writer (like Osborne) can still be master, rather than servant, and master of a much larger kingdom than in the theatre. It is almost certain, however, that there will be points of disagreement or differences of taste in any television production. Inevitably the writer will experience a twinge of paranoia on seeing his creation in the hands of a group of strangers. Often he may be blissfully unaware of the production difficulties which have led to changes between the initial script and the end product. For a few writers like Terson, however, the organic genesis of a play in production is a natural process.

Peter Terson's unflagging optimism and application should be held up as a shining example to any aspiring writer who loses heart after a couple of rejections. Terson's road to success was paved with them. His first submission to the BBC was in May 1958, with a play called *Big Racy Man*, about a shipyard worker. At that time he was living in Northumberland and was a young games master, writing under his real name of Patterson. The freshness of his dialogue and characterization were immediately recommended by the BBC script readers to Donald Bull in the script department. But between that time and 1962 none of the thirteen plays he sent into the BBC was produced. Two scripts were, in fact, paid for, *Big Racy Man* and *A Coat of Whitewash*, but no one could find a way to structure these big sprawling works into produceable plays. Donald Bull even wrote to Terson, in 1960, saying, 'Without professional collaboration, I do not think you will get to the point where you can sell your work. There is a great gap between what you can do and what is required of a professional playwright.' Bull then recommended that Terson find a collaborator. What he obviously 'could do' was pour out eminently speakable and enjoyable comic dialogue and create comic morality figures much in the style of a Jonsonian comedy of manners. The problem was how to catch these characters and harness them to a workable dramatic framework.

Luckily for Terson, at this point he was taken up by Peter Cheeseman and, on an Arts Council grant, became resident dramatist at Stoke-on-Trent, where his work could be shaped with the help of Cheeseman and the company. His first play produced there was *A Night to Make the Angels Weep*, and seven more followed between then and 1971. In 1967 he began his association with Michael Croft and the National Youth Theatre, a natural outlet for his fresh, ebullient style of writing.

It was in 1967, when the BBC bought the National Youth Theatre production of *Zigger-Zagger*, Terson's play set in a football stadium, that I first met him. Nine years had, in fact, elapsed since his first submissions to the BBC. I asked him if he had any ideas for a new play and immediately commissioned *Mooney and his Caravans*, which was screened a year later[1] and followed by

[1] And subsequently put on as a stage play at the Hampstead Theatre Club.

The Last Train Through the Harecastle Tunnel, commissioned in 1968 and transmitted in October 1969.

The first thing that struck one about Terson was his tremendous energy and enjoyment of life, both of which characteristics over-flowed into his work. He came from a working-class background, but was totally devoid of any chip-on-the-shoulder complex about this, while obviously respecting the 'natural' life of people who work with their hands and the land in preference to the sophisti-cated life of the city dwellers. His attitude to the working classes had been compared to that of Tressell,[2] 'a mixture of contempt and pity, seeing them as prisoners, doomed to be either cannon or factory fodder'.[3] To my mind, it is much more that of a benevolent satirist seeing people trapped by their own conditioning and their own comic characteristics into a specific way of life.

Mooney and his Caravans told the sad tale of Charlie and Mave, newly-weds, who wanted to better themselves and escape from council-estate life into the Cotswolds. Their interim step was to rent a caravan on Mooney's site; the site, as one critic, Irving Wardle (*The Times*, 18 May 1958), so aptly remarked, gradually emerges as a miniature police state with Mooney controlling the couple's behaviour, what they eat (the camp shop charges more than any-where else), seducing the wife and finally turning them out. Throughout all these events, the husband's foolishness and the wife's snobbishness blind them to their own exploitation. It was, in fact, a mini political allegory.

The Last Train Through the Harecastle Tunnel showed the strength of a man with an obsession, in this case, train-spotting. Terson described the idea for the play to me in a letter as follows: 'I have a super play about a youth who is a train-spotter and goes to be on the last train through the Harecastle Tunnel; before he goes, his world seems ridiculous, and the world of his colleagues at the office seems immensely important; by the time he has come back we realize that *his* world is immensely important, and the rest of the world ridiculous.' On his journey the naive Benjamin encounters a number of people who, attracted by his innocence, are led to confide their problems to him, while he remains secure in his obsession.

[2]Robert Tressell wrote *The Ragged-trousered Philanthropists*, an early socialist work which was televized on 'Story Parade'.
[3]*Sunday Times*, 24 January, 1971 (reviewed by John Mapplebeck).

2 John Le Mesurier and Richard O'Callaghan in *The Last Train Through the Harecastle Tunnel*.

Terson was, in fact, writing about situations he had actually experienced and observed at first hand; all his plays start off on this basis. He had met both the train-spotter and the caravan-site victims. I was to discover only just in time that they were, in fact, still carrying the names of their real-life counterparts. In fact, so unable is Terson to divorce himself from reality that he usually gives his characters real-life names and, on one occasion, presented me with a fascinating play, only to take it back saying it could never be done as everyone was real and would sue. In the course of looking for new aspects of life he has gone to live with the gypsies (and been beaten up by them) and spent months with a touring ballet company. His scripts, badly typed on the back of previous scripts, all give the impression of having been written under a haystack or, indeed, on the barge where he lived for some time. Terson, himself, is only too aware of the untidy nature of these scripts in form, as well as appearance, and waits for the next step of production to knock them into tighter shape. But, in the case of both plays mentioned, the morality-play structure was clearly

91

visible through the untidiness. It was up to those working on the productions to cut away the undergrowth and get at them.

The most important ingredient of both these plays was to find the right comic style in which to play them; in both instances, the directors and myself (James Ferman for *Mooney*, Alan Clarke for *Harecastle*) decided on actors who were basically comedians – John Alderton and Richard O'Callaghan – and on a 'comedy-of-manners' stylized presentation: heightened reality. Both were done in the studio with small amounts of filming. Audience reactions, as usual, were mixed, and once more pointed to the fact that any play which departs from a totally realistic convention causes a large section of the audience to be baffled and, consequently, annoyed. If they took the goings-on in these plays literally, then the characters were unbelievably naive. The tenuousness of the plots annoyed them; the morality themes got through almost subconsciously, but they wanted something more concrete to grasp. The critics, on the other hand, were almost universally appreciative of the originality of the two productions and of Terson's intuitive insight into his characters.

A more specific but less happy example of democratization was Roy Minton. In March 1968 I commissioned a play from a writer who was new to me. Roy Minton, who was living in Norwich at that time, had submitted scripts to the BBC since 1965 but had only, so far, been produced on ITV, who had done a thirty-minute play of his. Previous correspondence between Minton and BBC script editors made interesting reading. When one script editor had kept a submission too long, he had been warned in a letter rich in four-letter words that Minton would come down to London and 'sort him out on a personal basis'. As a very consciously working-class writer Minton supposed that the BBC was 'only pin money' for the editor: an attitude to all those whom he considered more privileged than himself which was to colour a lot of his work.

Minton came to see me with what I considered to be a good and lively idea: a description of a weekend outing in Blackpool for a charabanc full of Nottingham miners. He told me he had, at one time, been in the mines himself and I got the impression he knew the subject well. The first draft of the play came in three months later. It was a vast, sprawling script, which would probably have run about a hundred minutes in its entirety. At the same time, much of the dialogue and characterization was extraordinarily fresh and funny. The plot, in so far as there was one, began realistically and dissolved into fantasy as one by one the colliers decided to 'drop out' in Blackpool and the publican who had organized the party eventually returned to Nottingham alone, on an empty bus. Several drama directors gave me their opinion that it could not be made to work, while the Head of Plays opined that it was 'just a possibility' if cut down to half its size. He felt, too, that the serious background of increasing pit closures which Minton had intended was entirely lost in the script.

Not long before I received this script, a documentary director named Michael Tuchner had come to see me, saying how much he would like to work in the Drama Department. Tuchner seemed to me to share the same ebullience and curiosity about life as Terson and I had been proved right when I viewed his work. He had begun on *Tonight* and had made many programmes with Malcolm Muggeridge and Alan Whicker, including several whose sublime sense of the ridiculous caused me to laugh almost as much as the *Benny Hill Show*: *Paris Fashions* with Whicker, *The Making of Grand Prix*, showing Frankenheimer going berserk on location, *The American Way of Sex*, all showed Tuchner to have a marvellous ability to pick out people's idiosyncrasies: selecting from reality to produce comedy. When Minton's script *Sling Your Hook* arrived, it struck me that Tuchner might be an ideal director. It was true that he had never worked with actors before. This aspect would provide an element of risk, but the characterization in the piece was bald and broadly comic; intense, sensitive performances were not called for. What *was* obvious was that Tuchner could handle film superbly well, could cut it with a great feeling for pace (he was himself an ex-film editor) and had an outstandingly humorous approach to life. I felt, also, that he would be much able to utilize the existing documentary background of Blackpool to advantage than a drama director who was used to artificial filming conditions set up with the help of a designer. It was a hunch which I followed and, in my opinion, it worked supremely well.

Minton, however, from the moment he and Tuchner and I set out on a 'recce' of Blackpool, was determined to disagree. He was not happy with the idea of a director who had never worked with actors before. On arrival in Blackpool, we were to find that many of the locations, as described by Minton, were no longer in existence (he had not, it turned out, been there for years). Substitutes therefore had to be found. Requests to change the script to accommodate the substitutes and to cut it down to the seventy-five-minute length at which it had been commissioned were greeted with non-compliance, as Minton felt the entire script should be shot without change.

We started to film *Sling Your Hook* at the end of September, in Nottingham. It began with the miners coming up from the mine shaft, released for their weekend. It then showed them leaving the pub in Nottingham, all of them fairly young except for Joe, the publican (played by Michael Bates), and Oliver, his querulous friend (played by the north-country comedian Joe Gladwyn).

The next part of the filming, which I shall remember to my dying day, took place inside the charabanc. For what seemed like days, I lay at the back of the coach, staying out of shot amongst crates of brown ale, while we drove back and forth between Nottingham and Blackpool. The enormous cast had so entered into the spirit of the piece by the time we had arrived that it was almost impossible to believe they were not the swearing, drinking, temporarily liberated group of miners they were playing. Their luggage also included a basket of pigeons which Joe, the landlord, kept on his bed and which were released on the beach, one pigeon obligingly relieving itself just as the shot was being taken.

The sheer Giles granny/Donald McGill aspect of Blackpool was then captured by Tuchner as he went along and although the script was never rewritten or altered, Tuchner and I had to cut it and alter locations as the production demanded. I was, for instance, to write to Minton in October explaining that a scene in a bowling green had been cut because when we came to shoot it the green was 6 ft under water.

The play, which was transmitted in April 1969, was enormously successful in terms of viewing figures, audience appreciation and the critics. The audience reaction index was 71, well above the average of 52 for the previous and current series of 'Wednesday Plays'; the viewing figure of 8.5 million was also extremely high. Peter Black in the *Daily Mail* (3 April 1969) described it as 'a splendid outing to Blackpool . . . cheerful and funny, as well as authentic', while James Thomas, in the *Daily Express*, called it 'A human document with heart and real humour. It finally restored to "Wednesday Play" the originality which made it famous.' Any adverse criticisms were directed at the fantasy element of the play – it was difficult to swallow the defection of all the miners – but some recognized it as an allegory of the future in terms of pit closures.

Minton's initial discontent turned to grudging pleasure at the reception of the piece which he, on several occasions, asked to show to film companies as an example of his work. I commissioned a second play from him, *The Hunting of Lionel Crane*, which again was all shot on film by Tuchner, and transmitted in January 1970.

The play was about a deserter from the army who lives rough until he is discovered on the land of a wealthy squire and shot, while escaping, by the gamekeeper. The opening army scenes contained some of Minton's rough humour, but in the serious section many viewers and critics found it hard to believe in the blackness of the villains and the author's permeating resentment of the 'privileged' classes. Although the viewing figures were high for the season (7.75 million) and the reaction index was 64, many viewers said that an otherwise good play was 'ruined' by a ridiculous finish – a criticism which both the director and myself had tried to make on numerous occasions before the final production, but to no avail, so far as rewrites were concerned.

We were now both to be recipients of letters similar to those received by the story editor. The films had introduced Tuchner to dramatic production and brought him feature film offers. Minton had, in turn, received his most favourable reviews for any work to date, but his conviction that his work had not been properly served, a recurring pattern, brought our relationship to an end. Without 'democratization' the work could not have got on to the screen, but in this case the author could not accept the fact that the creative contribution of others had added immeasurably to the success of his original creation.

Chapter 9

The autocrats

The plays discussed in the last two chapters could be described as having a basically parochial British appeal, although the problems dealt with in Tony Parker's work (which has all sold well abroad) are, of course, found in other countries. I now come to three authors, John Osborne, John Mortimer and Peter Nichols, who, in the fields of theatre and film, have achieved an international status. Although they are very much chroniclers, satirists and social commentators on contemporary Britain, their work is, of course, well known and much performed abroad.

As soon as I came on to 'Wednesday Play' in 1967 I wrote to John Osborne asking if he would be interested in writing an original play for the programme. He replied that he would, in principle, but that other commitments were too heavy for him to start anything else at the time. Much to my surprise, for I had assumed that he was politely declining to write for television, he came up, over a year later, with the idea for *The Right Prospectus*. The idea was followed by the script, in June 1969.

I had never met John Osborne before I went to his house to discuss the script with him. I did so with a certain amount of trepidation, in view of his attitude towards 'democratization' and his renowned reputation for never doing rewrites on any of his work. The script was not an easy one to produce or direct. It had elements of everything: fantasy, satire and tragi-comedy. In it, a wealthy middle-aged couple (the husband a well-known man in the arts) decide to send themselves back to a boys' public school to find out how they could cope in such a society. The wife (one must believe) is entirely accepted as a normal pupil. Most of the lengthy and satirical speeches were written for a seventeen-year-old 'head boy' – not an easy part to cast. Although the dialogue was fascinating, there was little visual guidance as to where or how anything should be shot. At the same time, the script was undoubtedly one of the most unusual and interesting, in terms of ideas, that I had ever read.

My first meeting with Osborne was mainly about directors and casting, nearly all his suggestions being people he had worked with in the theatre. Understandably perhaps, as he had had little performed on television,[1] he did not seem to know the work of many television directors. One thing I do remember from the meeting was his close acquaintanceship with what the critics had had to say about the 'Wednesday Play' – at least, what they'd had to say that was uncomplimentary.

In the event, I asked Alan Cooke (who had also directed Osborne's *Luther* for television) to direct the piece and we all met again for lunch mainly to try to find out from Osborne which way, stylistically, the play should go. Our main problem was going to be to get the audience to accept the wife's integration into the school and to make the head boy's long speeches hold up for the time required without becoming static and visually unexciting.

Much to my surprise, it seemed to me that Osborne wanted to detach himself as much as possible from the production and to leave us to get on with it, trusting of course that nothing would be altered. Although I kept in constant touch with him throughout the production, telling him what was going on and inviting him to the read-through and to see the rushes and the rough cut and final cut of the film, he did not, in fact, come near, although he always replied with polite and encouraging notes. To a letter from Alan before we went into production, asking for clarification of certain sections of the script, he replied: 'Very often things are not clear because they are not meant to be clear.' He then offered to buy the play back, and what had begun as a mild and friendly letter ended in an angry outburst against the BBC and 'Its "Wednesday Play", which doesn't have much reputation anyway, and could do with a bit of prestige, even if it might be a bit spurious.' A sentiment which, did he but know it, was not entirely foreign to me. We decided therefore to proceed, as best we might, without further requests for clarification.

[1]His only other work specifically written for TV was *A Subject for Scandal and Concern*, which was put on by the BBC in 1960, with Richard Burton in the lead.

Luckily for Osborne, he was not involved in the practical difficulties of mounting this particular production. We realized that the only way to do the piece authentically would be to film it entirely in a real public school, using the real boys as extras and putting our cast among them. The problem was to find the school. We came in the wake of Lindsay Anderson's film *If*, which had so offended the Headmasters' Conference that all headmasters who were members had been advised not to allow a film unit into their schools, and not to do so under any circumstances without consulting the public relations officer of the Conference first.

One snowy, freezing day Alan Cooke and I set out for Cambridge with a copy of the script to show to the public relations officer of the Headmasters' Conference (himself a headmaster of a school in Cambridge) in the hope that the fame of the author and the satirical nature of the script would convince him that we were not seriously attacking the public school system and that we should be allowed into a school to film. Our reception was as icy as the weather. After the script had been read, we were told that it was obscene and that all headmasters would be advised not to let us in. The obscenity, presumably, was in some references to masturbation in one of the long speeches delivered by the head boy.

We now had to find a headmaster brave enough to defy the Conference and let us in. We had the additional problem that John Osborne had written the wife's part for his wife Jill Bennett and that, in order to have her in the cast, we had to find a school near London because she was starring in a theatre play in London and would have to return every night from filming in time to be on stage. At last, the tireless production assistants found a suitable school near Guildford where the headmaster, an admirer of Osborne's work, proudly told us that he took orders from no one and would let us in. The set designer began to take his measurements of the school and the costume designer began to make school uniforms and badges to tone in with those of the school.

Over the following few days, however, the board of governors of the school must have decided that the headmaster's decision had been ill advised. With no explanation, we were told that it would not be possible for us to film there after all. We were now left with a pile of the wrong uniforms and a leading actress who could only film at a certain distance from London. Our only possible alternative school was one in north Devon where the headmaster was willing to let us in, for which decision he was later to get into serious trouble.

The problem of the leading actress was 'resolved' by her agent demanding that she be paid handsomely for *not* being in the film, although no contract had been signed, and by our having to replace her at the last moment through no fault of our own. The budget was now seriously impaired by having to pay for two leading actresses.

At long last we began filming, in freezing weather in March 1970. After a couple of weeks we all began to feel very much like the couple in the play, as though we, too, were part of the closed society of the school. When the bell rang, one's instinct was to collect one's books. The young assistant film editor (we had a mobile cutting room parked in the middle of the school grounds) was, in fact, hauled out of a telephone booth by a master and reprimanded for smoking; the boys fell on our location catering van at tea-time, stuffing their pockets with sandwiches and cakes while George Cole and Elvi Hale, the two leading artists, began to look more and more at home in the school dining room dressed in uniforms eating baked beans – their greatest ordeal being a cross-country run in icy rain in which the wife (as in all other fields) came up trumps while the husband fell miserably behind.

By a curious coincidence, it turned out that John Osborne had himself attended a public school in Devon not far from ours and had played games against our school. It was from this school that he was expelled, at the age of fifteen, for hitting the headmaster back after he had been hit (described in an interview with Terry Coleman in *The Guardian*, 12 August 1971). But the play was by no means anti-public school. Like all Osborne's work, it had a sense of regret for certain passing values, a wistful middle-aged look back at youthful experience, and it had many satirical observations to make on the school system and the way people choose schools for their children from 'the right prospectus'. Take, for example, this extract of the discussion between Mr and Mrs Newbold as to which school they should choose for themselves.

> MRS NEWBOLD: Well, I'll tell you this, we're not going to one of those scruffy boy and girl places where they all smoke and have affairs and call the teachers Alf and Mary.
>
> NEWBOLD: No, I don't fancy that. Think who you'd meet. The parents, I mean.

MRS NEWBOLD: Poets who go around talking to young people, women who read *The Guardian*.

The Right Prospectus went out in October 1970 and was repeated in December of the following year. Of it, Sean Day-Lewis said in the *Daily Telegraph*: 'For me, *The Right Prospectus* was not merely the most distinguished original television play of the year, but one which will linger uneasily in my mind for years ahead.' When the play went out, I heard nothing from Osborne and was overcome by a great uneasiness. We had had, in the course of editing the film, as is inevitable in this medium, to cut sections – especially the very long speeches of the head boy. I wondered if this was the reason for the silence.

To my astonishment, however, after the play was repeated, I received a card. 'Seeing *Right Prospectus* again,' wrote Osborne, 'I was struck by the care and skill that had gone into it. Also the very strong and sustained lyricism, regret and melancholy of it – simple and no jokiness. Just thought I'd tell you as I was a bit captious before and possibly ungenerous.' It seemed that the carefully guided 'democratization' had worked. Even the author recognized that his intention had been honoured and all attempts had been made to realize it.

John Mortimer was an author whom I had met briefly in 'Armchair Theatre' days and who, as a personality, comes nearest to Renaissance man of anyone I have encountered; his conversation bursting with life, wit and an interest in every conceivable aspect of human experience. He has said of himself (*Daily Telegraph*, 10 March 1970): 'I have a very low threshold of boredom. That's why I do many careers.'

Unlike the majority of writers on the list, he comes educationally from an upper middle-class background, having been educated at Harrow and Oxford before being called to the Bar. Unlike most of the writers on the list, too, he has always pursued another profession, the law, while writing incredibly prolifically, and his fields of writing range over novels, the radio, ballet, many film scripts and, of course, stage plays. When asked by an interviewer in *The Times* (7 March 1960) about his position in the theatre and the influences on his writing, Mortimer replied: 'There's no group I feel strongly connected with. I admire Harold Pinter's plays and N. F. Simpson's, but I think they're writing for a smaller audience than I am. I'm pretty much in agreement with the opinions of writers like Arnold Wesker and John Osborne, but I wouldn't write in the way they do – not after the realists of the 1930s, the Clifford Odetses. Also I think they assume a tremendous weight of public opposition that isn't there. But I don't deny influences; they're very important. Dickens, the Russian novelists, Chekhov – they've affected me. So have the law courts.' Elsewhere, he has said (*Sunday Times*, 14 October 1962) that the law keeps him in touch with real people and enables him to indulge the talent of a frustrated actor and (*Evening Standard*, 7 April 1966): 'It teaches you also, the way people talk, I love some of the dialogue you hear in court.'

He is also remarkable among playwrights in being an optimist. 'I use comedy because it's a better weapon than frontal attack. I want to give the audience the shock of recognition in which they see the actors reflecting their own behaviour and laugh at it. I want to open their hearts,' he has said. 'Comedy is the only thing worth writing in this despairing age, provided it's comedy which is truly on the side of the lonely, the neglected and unsuccessful and plays its part in the lone war against established rules, and against the imposing of an arbitrary code of behaviour on free and unpredictable human beings.' (*Spectator*, 18 April 1958.)

Again, as soon as I came on to 'Wednesday Play', I approached John Mortimer to ask if he would write for the programme. He was not, of course, a stranger either to television or the BBC, having already had eight plays produced, on both radio and television, since 1957, as well as several on ITV. He immediately came up with an idea for a play related to the new divorce laws.

Mortimer's idea, like Osborne's, was, in a sense, a fantasy. *Infidelity Took Place*, as it was called, concerned a happily married couple, Molly and Bill Panett. Their only problem was that, as they were both highly successful professionals, their tax position was very disadvantageous. Their accountant therefore advised them to get divorced and live together as two single people.

Molly, a scatterbrained painter, goes to a divorce lawyer, Leonard Hoskins, armed with various false grounds for divorce. But Hoskins, a mother-ridden bachelor of forty, sees in her a suitable mate and in himself a knight in shining armour rescuing her from a dragon husband. Hoskins eventually discovers the truth and is thoroughly disillusioned by the dishonesty of the couple, though practising similar deceptions himself daily in the name of the law.

John's description of Hoskins, in his synopsis of what the play would be about, was wonderful indeed. 'His suede shoes are shiny, his RAF tie is threadbare, his macintosh pockets bulging with divorce petitions . . . the crumbs of the pork pie (which he has eaten in a crypt of the law courts) hang on his waistcoat.' He also has a 'set of automatic and extremely reactionary opinions'. The part was eventually played to perfection by John Nettleton – a personification of shabby narrow-mindedness.

Like Osborne, Mortimer was 'taking the mickey' out of some of the Sunday supplement people, but in a far more loving way. Here is a sample of dialogue from the play.

> MOLLY (having made some money): 'I thought I'd have a new boiler in the cottage and a washbasin in the upstairs loo, and next year's MG and go to Klosters for Christmas . . . Oh, and I want a tidy bin with Union Jacks on it.

And here is John's picture of the divorce lawyer (when asked about grounds for divorce by Molly): 'Basic menu is . . . disaster for three years, adultery or cruelty with injury to health, eye or limb. I mean leaving aside such little *à la carte* capers as incurable insanity, epilepsy, pregnant by another man at the time of the ceremony or nonconsummation. . . . No hope, I suppose, of nonconsummation?'

The play was commissioned in June 1967, delivered in November, with rewrites, and produced in March and April 1968, with Michael Hayes directing. It was transmitted very soon after recording, in May 1968. The production was all in the studio, with short filmed inserts, and like all John's plays, it provided excellent acting parts. Like all his plays, it also commanded a high audience viewing figure (8 million), although comments from the audience – as with the Osborne play – complained of the fantasy element in the script. Again, there seems to be a large section of the public who are unwilling or unable to open up their minds to anything other than direct realistic portrayal of the life they see around them.

Like Osborne and Mortimer, Peter Nichols is, of course, a leading portrayer of contemporary England, though in perhaps a more directly autobiographical way than either of the others. Unlike them, he seems to pursue a more realistic line on television, leaving the more experimental forms and stylized satire, such as are found in *A Day in the Death of Joe Egg*, *The National Health* and *Forget-Me-Not Lane* for the stage. All three of these plays do, in a sense, contain the same elements of fantasy as *The Right Prospec-*

tus and *Infidelity Took Place*. His television plays do not. *Hearts and Flowers*, which I commissioned from Nichols for 'Play For Today', was written, so he has said (in an interview in *The Times*, 31 March 1971), as a 'footnote' to *Forget-Me-Not Lane*. 'I started to write this one, got bogged down, so turned aside to write a television play about the death of the man I was trying to write about in the stage play – the father, who's already dead when the funeral play begins.'

Nichols, unlike the other two writers, did in fact, serve his apprenticeship in television after having been an actor and school-teacher. His first television play *Walk on the Grass* won the BBC West Region Television Play competition and was screened in 1959, while *Hearts and Flowers*, transmitted in December 1970, was his sixteenth for the medium. In many cases the television plays have been, as Nichols himself has described it, 'essays' for stage plays. *The National Health*, for example, began as a television script called *The End Beds*. In each case, the television version has been more directly realistic and less strongly satirical than the stage works, Nichols being aware that he was writing for two different types of audiences.

Take, for instance, the following remarks from Nichols characters in *Hearts and Flowers*. Tony, a television personality and interviewer, and Bob, his brother, a provincial architect, are at their father's funeral, surrounded by an assortment of elderly relatives and friends as well as a beautifully observed delegation from their father's place of work, all mouthing platitudes. As the funeral procession drives through the cemetery, the following comments are heard on the elaborate tombstones that loom into sight (Marie is the widowed mother, Eric a pedantic cousin):

ERIC: I could spend a week amongst these monuments without losing interest.
MARIE: That's nice and cheerful.
ERIC: They represent a broad spectrum of the visual tastes of the eighteenth and nineteenth centuries.
BOB: That one there reminds me of the Elephant House.
TONY: Superb location for a film.
BOB: I'd bulldoze the lot and make it into a children's park.
ERIC: But surely, as an architect, you'd deplore the loss? What about that hideous council estate we passed?
BOB: At least it houses living people . . .

TONY: Look at the class distinction – carried to the grave. These monstrous memorials here and – up on the hill – the ordinary stones in serried ranks. Just as they were in life.

Thus Nichols gently mimics his characters – Tony, the poseur whose every remark is aimed at an unseen television audience, Bob stolidly practical, Eric in his ivory tower, Marie mouthing cheerful, working-class platitudes. Much less strong stuff than Osborne's, much less stylized than Mortimer's and obviously immediately recognizable to the audience.

Of this production I have little to say. At the time it was rehearsed and recorded (it was a studio production with a little filming) I was totally preoccupied with the filming of *Edna, the Inebriate Woman*. I had invited Christopher Morahan to direct the play, knowing that he and Nichols had worked together very closely in the past. There was little for me to contribute. Nichols's script was totally workable, Morahan was superbly organized and was working hand-in-glove with an author he knew well and respected. Once we had agreed on casting, I disappeared until the final run-through at rehearsals and in the studio.

Of these three plays, *Hearts and Flowers* appeared, from the readers' reports, to 'have hit the gold' as a piece of credible writing. It was easier for an audience to accept than the other two, being totally realistic. People's main enjoyment lay in the closely observed small part characters and the closeness-to-home quality of the play. At the same time, other escapists in the audience objected to such a depressing subject being treated at all in drama.

Why are there not more plays on the list by these three authors? The answer is simple and obvious: all three can make more money and gain more lasting acclaim in other fields. The financial rewards of the one-off play for television, in England at least, are slender and can never hope to match those of a successful stage play or film script. On the other hand, television is an outlet for all these authors for certain scripts they want to write which will not extend to the other media.

Chapter 10

The 'blockbuster':
Edna, the Inebriate Woman

I mentioned in the last chapter that, at the time we were rehearsing Peter Nichols's *Hearts and Flowers*, I was involved in the filming of *Edna, the Inebriate Woman*. For a long period, in fact, it seemed to me that I had never been involved in anything else.

The history of *Edna* began for me in January 1968 when I wrote to Jeremy Sandford asking if he'd be interested in writing a script for 'Wednesday Play'. His agent had mentioned to me that he was researching into the life of gypsies in England and it was on this subject that I first approached him – at the same time trying to get from Gerald Savory, the Head of Plays, an assurance that if I commissioned such a script, I could produce it all on film. Obviously, one cannot show the life of the gypsies within the four walls of a studio. Nothing came of this script for another year, there being some talk of a possible feature film on the subject.

The following December I met Sandford, who put to me the idea of writing a trilogy of plays linked with his famous *Cathy, Come Home* by the title 'In the Time of Cathy'. It was to show three aspects of intolerance. One play was to deal with the gypsies and their maltreatment by society; another, *Arlene*, was to handle the plight of unmarried mothers. (On both these subjects he had already written a number of newspaper articles.) The third play was to be called *The Lodging House*. It was to be a sociological study of a doss-house for women vagrants and drunks.

The trilogy was commissioned together, the understanding being that the gypsies script would be made all on film, while *The Lodging House* (which would have a structure something like Gorki's *The Lower Depths*), confined as it was within one lodging house for old women, could easily be done in a studio. The action

3 Patricia Hayes in *Edna, the Inebriate Woman*.

was to centre around an announcement that the lodging house was to be closed and the inmates turned out into limbo.[1]

The script of *The Lodging House* was commissioned in December 1969; the first draft was received the following May and the final draft paid for in October 1970. Between the delivery and

[1]In the end, this constituted one short scene in *Edna*, when she bids adieu to a beetle-infested lodging house.

acceptance dates, countless cuts and rewrites and 'amendments' were made.

When the first draft, now retitled *Edna, the Inebriate Woman*, arrived on my desk, a simultaneous feeling of elation and faintness overcame me. Was this seriously meant to be the all-studio play I had commissioned from Jeremy? The first 'amended' version, presented after I had asked for cuts and reductions of the cast, still ran, in Jeremy's typing, to ninety-four pages, and in the BBC typist's version it came out to 130. The cast ran to ninety speaking parts, apart from hosts of non-speaking extras. Almost every scene took place in a different location and almost every page contained another scene. Where was I going to get the film allocation, the money or the time to bring this to life?

My feeling of elation came from the fact that, massive, sprawling and untidy though *Edna* was, it conveyed a marvellously vivid picture of Dickensian low life in modern times; it contained a strong central character who had much humour; it also had some deeply touching moments.

The work of Jeremy Sandford and Tony Parker has often been compared because they both deal with subjects of sociological interest and importance. Yet no two writers could be more different in their approach. Parker's work is always immaculately researched and always attempts to present a totally impartial picture; the author stepping back to let the audience draw its own conclusions. The accuracy of his work has always been attested by the Home Office, the children's welfare organizations etc.

A script by Sandford, on the other hand, is like an impressionistic painting. The total effect conveyed has great emotional impact; the details, on close inspection, are blurs and blobs. As anyone who saw *Cathy, Come Home* will know, Sandford, unlike Parker, is blatantly propagandist. The authorities have not always been so well disposed to his work. After *Cathy, Come Home* was screened, there were many protests about the inaccuracy of its statistics about the homeless and its portrait of the authorities. On its second showing, 2 million council members and officials were asked to watch and see how many mistakes they could find in it. Mr Laurence Evans of the Local Government Office said, 'This play is full of blunders and omissions.' Another official complained of factual inaccuracies and another of the deliberate misrepresentation of officers of a public authority as 'gangsters', especially in the scene where the children are wrenched from Cathy on a station platform. At a later showing, most of the background comments giving statistics were, in fact, omitted. There is no doubt, however, that *Cathy* would have had much less impact had a more evenly balanced picture been painted.

Sandford's own working technique is also impressionistic by comparison with Parker's painstaking research. In a *Sunday Times* article on 6 September 1970, Sandford gave his account of how he researched *Edna* (and the book on the same subject, *Down and Out in Britain*, which contained many of the characters also found in *Edna*). 'To gather material he grew his beard, bought some old shoes and a mac and joined the men down on the Thames embankment.' 'For two separate occasions of two weeks,' said Sandford in the interview, 'I submerged myself in that nether world.' To all intents and purposes he became, himself, a temporary tramp.

Questioned (after *Cathy*) by Robin Douglas Home (in an interview in *Woman's Own*, 28 August 1967) about why he, who came from an upper-class background, was educated at Eton and Oxford and married to the daughter of a millionaire, chose to write about the poor and not the rich, Sandford replied with great honesty that his basic motivation was curiosity. 'The upper classes are completely written out . . .' he said. 'To write about an area of society which has mainly been ignored – that is much easier to do in that it's virgin territory. It wasn't any desire to plumb the social depths, so to speak, which led me to do something so uncharacteristic. It was just curiosity.'

Sandford's entire career had, in fact, been marked by an aura of eccentric curiosity. His life at Oxford has been well documented. 'At Oxford, Mr Sandford was a leader of the smartest set the university has known since the 1920s,' said an article in the *Sunday Express* on 6 January 1957, written at the time of Sandford's engagement to heiress Nell Dunn. 'His rooms were papered in scarlet and gold. His bed was over his bath and it was his practice to discomfit "tedious visitors" by turning on the taps to drown their small talk.' According to another article in the *Financial Times* (26 September 1963). 'He lived in a crumbling mansion on the river, called The Folly, kept hard-boiled eggs in a chandelier, took a punt-load of costumed musicians on to the Cherwell for a night-long performance of Donizetti, and managed to do brilliantly too. "He was so much a figure of fantasy," says a friend of the time, "that it was hard to remember he really existed." Frequent reminders for the doubtful appeared in the columns of the *Tatler*.'

Sandford's debut on radio belongs to this era. In 1956, at the age of twenty-five, he made a contribution to the Third Programme with a piece about a machine that wrote love letters. This machine, MUK, was 'originally designed to deal with business problems rather than love,' said Sandford to a *Daily Mirror* reporter, when questioned about the programme (19 December 1956). 'To use it for love letters you need a rather paternal attitude towards it . . . I am of a loving nature. So it was not hard for me to give the machine loving ideas . . . I believe I understand machine language like some people understand dog language. I am working now on an idea for mechanical concerts given by mechanical birds . . . I am also training a nightingale to sing human songs.'

From this early rarified Ronald Firbank atmosphere Sandford was led, obviously by curiosity, to make a very eccentric move. When called up for National Service, instead of taking up a commission, he joined the RAF band in Germany, playing first clarinet and getting his first entrée into the life of the 'working classes'.

Out of this experience came Sandford's first play, *The Dreaming Bandsman*, which was transmitted on the BBC Home Service in September 1956 and then turned into a stage play. The latter, directed by Ted Kotcheff, was put on at the Belgrade Theatre, Coventry, in July 1960. The play concerned four army musicians who form a jazz combo, dream of imaginary futures and pasts and stay on in the army while supposedly looking forward to being demobbed. Like all Sandford's work it had tremendous production demands, with the City of Coventry Police Band marching up and down the stage for much of the first act.

The *Manchester Guardian* critic, Gareth Lloyd Evans (13 September 1960) was outraged by what he called this series of 'undramatic, inchoate scenes'. 'Have you ever,' he asked, 'had an invitation to a party at a swish place with the best people and found yourself gulping beer in a public lavatory with the graffiti being howled at you?' Robert Muller, then drama critic for the *Daily Mail*, was the only one to recognize in it the vitality that marked all Sandford's work. He described it as being 'such attractive bad taste' and as 'having all the airs and graces of an "Armchair Theatre" product. It is "contemporary" (Americanized), "vital" (sexy), "frank" (rude), and "efficient" (insubstantial).'

In 1959, two years after their very much publicized marriage, Sandford and his wife, Nell Dunn, moved from their fashionable flat in Cheyne Walk, Chelsea, to a block of condemned houses in

Battersea. Sandford, described in the *Daily Express* (12 November 1959) as a 'surrealist writer', said he was anxious to experience life 'with real people' while his wife, who took a job wrapping chocolates in a factory, said that arriving in Battersea was 'like arriving in Mexico' (*Sunday Times*, 8 January 1967). 'I felt happy and relaxed straight away, I still do. I prefer working-class people.'

It was after this move that Sandford began writing articles (*The Observer*, 1961; *The People*, 1964) about the homeless, inspired by the plight of a neighbour who lost her home and had been put into Newington Lodge, an LCC accommodation centre for homeless families. The script of *Cathy, Come Home* followed.

'By the time we finished working on it,' said Sandford (the 'we' being himself and Ted Kotcheff, who had consulted closely with him on it), 'we hoped it would appear as a document in the 1964 General Election, as an indictment of Toryism, but we were unable to find anyone to back it.' (*Morning Star*, 3 December 1966.) Both Sydney Newman and Peter Luke, then producing 'Wednesday Play', turned it down on financial, 'structural' and political grounds. 'One commends his crusading spirit but this is documentary stuff . . . The "Wednesday Play" is not a political platform,' was Luke's response, quoted in a rejection letter from his story editor, David Benedictus. There were also practical and organizational difficulties involved.

The play, which, as most readers will undoubtedly know, dealt with the story of a young couple and their children, rendered homeless by unemployment and eventually torn apart as a family, was eventually filmed with enormous success by Ken Loach and Tony Garnett in November 1966.

Sandford and I had discussed the possibility of Kotcheff directing the gypsies script. I now wrote to him in Australia, where he was filming, and asked if he would be interested in directing *Edna*, always bearing in mind that it must be reduced to a financially viable size. I felt that Kotcheff would have the same warm, humane approach to the subject as Sandford; the problem would be to control the size and shape of the project.

With the lever of Sandford's past success and by sacrificing one other film production for the following year, I managed to convince Gerald Savory to give me an enormously enlarged budget for *Edna*. In fact, the final budget was to be well over twice the normal one for a filmed 'Wednesday Play', and the number of filming days almost twice as long.

A tremendous three-way tug-of-war was now to develop between Kotcheff, Sandford and myself as to the size and shape of the script and how many characters were to be cut. The 'amended' script (second from the original) of October 1970, from which we started out, ran to 130 pages; the transcript of the film, as it went out on the air (typed on identical paper, but marginally tighter), ran 33 pages. The rough-cut ran 136 minutes, the programme on the air 90 minutes; the original number of speaking parts was approximately[2] 110, the final number on the air 44. Between the beginning and end product lay a very tortuous path indeed.

The first draft of *Edna* had contained, at various intervals, a disembodied voice which commented at great length on the happenings in the script and quoted statistics. Edna also turned to the audience and commented herself on her plight. Both Kotcheff and I felt this was a great mistake dramatically and I, in particular, remembering the accusations of inaccuracy in *Cathy*, was nervous of such a contrivance. In fact, one of my first requests to the two production assistants was to check all the facts as carefully as possible. At any event, we decided to drop the voice completely feeling that, this being drama, not documentary, the events should speak for themselves. The same applied to Edna's addresses to the audience.

As soon as I had got the go-ahead on *Edna*, I began to line up the team of people who I thought could best bring it into being. The role of production assistant in a filmed television production is one of the most neglected and anonymous and also one of the most important. Very often, it is the production assistants who find the locations which make the film look the way it does; very often they will have lined up the extras who look so authentic; only through their organization does the entire operation work. Had I been at the awarding end of the prize-givings for *Edna* (which won many prizes), the two production assistants, John Bruce and Chris Baker, would have been among my first candidates.

Not only was I lucky enough to manage to get these two PAs, I also got the cameraman I most wanted – Peter Bartlett – who had done a great deal of distinguished documentary work and had shot the famous *War Game* film. I knew Peter Bartlett would be able to capture just the right documentary flavour and I knew that Peter

[2]Approximately, because in some cases the number of characters was indeterminate.

Edwards, the sound man, who usually worked with him, would be able to record sound beautifully in the most difficult of conditions.

Armed with this basic nucleus of people, as well as a good costume designer (who would not turn the characters into musical-comedy tramps), a good make-up supervisor (who would try for naturalism) and a good designer, one was half-way there. The other most important person was the film editor. In the case of such an amorphous production as this, the editor is, of course, a key person; it's his skill in selecting and pacing which can make or break the interest of the material. For Peter Coulson, the job of reducing 136 minutes to ninety, in consultation with Kotcheff and myself, was a considerable one. The form of the play was, in fact, largely hewn out in the cutting room, as it is in many such 'documentary' works.

By the time Kotcheff joined the production, at the end of September 1970, the production team had been lined up and had started work. Voluminous notes (printed in the appendix to give the reader some sort of idea) had passed between him and me and Sandford about cutting down the characters and locations and giving the script more dramatic progression. One of the problems was that Sandford had become infatuated with a lot of the incidental characters and at certain points went off at such tangents with them that one totally lost track of Edna herself. Originally, for example, an entire soup-kitchen sequence took place without any trace of Edna (in the end we amalgamated it with another scene to include her). When Edna arrived at the hostel, Jesus Saves, Sandford digressed at great length on the life histories of almost everyone there. In the courtroom where she was charged with being drunk and disorderly, before getting to her case, he described in detail two other cases that preceded hers. In theory, of course, this might provide good background atmosphere. In practice, it was making an already over-length script even longer. In practical terms it was requiring the budget to pay for yet another actor. Artistically I felt it was entirely wrong in diverting the audience's attention from Edna herself.

Whenever Sandford and I agreed to drop one character, Kotcheff would become infatuated with him or her and stick her back into the script. Or Sandford would drop one character and write in two others. As a result, by the time we started filming we had still reached no agreement and a large number of minor parts had still not been cast. Sometimes, after a long day's filming, Kotcheff, the two production assistants and myself would have midnight sessions deciding how many people (nuns, tramps, social workers etc.) we needed for one day ahead. Panic-stricken, I would interview a stream of actors the following day, select some and ship them down to the location to perform there and then, without Kotcheff even having laid eyes on them.

On one such occasion, I had to find, at twenty-four hours' notice, four men to act in the most low-life scene of the play (where Edna encounters a group of meths drinkers in a 'derry' – a derelict site). They had to swear and fight and mouth obscenities. I can remember interviewing some eminently respectable elderly actors and being half ashamed to ask them to read their lines to me, or to explain to them that they'd be needed immediately and in the most sordid location any actor could ever have worked in. Our filming, in November and December, was nearly all in the coldest and most squalid conditions one could imagine.

The casting of Edna was, of course, the most important decision we had to make. Kotcheff and I were in complete agreement that we should look for a comedienne. If Edna herself were too downbeat and tragic, the production might become unbearably depressing; besides, as written by Jeremy, the character was very funny. Some interesting remarks have been made on the subject of *Cathy*, in this respect; there were criticisms that the heroine of the play was much more glamorous than her real-life counterpart would ever have been. 'But,' said one reviewer, 'if Cathy had been more realistically portrayed as a foul-mouthed working-class scrubber and her pretty, appealing children had been replaced by appropriately snotty-nosed delinquents, then the sympathies of the good, honest, hard-working and decent British people would have remained dormant . . . like Dickens before him . . . the play's author has recognized our incapacity to sympathize with people who happen to be ugly or coarse or nasty' (*Granta*, the Cambridge University journal). Equally, if Edna had just been ugly, smelly, and a nuisance, without also being funny, it would have been difficult to arouse people's sympathy for her plight.

The actress Kotcheff most wanted to cast was Kathleen Harrison; I disagreed. Although I had always enjoyed her performances, I felt she was too much of a 'genteel' cockney ever to be convincing in this part. The thought of Patricia Hayes, Benny Hill's ugly lady stooge (as she appeared in the show), had occurred to me early on but I had never seen her taking a straight part; Kotcheff had and felt she could do it, but an availability enquiry revealed that she was booked up doing sketches with Benny Hill at the time we required her.

On a memorable cold evening early in our planning period, therefore, Kotcheff and I set off for Wimbledon to visit Kathleen Harrison and tell her about the part. As I did not know the way, Kotcheff, who is one of the world's wildest drivers, told me to follow him and immediately proceeded to smash into another car at Shepherd's Bush Green while turning round to see if I was behind him. Eventually we reached Miss Harrison's house. She entertained us to sherry, wearing a frilly blouse and looking the personification of a sweet, refined, middle-class lady. My heart began to sink at the thought of describing the various activities required of Edna, like taking a shower and being deloused at the 'spike', drinking and swearing in the derry with the meths drinkers etc. The situation was not helped by the fact that Miss Harrison, who was absolutely charming, also appeared to be slightly hard of hearing so that her conversation with Kotcheff ran something like this.

'What did you say dear, a tramp?'

Kotcheff, shouting in his best Canadian, 'Yeah, a drunken, filthy old tramp.'

'Would I have to mix with really dirty people, dear? You see, there are children in the house, my grandchildren.'

Eventually we departed, leaving a script behind for Miss Harrison to read and with a silent prayer in my heart that she would turn it down. I did not want to be a witness to her standing in rags in a December storm amongst a group of tramps. Needless to say, she declined the part on the grounds of her age and the physical hardships it would entail, for which no one in his right mind could blame her.

At the same time I hit on the idea of calling John Robbins, the producer of the Benny Hill show, whom I had known years before in 'Armchair Theatre' days and begging him to see if there might be some way of releasing Patricia Hayes. It would be a marvellous opportunity for her, and both Kotcheff and I felt she would be tough enough to stand up to the requirements of the part. After begging, cajoling and pestering, John agreed, with Benny Hill's approval, to reschedule all the sketches that involved Patricia Hayes and to release her to us.

Other parts were not easy to cast either, especially if the artists read the descriptions of themselves in the script . . . like Trudi, an exhibitionist nymphomaniac who exposed her private parts to Edna at the hostel; or Irene, a big, bull-like lesbian who smuggles Edna into a terrible woman's doss-house and hides her under the bed.

At one point, I even robbed one of my other productions for an 'instant' prosecuting counsel. One Sunday we were in the studio for the last day of *Hearts and Flowers*. I rushed up to Geoffrey Segal, who was playing in it, pushed a script of *Edna* into his hands on the studio floor, and asked him if he could learn the part of the counsel for the courtroom scene, in which it is decided that Jesus Saves should be closed down. The following day, fresh from *Hearts and Flowers*, he arrived at Chiswick Town Hall, word perfect, to appear in *Edna*.

The hunt for locations, initially made by the two production assistants, was mainly concentrated in the East End of London. One of our most used locations was an abandoned Salvation Army hall, called Congress Hall, in Hackney. It was, of course, entirely unheated and was alternately converted by the designer, aptly named Evan Hercules, from prison to dormitory to Victorian court-room (for flash-back sequences of Edna's early life). Jesus Saves, the hostel where Edna almost finds salvation (which was based on a real Christian Action hostel), was around the corner from Congress Hall, in an empty house in Mayolo Road, Hackney.

Some of my most vivid memories of *Edna* are connected with this house. There were three occasions when we used 'real' people mixed in with the cast. As a rule, Equity, the actors' union, will not allow this, but in certain circumstances when one has exhausted all suitable Equity members or when special skills are required, one can 'get away with it'. It would have been impossible to have found some of the faces we needed amongst actors. One of the groups we used were some actual inmates of the Christian Action hostel, who became the film inmates of Jesus Saves. They included a number of girls of such extreme lesbian appearance that they resembled a gang of teddy-boys; their dress (striped waistcoats and trousers) and haircuts and general manner were of the teddy-boy era. Most of them were also on drugs. In a scene where Edna wakes up on her first morning at Jesus Saves, she meets the inmates for the first time. For this scene, Kotcheff suggested to the girls that they should do what they would normally do every morning on first waking at their hostel. Wardrobe department had brought a selection of night-clothes, men's and women's. 'What shall we put on?' they asked.

'Whatever you'd normally wear,' said Kotcheff, 'there are plenty of nighties there.' 'Will you do me a favour, guv,' said the largest of them, 'can you see me in a nightie?'

They all appeared in men's pyjamas and, as a first-thing-in-the morning activity, began to roll up their shirtsleeves and compare hypodermic marks. Our filming activities were occasionally interrupted by one of them having hysterics upstairs, while all the time we were watched by a silent spectator, a person of totally indeterminate sex, the unhappiest-looking human being I have ever seen.

On such occasions, and when we filmed a soup-run scene with actual men from the Hammersmith Rowton House, I began to have serious qualms about what we were doing. It was true that, for the men, it meant a hot meal (from our location caterers) and some money, but to use them and the girls from Christian Action basically as human exhibits was of dubious morality. There is no doubt that, on such occasions, voyeurism plays its part. We filmed the soup-kitchen scenes on a freezing night in the nether regions of Notting Hill, and I can still picture Jeremy on one of his flying visits to the filming, standing wild-haired and radiant amongst the Rowton House men, lined up for a tray of BBC dinner. When several of them actually began to ask about the possibilities of a job, my guilt loomed even larger.

Women down-and-outs seem, as a whole, to cope better than men. The other group we used were the women who occupied the doss-house into which Irene smuggled Edna. Our doss-house was, in fact, made up by the designer in a house in Blackfriars Road which had only recently been abandoned as a council-approved dormitory. The women came from a similar house which was still in operation and, despite their miserable lot and their almost uniformly grotesque appearance, seemed like a bunch of schoolgirls enjoying 'girl talk'. So sordid was this particular location that the prop men, after working there, sent in bills for new clothing, claiming that they had had to burn theirs as they were infested.

My second reason for remembering Mayola Road so well was a row of volcanic intensity which took place there between Kotcheff and myself. Relations between producer and director are, of course, entirely a matter of personality and never the same between any two people any more than they are in marriages. As Kotcheff and I had known each other since our teens, there was no formality lost between us, but other members of the unit did not, at that time, appreciate the fact.

I arrived at Jesus Saves one morning to find that the prop boys had set up one room for a dormitory scene and the cameraman had lit it, but, at that point, Kotcheff changed his mind and decided he would shoot in the kitchen instead – a scene in which the inmates carry large boxes of horrible-looking meat and bones into the kitchen and Josie, the social worker, describes how this meat has been donated to the hostel by a friendly butcher.

Time and money were running short on the production and Kotcheff, to ensure good results, was using a very high shooting ratio ('taking' almost every shot a considerable number of times). I was seriously beginning to wonder if we would ever be allowed enough money to complete the film and was blackly pondering this question and that of all the extra characters I had wanted to cut from the script before we started and who would now end up on the cutting-room floor, as I drove down to Hackney through freezing, foggy weather. The house was small and, on my arrival, I found it in a state of chaos with prop men and camera crew at a loss where to go next, screams of drug hysteria coming from upstairs and a bewildered-looking cast hoisting boxes of meat that was turning high under the lights. I decided that the time had come to tackle Kotcheff on the subject of shooting ratio and on the cost in time and money that such changes of mind incur. Amidst the bones we shouted and railed at each other, dressed like scarecrows. 'I've made feature films' was the import of his argument. 'I don't need you and your lousy little television shows.'

'You are the most disorganized director I have ever worked with,' was the import of mine, 'this scene is a disgrace.' Meanwhile, an ashen-faced cameraman and production assistant mulled around in the background, pretending not to listen.

Several such scenes, usually ending in hysterical laughter as we realized the utter ridiculousness of our situation, were to take place throughout the filming but, unfortunately, without any truly beneficial effect upon the shooting ratio or budget. Kotcheff's theory was that, with such documentary material, the only way to achieve results was to cover oneself for all eventualities. Out of thirteen takes, he was bound to find one good one. If he shot four peripheral characters, there was bound to be one worth preserving. Only after 136 minutes had shrunk to ninety, and the corpses of numerous celluloid characters lay on the cutting-room floor, did he agree that they could have been cut from the script before we started shooting.

Apart from the preliminary script discussions, *Edna* officially took from the end of September 1970 to the end of March 1971 to plan, film and edit. A feature film, which it resembled in proportions, and complexity, would certainly have taken at least as long. For television it was something of an epic.

Edna was transmitted in October 1971, almost a year after we started shooting it. It was repeated the following March, having won the SFTA[3] awards for best production and best actress of the year; the Writers' Guild awards for best original television play and having been selected as the Critics' Circle choice for the best television play of the year. As I sat, wondering how to account for the vast overspend and how to break it gently to several other directors that there was no money for their shows, I asked myself, 'Could it have been as successful without the chaos? Could we not have controlled it from the outset by cutting the script and characters and reducing the takes?' I also wondered if this really was the best-written, best-directed, best-acted play I had ever produced, or was it the subject that made it seem so and the superb work of the production team that had made the backgrounds so real and full of life? These were questions to which one would never know the answer.

Two things were certain, however. *Edna* had been an unusually exhilarating filming experience; it had also drained the coffers dry. Surely Edna was the most expensive tramp the British public had ever had to support!

---

[3]Society of Film and Television Arts, now called BAFTA, the British Academy of Film and Television Arts.

Chapter 11

The world of the novelist: William Trevor, the 'gentle gerontocrat'

At the opposite extreme to the inarticulate world of *Edna* is the world of William Trevor's plays. It is an imaginary landscape inhabited mainly by genteel eccentrics: decaying generals, fat schoolmasters' wives, lonely junk men who listen to *The Archers* for company, deserted middle-class women of all kinds. What they all share is a high degree of articulateness. They are all given to pouring out the stories of their lives in poetic lists and inventories of pain. No television writer has written such bravura parts, especially for actresses, as Trevor.

As mentioned in Chapter 5, I first encountered William Trevor in 1964 when I bought the rights to his novel, *The Old Boys*, for 'Story Parade'. The book, which was adapted for television by Clive Exton, dealt with a group of sixty and seventy-year-old men who were still carrying on their public school battles even to death's doorstep.

By 1964 Trevor had, in fact, already made a start at writing plays. Alastair Sim, after reading *The Old Boys*, had commissioned him to write *The Elephant's Foot*, a stage play about a couple in their seventies. It was put on at the Nottingham Playhouse in April 1964, with Alastair Sim directing and starring.

Trevor's distinctive speech patterns, his 'odd ceremonious dialogue and unnervingly vivid characterization', have been aptly attributed by one reviewer (W. L. Webb, *The Guardian*, 1 May 1965), to his childhood influences. 'Trevor is Anglo-Irish, the son of a bank manager, born on Empire Day 1928, into the defensive and socially fossilized world of post-Revolutionary Anglo-Ireland.' 'Socially fossilized' is, indeed, what most of his characters seem to be. And, to begin with, in Trevor's writing, they were mainly old;

hence he acquired from the same reviewer the title 'gentle gerontocrat'.

Under his real name of Trevor Cox, he began his professional life, after graduating from Trinity College, Dublin, as a sculptor and carver. In 1956 he had a successful exhibition at the Dublin Painters' Gallery and was joint winner of the Irish section of the Unknown Political Prisoner competition. But financial pressures led him away, to teaching and then to advertising. His first novel, *A Standard of Behaviour*, came out in 1958, but its failure with the critics so discouraged Trevor that he did not write anything more for nearly four years. Then came a series of stories about the old, published in the *Transatlantic Review* and *London Magazine*, which contained the germinal scenes of *The Old Boys*. If this was a funny book it was also deeply pathetic, inspired, as Trevor has said, by his resentment at the way the old are treated nowadays – as though they were children.

Like Jeremy Sandford, Trevor has said he writes out of curiosity. But, although he has been known to move himself into a seaside hotel off-season in order to observe the old in their natural habitat, most of his curiosity is internal. 'One does tend to write out of curiosity. I'm always aware of my inquisitiveness about characters that I've invented. You make them talk, and see what happens.' (*The Guardian*, 1 May 1965.)

Like Peter Nichols, Trevor usually develops the same idea along several different lines: in short story form and as a television play; even, perhaps, as a radio play. Some of his works have also ended up on the stage. *A Night with Mrs Da Tanka*, for instance, was ecstatically reviewed when it was put on at the King's Head pub-theatre in June 1972 without any of the critics ever appearing to realize that it had been a television play four years earlier. Of his method of transforming stories into television plays Trevor has said: 'If you turn a story into a television play, you've lived with the people. You know them and you know the situation. So you look at it with both a fresh eye and a weary eye because you know exactly what they're like, and then you wonder whether you're right. You don't have to invent your actual characters. You have, of course, to invent everything else. It's got to be replotted every time – every single thing.'

As soon as I came on to 'Wednesday Play' I approached Trevor to ask for a contribution to the programme. I felt that his type of writing would make a welcome contrast to the plays of social realism which formed the mainstay of the programme. I believed that, as his novels abounded with such excellent dialogue, he would take easily to writing in dramatic form. In fact Brian Brooke, who had been my assistant on 'Story Parade', had already commissioned one script, *The Baby Sitter*, a macabre story about a couple who keep an old person in place of a baby and employ an unsuspecting baby-sitter to look after him.

When we met, Trevor proposed an idea which was, in some respects, an offshoot of *The Old Boys*. The story, entitled *A Meeting in Middle Age*, was to be told through the person of Swingler, a seedy private detective who had featured in *The Old Boys*. Swingler was to engineer the coming together of two lonely, middle-aged people: Mrs Da Tanka and Mr Mileson. In Trevor's original synopsis, Swingler, who is employed by the vulgar, thrice-married, fifty-year-old Mrs Da Tanka to arrange her latest divorce, persuades Mileson, an inhibited, elderly, bachelor civil servant, to act as co-respondent. Mileson does it simply for the money and on an assurance that he will not have to actually 'do' anything other than be found in Mrs Da Tanka's room. A rendezvous is arranged at a seaside hotel, but loud, unhappy Mrs Da Tanka cannot control herself from pouring out her vulgar life-history, which upsets the withdrawn Mileson. Swingler observes these two lonely people, who might have helped each other, departing for their respective lonelinesses.

A Meeting in Middle Age was commissioned in May 1967. By the time it went into rehearsal, in January 1968, as *A Night with Mrs Da Tanka*, it was a very different play from the one originally planned. Swingler, on whom I had never been very keen, had been abolished, as Trevor had found him superfluous when he came to write up the two central characters. Mr Mileson had also undergone a considerable change. Instead of being a paid co-respondent he had become a shy, romantic elderly bachelor, who went every year to the seaside hotel where, in his childhood, he had fallen in love with a little girl called Cynthia. All his life he had pined for Cynthia, and his annual journey had become a sort of pilgrimage to her shrine.

Mileson's pilgrimage is desecrated by Mrs Da Tanka, whose arrangements with a professional co-respondent have gone awry. By devious means, she lures the terrified Mileson into her bed-room and proceeds to destroy all his illusions, even claiming to be his long-lost Cynthia herself. Here is an example of Mrs Da

Tanka going about her awful business of destroying Mileson's world:

'Cynthia's dead, love . . . I didn't mean dead in a grave somewhere. She's dead as far as you're concerned, Mr Mileson . . . You've never spoken to anyone else about Cynthia because Cynthia is a sacred subject. And whenever you think of her, you think of death too . . . I've broken the spell. I've told you home-truths you didn't want to hear. She got her sex where she could find it, with anyone else except yourself.' And (addressing a photograph of Cynthia): 'That face is not the face of a woman who goes without sex.'

The search for the right Mrs Da Tanka (as for most of Trevor's heroines) was a difficult one. Eventually the director, John Gorrie, and I lit on Jean Kent, the ex-movie star who had done little television. She seemed to us to be able to combine the characteristics of a woman who had obviously been both very beautiful and sensuous and was now somewhat larger than life. Opposite her, Geoffrey Bayldon was suitably slight and frail as Mileson. One of my memories of this production is connected with James Mossman, the political commentator who later committed suicide. James Mossman became hypnotized by Jean Kent's performance on the studio floor as, dressed in a chiffon pyjama suit, she seized a shrinking Geoffrey Bayldon by the tie across the hotel dining table. I had commissioned Mossman to write a play and, as he had never seen a drama production, he asked if he could drop into the studio for an hour. He ended up staying for most of the three days we were there, laughing copiously most of the time.

The filmed sections of *Mrs Da Tanka* were shot in Hastings on the first four days of January 1968. Four years later, in March, we were back in this haunt of the lonely and elderly, filming Alastair Sim walking down the promenade as General Suffolk in Trevor's *The General's Day*.

I had asked John Gorrie to direct both these plays. What they most required was a director who could elicit star performances from the actors: a director who would understand the antiquated world of Trevor's writing and not try to 'jazz' it up with trendy inventions, Freudian interpretations or tricksy shooting, and who would be sympathetic to the problems of the middle-aged and elderly found in both these plays, as well as being able to bring out the comedy elements. I knew that Gorrie was not the sort of director who puts his own shooting style above the author's intentions but one who tries to get to the core of what the author means. If badly acted or allowed to 'go over the top', some of Trevor's lines could easily become melodramatic. I knew that Gorrie would bring them out of the actors in a controlled and subtle way that would never let this happen. Part of a producer's function is always to watch out for these dangers in rehearsal, when everyone else is too near the piece to be objective.

The General's Day was, in some ways, the obverse of *A Night with Mrs Da Tanka*. A repressed spinster has her illusions shattered by a more earthy man. General Suffolk, a retired seventy-year-old general, had once been a great ladies' man. Now in his seaside retirement, he has problems with his sinister charlady, Mrs Hinch (played by Dandy Nichols), who shows signs of wanting to move in permanently. He believes that Miss Lorrimer (played by Annette Crosbie), a shy creature who has never grown up, may be a means of rescue. If she will agree to move in, Mrs Hinch won't be able to; and Miss Lorrimer worships the General for his heroic past, even finding his past affairs, recorded in his photograph album, an agreeable part of his romantic image. But when Miss Lorrimer finds out that the General has actually had an affair with

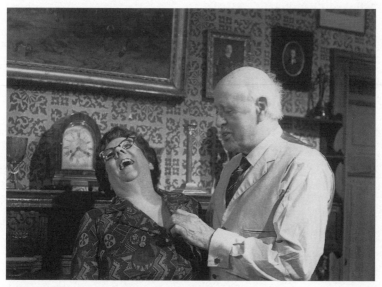

4 Dandy Nichols and Alastair Sim in *The General's Day*.

123

the dreadful Mrs Hinch, her illusions are well and truly shattered. She cannot bear to think that there's life in the old boy yet.

'You've held between your hands thousands and thousands of lives. You've charted the boundaries of nations,' she says accusingly to the General.

'I wasn't sober one night,' he tries to explain.

'Who cares if you were sober? With tooth and nail you have defended this island, laying down your life over and over again. And now you end with Mrs Hinch.'

In both plays, Trevor's 'socially fossilized' characters are found walking along seaside promenades dreaming about the past. The General, as he walks, hears his old regimental marches and dreams of battles past; Mileson remembers Cynthia. In both plays the places of entertainment are hotel lounges where ancient trios play 'Lavender Blue' and 'The Arcadians', while the elderly plan their outings. It is an England where 1914 and 1970 seem to coexist in time; an England fast slipping away for good.

As well as a tremendous sympathy for the old, Trevor has also shown in his work an amazing understanding of his women characters and their feminine intuitions. *The Mark II Wife*, *The Italian Table*, *O Fat White Woman* and *Access to the Children* all deal, in depth, with the tortures of women whose men have deserted or betrayed them.

I commissioned *The Mark II Wife* in February 1968. As soon as *A Night with Mrs Da Tanka* went into rehearsal, it was apparent to me that Trevor was as natural a dramatist as he was a narrative writer; his characters sprang to life in the acting, despite the literary quality of their lines.

The Mark II Wife, which also underwent many changes before reaching its final form, concerned Anna Mackintosh, a handsome, but ageing, woman who appears at a fashionable party given by some people called Engelfield. To everyone's embarrassment, Anna begins to confide her personal life to the party guests. Everyone flees except for an elderly couple, General Ritchie and his wife, who allow themselves to be drawn into Anna's tale of how she knows her husband is about to leave her and take a new 'Mark II wife'. She even predicts that he will turn up at the party with this new 'intended'.

General Ritchie (very different from Alastair Sim's randy General Suffolk) hates parties and only longs to get home to *A Book at Bedtime*, but his wife reminds him that she, too, once felt like Anna

5 Faith Brook in *The Mark II Wife*.

when he had an affair. Then, just as the Ritchies have convinced everyone that Anna's plight is probably real, Anna, having phoned her psychiatrist for reassurance, says it's probably only her imagination. She leaves the party just before two new guests arrive: the Engelfields' beautiful young daughter[1] and her 'darling Edward Mackintosh'. Anna's intuition, it seems, had been true.

In *The Mark II Wife* Trevor had written a play which was far more technically demanding than *A Night with Mrs Da Tanka*. The basic problem, of course, was how to keep the party going for seventy-five minutes while playing all the main action against it; how to balance what was going on inside Anna's memory and imagination with the action around her; how to show her viewpoint of the party guests and theirs of her. It needed tremendous technical virtuosity on the part of the director to bring this off.

Philip Saville seemed to me the director most likely to be able to cope with the problems of transferring *The Mark II Wife* to the screen. I had known him from 'Armchair Theatre' days and had previously invited him to direct *The Machine Stops*, an E. M.

---

[1]Played by Joanna Lumley, one of her first television parts.

Forster science fiction story which was the most complex and technically demanding script I have ever had in my hands. Saville had revelled in such problems as having a fully practical monorail in the studio, duplicate sets built like honeycombs and numerous, extraordinarily complex, special effects. The result had been extremely successful; the piece won first prize in a festival of science fiction films against such entries as *Alphaville* and, more important, had brought forth a letter of praise and gratitude from E. M. Forster himself. I was certain, therefore that Saville would be able to handle the seventy-five-minute party. The only drawback with directors who veer in this visually inventive direction is that they may become so involved in technical pyrotechnics that the writer's storyline and basic intention get submerged. It is, of course, the producer's unenviable job to stop this from happening as well as to try to stop a director introducing his own hang-ups, sexual or otherwise, into the piece in a way the writer never intended.

Our first step with *The Mark II Wife* (which was one of the last 'Wednesday Plays' in black and white) was to request to record it on film, rather than on videotape (a process which is not yet technically possible in colour). Saville, more than any director I know, has always used film techniques in an electronic studio. For example, in *The Mark II Wife*, he shot a number of scenes several times over: first from Anna's point of view, then from the viewpoints of different guests. The scene could then be edited like a film. Electronically, one would have shot the different viewpoints on different cameras; editing there and then by cutting from camera to camera. As mentioned, before, another trick Saville has always favoured is that of giving himself the widest choice of angles possible from which to shoot by building duplicate sets. In *The Machine Stops* the two leading characters leapt from duplicate set to duplicate set between shots, so that they could be shown with maximum visual variety. Saville's first action at rehearsals (an unnerving one for many actors) is to go around looking at them through a viewfinder; the shots are in his mind before he has even started.

By recording *The Mark II Wife* on film, it was possible to edit it and dub the sound in a far more intricate, filmic way than would have been possible on tape. The sets, camera-work and sound all contributed to its success, as did the operatic performance of Faith

Brook as Anna. In this second play Trevor had written a much more expensive and complex piece, without, perhaps, having realized it.

O Fat White Woman, also directed by Philip Saville (in August 1971), again had many production problems. The story, set in a private school for boys, dealt with the awakening of the headmaster's wife, Mrs Digby Hunter (played by Maureen Pryor) to the realization that her sadistic husband has actually caused the death of one of the boys. As the play was entirely located in the school (which was shot in the studio, apart from some brief film inserts), the first problem was to find enough good child actors to carry it off and to get them licensed by the Inner London Education Authority in time for the studio dates. Trevor had written some extremely complex scenes, as, for example, one in which the sadistic Major Digby Hunter makes the boys recite Latin in chorus. There was also another party scene, in which Mrs Digby Hunter picks out her husband and another woman, Miss Roan, amongst the crowd, and guesses that they are having an affair. There was also the problem of conveying the effects of brain damage and double vision from which the boy, Wraggett, suffers after the headmaster has dealt him a fatal beating. The latter was achieved by putting mirrors on the sides of the camera and through the use of special lenses. Design, style of shooting and sound once more played an important part in conveying the inner life of the central character, who surrounded herself with fuchsias and food to obliterate the reality of the horrible goings-on around her at the school.

In all Trevor's plays, there is always an inner and outer life existing simultaneously: not only a gift for the leading actors but also, visually, for the directors. In *Mrs Da Tanka* it lay in Mr Mileson's memories of childhood scenes with Cynthia; in *The Mark II Wife* in Anna's memories of her wedding day and visions of the imagined 'other woman'. In *The Italian Table* (originally entitled *The Heart in the Breast of A. R. Jeffs*) the central character, a recluse junk man (played by Leonard Rossiter) dreams of himself dining in splendour with the beautiful, betrayed housewife, Mrs Hammond, from whom he has bought the Italian table – a beautifully tragic-comic scene, shot initially by the director, Herbert Wise, in a rubbish dump which pans out and dissolves into a 'posh' dining table. All Trevor's plays end with grand operatic arias from

6 Leonard Rossiter as the junk man in *The Italian Table*.

the leading characters. Here are some of Trevor's creations, assessing their own unhappy lives in the style of *The Love Song of Alfred J. Prufrock*: 'I grow old . . . I grow old.' Mrs Digby Hunter describes her life to Miss Roan, 'the other woman', thus: '. . . and now I'm forty-six years old and run to fat. I train girls from St Edna's Orphanage and even still feel shy of them. On the telephone, three times a week, I order from the local shops, vegetables and cooking apples, bacon, sausages, mince, chops for fifteen boys. I've become a dab hand at making shepherd's pie. I stand in this room while people drink their drinks and chatter on. I stand in the gardens once a year when there's a fete for charity and everyone comes from all around. I go about with Meals on Wheels. I say a few words to Brownies, I give out prizes because they ask me to. I grow my fuchsias. I pick my flowers. That is my life.'

Mr Jeffs, the junk man in *The Italian Table*, expresses to Mrs Hammond the futility of his calling and his life thus: 'People come to me asking for fashionable objects for their houses. Drapers' dummies, prints of Queen Victoria, enamel signs with fingers pointing, old irons, swords, helmets, hats. Anything that comes from the past and is curious. "Junk man, go out," they say, "and find us something to make us smile." They came the other day, three men and a woman, and asked me to get them corsets. Edwardian corsets can now be placed behind framed glass and hung upon a wall. Bygones they call them, the latest thing. My God . . .' And later: 'I have no friends. I have never in my life had friends. Junk man die, is what they say, Junk man die, so we never have to see your face again. Who cares, Mrs Hammond, who wants to know . . . My life is broken chairs and clocks that don't go, croquet sets and stained grey cushions. Every day of my childhood I was beaten for eating my fingers.'

In every one of Trevor's plays there is such an opening of the floodgates, such a catharsis. A crisis occurs and one character pours out his welled-up emotions to another, chronicling his entire life in a speech. Theirs is a heightened reality which needs extraordinary acting performances to bring it off.

Trevor once remarked humorously to an interviewer that his books were getting younger all the time. Pointing out that *The Boarding House*, which followed *The Old Boys*, dealt with the middle aged, he said, 'At the moment, I'm writing about lonely housewives and soon I shall go right down the scale and write about the kindergarten' (*Observer*, 4 July 1965). In terms of his television commissions, the prediction was to come true. *Access to the Children* (1972) dealt with the divorce of a youngish couple and included that production nightmare, two large parts for small children. His latest play, *Eleanor*,[2] deals with a girl of fifteen. The 'gentle gerontocrat' shows signs of becoming an 'infantocrat'.

[2]Played by Pauline Quirke, of *Birds of a Feather* fame, in one of her first parts.

Chapter 12

Making up a season: variety and budget

In the last six chapters, I have tried to describe the differences in techniques and inspiration of various writers who have contributed to the programme, and to convey some of the attendant production problems and explain how they were dealt with.

It may be interesting, now, to go back to the list in Chapter 7 and to the more general problem of how a season of plays is made up. What is the history of the remaining plays on the list? Why were they commissioned and produced? In asking this question one should, of course, also bear in mind that this list shows only the commissioned plays which actually got on to the air. There is also, of course, a list of plays which didn't get on for one reason or another. It is inevitable that, if one is looking for a season of original plays, one has to over-commission in order to have the freedom to experiment with new writers and to ensure that there will be something suitable to be transmitted. I have mentioned, for example, a commission from James Mossman, who wrote a deeply moving but totally unproduceable first play: unproduceable in that it was basically written as fiction, not drama, and would never have 'played' on the screen. Other examples of commissions that were not produced range over first plays by novelists and journalists, and a play from the actor Kenneth Griffiths which depended on the participation of a famous film star who could never be pinned down to be in it. A commission, therefore, does not necessarily guarantee a transmission.

Apart from the pressure of time, the two main problems a producer has to consider in making up a season of plays are whether there will be enough variety and that the plays can be done on the annual budget. A production like *Edna*, for example, not only uses up a lion's share of the annual budget, it also makes great inroads into the resources of the servicing departments, which may consequently not be able to service other productions. Servicing is, therefore, another problem, as is the ratio of film to studio productions. Studio shows are automatically cheaper than films for a variety of reasons – one being an Equity agreement which puts up actors' fees on filming. The length of time that staff are needed on films is also considerably longer than on studio productions.

As some readers who are not involved in television may still be mystified as to exactly what the differences are in the techniques of making a play on film and in an electronic studio (even the critics seldom appear to be aware of the differences), I will give a much oversimplified explanation.

The method of making a play on film, for television, is precisely the same as in the film industry except that most television plays, at the BBC anyway, are made on 16 mm rather than 35 mm film, which means obviously that they are cheaper to make and require smaller crews.

The technique of shooting on film is to build up a scene, shot by shot, each shot being re-lit by the lighting cameraman. If, for instance, a scene shows a man and a woman having a conversation across a table, the film material that is shot will probably consist of the whole scene shot in close-ups of the man, the whole scene shot in close-ups of the woman, part or all of it in mid-shots of both and some long shots or medium-long shots establishing them together. Each of these shots will be filmed separately and many times over to cover various acting and technical faults, with long waits between shots while the different angles are re-lit by the cameraman. There is only one camera and no one sees the results of the shooting until the next day when the film has been developed. At 'rushes', the director and producer decide with the editor on which 'takes' are best and the scene is then built up by the editor from the selected takes. The close-ups, long shots and mid-shots are then welded together in the cutting room.

If this same scene were being shot in an electronic studio, the technique would be entirely different and much faster. The director will have at his disposal as many as six cameras, all operating simultaneously; it is up to him to place them in such a way that he can get maximum coverage of the scene. He can then shoot the scene in one whole piece, achieving at the end of it the entire sequence 'ready edited'. The lighting man will have lit the area of the studio in which the scene takes place and seldom needs to do any re-lighting during the course of it. In the gallery, above the studio, the director will have six monitors showing him the picture which is on each of the six cameras on the studio floor. At one glance, therefore, he can see a close-up of the woman, a close-up of the man, a two-shot of them at the table; possibly a high-angle shot looking down on them, etc. Out of this selection of pictures he can choose how he wants the scene to run; where it is most important to have the woman's reactions, where the man's. The camera script has already been made up on anticipated choices, but it is very often considerably changed when the director actually sees the pictures in front of him. There is always a fluid situation when the play gets on to the studio floor; certain problems arise with sets, sound etc. which could not have been anticipated and need adjustments; certain unscripted shots are offered by the cameramen as more aesthetically pleasing than others, etc. Unlike in film, therefore, everyone – the director, the producer and all the people in the gallery – can immediately see exactly what pictures are available to choose from. When the choices have been made in camera rehearsal, the vision mixer, by cutting from one camera to the next, produces the sequences, thus doing the job that the film editor would be doing for film. This system is obviously much faster and much less nebulous, in terms of decision-making, than filming. The arguments against it are that the studio lighting can never be as subtle as film lighting, where every shot is re-lit, and that, once a choice has been made, it is pretty final. Recently, outside-broadcast units (i.e. mobile videotape units) have been increasingly introduced into drama productions to take the electronic technique outside the studio (previously they were used mainly for sports and current events). As yet, they cannot match in subtlety or mobility the single film camera. It is up to the producer, therefore, to decide which plays will be best made on film and which electronically.

The producer gets an overall budget for his year's productions. Usually the sum of the average budget is agreed as follows. The producer offers a programme budget estimate – an assessment of how much he estimates a seventy-five-minute programme in the studio and a seventy-five-minute programme on film ought to cost. This estimate, usually costed by a production unit manager, in consultation with the producer, taking into consideration all the elements that go into a production – cast, sets, the 'man hours' of all the staff involved, equipment etc. – is then taken by the head of the department to the programme controller. Between them they decide whether the 'PBE' is realistic and whether they wish to expend that amount of money on that programme.

Resources are, of course, another problem. It is no use budgeting six films in a year if there are not enough personnel – camera crew, make-up and wardrobe etc. – available to service them. When these problems have been sorted out, the producer will know that he has £x to spend over the year on x number of productions: some on film, some in the studio. It is then up to him to find scripts which can be made for the amount of money he has. In every season there are inevitably plays with small casts, a minimal number of sets and little or no filming; very often these have been commissioned or bought to balance out heavy expenditure elsewhere.

The other problem, of course, is to make sure that one has not commissioned plays on subjects that are too similar; the aim is to get as many points of view and as many strata of society as possible represented on the programme.

What is the composition of the list found in Chapter 7, in terms of these considerations (always bearing in mind that the actual season on the air was balanced between these commissions of mine and those of Graeme McDonald, seen in the list in Chapter 6)? There is, for example, on the first page of my list a play by Errol John, a West Indian writer, *The Exiles*, and a play by an Australian writer, *All Out for Kangaroo Valley*, by Noel Robinson. These were both specifically commissioned by me because I felt that, considering how polyglot was the population of London, it would be both relevant and interesting to see England from the point of view of immigrants. I put it to both these writers that I'd like a play on what it feels like to be a West Indian (a sophisticated, educated West Indian in this case, as I felt the working-class West Indian had been well covered), or an Australian, living in England. Neither play was altogether successful – perhaps because the idea came from me rather than the writers themselves, or perhaps I had commissioned writers who were not 'hard-hitting' enough – but the plays did have the appeal of being 'different'.

Another unusual West Indian play which I bought was *In the Beautiful Caribbean*, which ended up being a studio equivalent of *Edna* in terms of cost, complexity and chaos. Barry Reckord, who wrote it, is one of the few black West Indian writers who can successfully write about white people. His play *Skyvers*, about the

7 Thomas Baptiste and Rick James in *In the Beautiful Caribbean*.

aimless life of a group of schoolboys about to leave their secondary modern school, had been a great success at the Royal Court Theatre in 1963, and was subsequently revived there and at the Round House. Reckord, a Cambridge-educated Jamaican, had already started writing *In the Beautiful Caribbean* as a stage play when I asked him if he would be interested in writing for 'Play for Today'. When he showed me the script, it was in a totally chaotic state: the seeds of a 'Brechtian' musical on the developing political consciousness of Black Jamaica. It seemed to me that there had been a certain number of plays about poor Jamaicans in England, but none that I knew of depicting the background from which they came and showing the poverty which motivated their emigration.

The other aspect of the play which appealed to me immensely was the music. At about the same time as Barry showed me the script I had met a young Trinidadian director, Horace Ové, who had made a film about Reggae music. After I had asked Philip Saville to direct the piece, we engaged Horace Ové to take charge of the music and commission a number of West Indian composers to write the songs. We also had in the studio a 'live' band of Rastafarians. It was only two years later that the production assistant had the courage to confess to me that part of the budget for 'studio food' on this production had been for 'pot' to keep this particular group going throughout recording.

Casting a West Indian play in England is not easy, especially when a number of the cast have to sing as well as act. The cast was enormous and included Calvin Lockhart, Ram John Holder the blues singer, and Louise Bennett, Jamaica's leading actress, whom we imported for the production. Rehearsals were like a non-stop West Indian party, with a large cuddly lady extra, called Lucita, arriving every day with a cauldron of West Indian stew for lunch for the cast. When we came into the studio at Television Centre, dressing rooms became small households from which emanated the smell of West Indian food, while Louise Bennett's small adopted daughter, and various other children of the cast, milled around constantly. In the circumstances, any hope of keeping a strict rehearsal discipline and routine rapidly vanished. For me, the production ended with a true crowning glory as a plate of West Indian curry was emptied over my head by accident in a Notting Hill restaurant after recording.

The impresario Oscar Loewenstein came to see the play in the studio and promptly commissioned Barry to write the stage musical version of it. In retrospect, one realizes that this was undoubtedly too ambitious a project to have undertaken for television, given our studio resources and the short planning period we had in which to mount what was virtually a folk opera. The stage was, perhaps, a better place for such a work, which called for crowds singing in chorus etc. By importing a Jamaican leading lady and by bending over backwards to be authentic, we learned (from audience research reports) that many of the audience had had trouble in understanding the language. However, the play remains in my mind as one of the most worthwhile and enjoyable experiments in which I have ever been involved. One critic, Peter Fiddick in *The Guardian*, went so far as to call it 'a sort of mini *West Side Story*, scaled down for television' (4 February 1972).

One of the most uniform characteristics of the writers whose work has been discussed in the previous chapters is their age; the majority were all in their mid- to late thirties at the time the productions were put on; none is much younger[1] and some reach the early to mid-forties mark. The significance of this fact, which I am

[1]Though David Rudkin was thirty-one when *House of Character* was put on.

trying to point out, is that basically they share certain attitudes and experiences which must be common to their generation. Of the entire list, in fact there is only one writer in his twenties, Peter Hankin, whose first play, *The Pigeon Fancier*, I commissioned and produced in the belief that he had the potential of developing into a good television playwright, even though this particular work seemed to hark back to D. H. Lawrence and early Alun Owen. Producers search for younger writers, but most of the younger writers in the small theatres are writing plays whose language and subject matter render them unproduceable during normal television viewing hours for what is deemed 'family viewing'. Their sense of construction also seems to be becoming increasingly loose. It has to be faced, therefore, that the majority of television playwrights who are capable of writing a good produceable script are middle-aged.

Two writers on the list who do not come into this category of mid-thirties to mid-forties are James Hanley and Maurice Edelman. Hanley, then in his seventies, had a considerable reputation as a novelist before his first dramatic work, *Say Nothing*, was produced at the Theatre Royal, Stratford, in 1962. It was described by the *Times* critic (15 August 1962) as, 'the most exciting and satisfying first play by an established novelist since *The Living Room*'. The memory of the television production of this play lingers in my mind as one of the most unforgettable 'viewing' experiences in terms of humour and emotional impact. (It was produced on 'Festival' by Peter Luke and directed by Philip Saville.)

It seemed to me important to try to persuade Hanley to contribute his unique viewpoint to the programme, which was so largely written by younger writers. He was a compulsive writer, with no sense of the commercial, and when I went to visit him at his flat I found him surrounded by dozens of unproduced scripts written, not on commission, but out of compulsion; most of them too experimental or too difficult to produce. Both *Nothing Will Be The Same Again* and *It Wasn't Me*, which were commissioned, had the same poetic, highly emotional, macabre atmosphere. In the latter, Hanley took a situation about which many television playwrights have written realistically: how to cope with the problem of an unwanted aged parent. In his hands, the subject was treated as a macabre, frightening allegory, in which a couple answer an advertisement by a company offering to dispose of such unwanted problems as an aged parent. Having arranged for his disposal, the

8 Derek Francis and Ronald Lacey in *It Wasn't Me*.

couple arrive home to find that the wife's father has died in his armchair; each turns, guilt-stricken, to the other, saying 'it wasn't me'.
    Maurice Edelman was, of course, well known as Labour MP for
Coventry and a suave political journalist. Then in his sixties, he
had written a number of novels and television plays, mainly dealing
with political subjects. I first met him at the time we did an adaptation of his novel, *The Minister*, on 'Story Parade'. It seemed
worth while to me to try to get a contribution from someone of
Edelman's background. In the event, *A Distant Thunder* was a
highly artificial and somewhat contrived piece about a refugee from
a concentration camp returning to haunt a respectable MP. It
belonged to the time of the well constructed play and, as such, was
picked on as old-fashioned by the critics. At the same time, for a
certain section of the audience, it provided a blessed relief from the
stark, realistic working-class drama that was allegedly the hallmark
of 'Play for Today'; one enterprising member of the audience, in
fact, telephoned me and got me out of the bath on a Saturday
morning to tell me so. Nancy Banks Smith, reviewing it in *The
Guardian* (27 November 1970) had this to say about it: 'New and
experimental drama? New and . . . No. An old-fashioned, copper-

bottomed, high-society coughdrop. Now coughdrops have their uses and it is probable that if *A Distant Thunder* were playing in Shaftesbury Avenue – with a knight playing the knight – there would not be too much coughing at the matinées.' In her assessment of its potential West End audience she was undoubtedly right, but perhaps not so right in thinking that this type of play should therefore be excluded altogether from a programme that allegedly represents all aspects of contemporary writing. Amongst the audience there are some (perhaps those who go to Shaftesbury Avenue matinées) who will find Maurice Edelman's world more real than Roy Minton's.

On the list are two plays by Alun Owen. As Owen was probably the best-known of the early generation of realistic television writers and his background is amply documented elsewhere, I shall not go into it. Suffice it to say that any young writer hoping to sell a script would do well to study one of Owen's; although his later plays, including the two on my list, *Charlie* and *Pal*, have undoubtedly lost the freshness and fire of his early work for 'Armchair Theatre', for pure sense of structure and command of dialogue they are unbeatable. Moreover, in the case of the two plays on my list, they were models of economy: both essentially two-handers and requiring very few sets.

Comedy, as is well known, is the most difficult branch of straight television drama to produce successfully. There is no question but that certain programmes, had they been played with a studio audience and with the broad style expected of a situation comedy, would have had an entirely different response than they got when played as straight drama and put out 'cold', without audience laughter.

The Fabulous Frump, by James Gibbins, was the only script I have ever bought on a recommendation from the BBC script unit and readers; it was also the worst-reviewed play for which I have ever been responsible. If a genie in a bottle were to appear and grant me one wish, I think it would be to have the chance to produce this play again with an audience, and with Benny Hill and Patricia Hayes in the leads; there is no question in my mind but that, with a live audience and the right cast and style of playing, it could have been wildly successful (it did, in any case despite the dire reviews, have an audience of 6.75 million).

The script of *The Fabulous Frump* landed on my desk, one day in April 1967, from the script unit, with two absolutely glowing readers' reports attached; a situation which seldom happens with an unsolicited script. James Gibbins, the author, was a features writer for the *Daily Express* in Scotland, and in 1966 had been one of the journalists cited by the Hannen Swaffer Awards Panel for original writing. He had, in fact, already sent one play to James MacTaggart in 1966, but it had been rejected.

The jokes in the script were, it is true, crudely written, and the characters were certainly not explored in depth, but the situation seemed to me immensely funny. The script opened to the sound of raucous coughing and to a first image of the heroine, Ella – an utterly masculine frump in her mid-forties – lighting her morning cigar. The phone rings and Ella answers, 'Fashion and beauty editor.' The rest of the script contained a plot straight out of Benny Hill. Ella decides the time has come to catch a husband and chooses Albert, the effeminate, mother-ridden head of a fashion house, as her most likely victim. In order to boost Albert's sales, she organizes a publicity campaign centred around a 'before and after' fashion show, recruiting tramps as her models and converting them into smartly dressed men. Unfortunately, her plan backfires when one of the tramps, Harold, becomes her rival for Albert's affection.

When I phoned James Gibbins in Scotland to ask him to come and see me and told him I wanted to buy the play, he was quite certain that one of his colleagues was playing a practical joke on him and, at first, ignored the request. He still seemed dubious when he arrived and, presumably, only believed it when he received the first pay cheque.

Two particular memories of this play remain. One was a day's filming in freezing cold in St Pancras cemetery, where Albert (played by Peter Butterworth), goes to visit the grave of his mother. For the mother's tomb, the director, Peter Hammond, had ordered from graphics department a photograph of Albert's mother which was made by dressing Peter Butterworth up in drag. When I arrived on the scene, Hammond himself, for want of a wind machine, was throwing leaves over the grave with such energy that it was difficult later to find any shots that didn't show his hand. My second memory was of Peter in the gallery of the studio, during a disastrous recording in which almost every shot needed to be retaken, deciding that the time had come to give up television. There and then he started going into the motions of leaving the gallery, so that I almost had to sit on him to keep him there and get him to finish the show.

What was the reaction to this play? According to an audience research report: 'Those who thought *The Fabulous Frump* touching and amusing (in an off-beat way) were far outnumbered by the rest of the sample, who complained that such characters as the fashion journalist, Ella Macy and the designer, Albert Gill, couldn't really exist.' A criticism they would never have made on a comedy show, billed as such, which would not have led them to expect stark realism in the characters.

As is well known, Willis Hall (whose writing background has already been mentioned in Chapter 3) most often writes scripts in collaboration with Keith Waterhouse. They were once aptly described by Bernard Levin as 'those ever-observant celebrants of the masses'. Team work, is, of course, quite frequent amongst comedy writers (Simpson and Galton, Muir and Nordern are other examples). In a joint interview with Robert Muller in the *Daily Mail* (6 June 1961), Hall and Waterhouse described their system of working:

HALL: When we're in the office, we sit down with our typewriters. A line of dialogue is suggested and thrown about. We never change the line in essence, but the other one may be able to top it.

WATERHOUSE: Nothing but dialogue gets down on paper. If an idea has to be written down, there must be something wrong with it. The first thing that exists for us is the character.

HALL: The people we write about really exist in our minds. We play a constant game of Happy Families. When a character is good and ready he gets tossed into a play.

Hall, in the same interview, described the theatre audience: '. . . basically people go to the theatre to see other people. They want to be entertained. They don't go to the theatre to be instructed . . . You can't tell them anything unless you're entertaining them.'

Here, therefore, are two north-country writers of working-class origin distinguished by the fact that they are dedicated, not to telling the world about the trauma of being a northern writer of working-class origin, but to entertaining.

Hall, whose own dialogue can often sound as funny as that of his characters and who was, for some years, banned from the BBC Club after being apprehended carrying out a large floral arrangement which he claimed he was going to lay on the grave of Donald

Baverstock's mother, came to me with an idea based on his own experience when he rented a house in North Africa only to find the Arab house boy living under the floorboards in the kitchen. In *The Villa Maroc*, originally entitled *A Certain Lack of Communication*, Hall dealt with this situation through the eyes of the Gifford family: father: mother and daughter, played in our production by George A. Cooper, Thora Hird and Anne Beach.

I despaired of a way to get this production done in December in England as it called for long, sunny beach scenes. Eventually, our PA came up with a scheme for taking the entire unit on a package tour to Hammamet for less money than it would have cost to film in England. The sight of Thora Hird, George A. Cooper and Ann Beach laden with Tunisian junk souvenirs on our return to Luton Airport, is not one I shall forget. They had truly become the Gifford family in the course of the filming, which almost didn't take place because our wigs and camera were confiscated by Tunisian customs until someone gave the right hand-out.

Both this and *Song at Twilight*, about a washed-up football manager who won't accept defeat, had a serious basis. But both were basically and deliberately written as sheer entertainment by a writer who obviously knew his audience well. Both plays got good reviews from the popular press. The *Mail*, *Express* and *Mirror* were all full of praise for *The Villa Maroc*, while the 'class' papers, apart from the *Sunday Telegraph*, which praised it highly, were semi-apologetic for finding such a superficial play entertaining and questioned whether such frivolity should have dared to make an appearance on 'Play for Today'. Once more, the reputation of the programme seemed to be working against it.

Two more plays on page one of the list were firsts. *The Man Behind You* (about a recluse), by Jeremy Scott, director of a television commercials firm, who had previously written in collaboration with another author for *The Avengers*, and *The Sad Decline of Arthur Maybury* (about a drunken schoolmaster), by director John Gorrie. *Happy*, a rural comedy in which we got Malcolm McDowell to star just before the release of *If* and his rise to film-star status, was ironically written shortly before the writer, Alan Gosling, committed suicide in a mental hospital.

Alma Mater was also a first 'Play for Today' by David Hodson, who had previously contributed to 'Thirty Minute Theatre', which is, of course, a good training ground for writers who may not yet be able to sustain a full seventy-five-minute piece. It, too, provided

9 Stephen Sheppard, Clive Francis and Oliver Cotton (*left to right*) in *Sovereign's Company*.

a comedy vehicle for Ian Carmichael, playing a lost soul who returns to England and sports day at his old school, after having been stationed abroad, and is astonished at the changes he finds.

Don Shaw, who wrote *Sovereign's Company* and *Ackerman, Dougall and Harker*, also came to 'Play for Today' after writing for 'Thirty Minute Theatre' and for Series Department, mainly for *Z Cars* and *Softly, Softly*. As with other graduates of *Z Cars* (John Hopkins and Troy Kennedy Martin are of course the most notable examples), Shaw's work shows a certain masculinity and concern for broader issues not found in the more introspective writers of single plays. Shaw, who has until recently taught in schools (including one for deaf children), was inspired to write *Sovereign's Company* by his own experiences at Sandhurst, which he left before graduating. It was an exposé of defunct military traditions and how the fear of an accusation of cowardice pushes a pacifist into a sadistic attack on another man.

For this production, which turned out to be enormously expensive, we had the problem of reproducing Sandhurst. The entire production was filmed at a deserted school near Windsor, where the designer built his own Sandhurst, down to the Indian Museum. Shaw's other play, *Ackerman, Dougall and Harker*, was also set in the realm of ideas rather than introspection. It was a morality tale about a young sales representative, crossing the Yorkshire moors as part of an initiative test on a sales course, and becoming gradually more and more disillusioned about the value of his job as he encounters different characters, including an illiterate shepherd who has been talked into buying a set of encyclopaedias in the belief that 'all knowledge is there'. Into this production, we (the director was Ted Kotcheff) tried to introduce a *Pilgrim's Progress*-like feeling by setting the tiny figure of the traveller against the vast expanses of the moors and making his encounters seem as though they had materialized from nowhere.

Another writer with a military background is Robert Holles, who wrote *Michael Regan*. Holles began life as a boy soldier, a subject dealt with in his novel *Captain Cat*. His work, which includes three novels, a film and numerous plays for ITV, as well as many episodes of series, is usually concerned with social issues or injustices in some field. *Michael Regan*, inspired by a true episode in the newspapers, dealt with an Irish labourer's revenge on a snobbish publican who had thrown him out of the pub restaurant for taking his jacket off. In the end, Regan barricades himself in his cottage with wife and child and has to be forced out by the police. Like Shaw's work, Holles's is less personally introspective and more orientated towards broad social issues.

One play remains on the list – besides those I am proposing to discuss in the next chapter – *The Long Distance Piano Player*, by Scottish novelist Alan Sharp, who has now become a Hollywood screenwriter. This play, about a young man trying to win the world record for non-stop piano playing, had, in fact, originally been a radio play. As such, like Broom Lynne's *Wanted, Single Gentleman*, it stood to have levelled at it the criticism that it was not original contemporary writing. However, to me it had two appeals: the subject was unusual and the script, at times, when the young man's futile pursuit obviously represented the monotonous routine of most people's lives, was moving. The other appeal was that of budget; it had a small cast and few sets. The most notable aspect of the production was, perhaps, the casting in his first part of Ray Davies of The Kinks as the piano player.

What I have tried to illustrate in this chapter is the variety of subject-matter and viewpoints found on such a programme as

'Play for Today'. All sorts of people, it appears, write television plays, but the preponderance, perhaps not surprisingly, is of writers who have at some time taught or acted (both professions give more leisure time than most), or who have written in other fields, novels or journalism. The 'natural' dramatists, like Terson and Minton, who tend to put their own experience directly into dialogue are rare, but, unlike in America, the majority of television writers are not university graduates. It's probably true to say that the trained 'intellectual' writer is in a minority.

Chapter 13

Experiments in form: the innovators

I have left until last the plays I discuss in this chapter because they provide the best illustration of works which are intrinsic to television. A few writers seem to have actually been generated by the medium.

Douglas Livingstone, after studying at Bristol University Drama Department and RADA became a full-time actor. It was while he was acting at the Globe Theatre in a long run of Peter Shaffer's play *The Private Ear* that he started writing. The long hours between performances have provided many budding writer-actors with the luxury of time to put pen to paper. Livingstone has gone on record as saying that he does not consider television drama to be a cross between the stage and film, but that there is still plenty of room for exploration of styles and techniques which can work satisfactorily on television.

His first successful script, which was televised by ATV, was *I Remember the Battle*, starring Patrick Wymark. By the time I commissioned *I Can't See My Little Willie* for 'Wednesday Play' in September 1960 Livingstone had already written about twenty scripts, all for commercial companies.

I Can't See My Little Willie was, on a realistic level, the story of a middle-aged local government officer, Arthur Palmer, who comes with his wife and son to his brother Frank's seaside pub to attend the christening of his niece. Numerous other members of the family also attend and there are various sub-plots connected with them.

Arthur is considered a success by the rest of the family. What they do not realize is that he has reached a 'middle-life crisis' bordering on a nervous breakdown. Events are being seen by Arthur in a peculiar way. He keeps thinking of his office life as a running

10 Avril Elgar, Frank Gatliff and Michael Graham Cox in *I Can't See My Little Willie*.

quiz show and competition in which a woman colleague, with whom he once had an affair, seems likely to win.

The most novel aspect of Livingstone's technique in telling the story was the introduction of a series of animated Donald McGill style seaside postcards, which our graphics designer made look like the characters in the play and whose captions reflected Arthur's views on his own life and the events befalling him.

Arthur's first move, on arriving at the seaside, is to buy some funny postcards and from then on they take over. All the action and all the other characters are interpreted through them. Arthur sees his brother's carefree pub, with its rowdy sing-songs, where all the old favourites like 'Danny Boy', 'Run, Rabbit' and 'I Can't See My Little Willie' are sung in chorus by fat ladies, as a paradise and a possible salvation. He begs Frank to let him become manager, but the entire family refuse to take the plea seriously. Eventually Arthur runs away from wife and son to lose himself in seaside postcard land.

The script, undoubtedly inspired by Livingstone's first-hand observations of his mother-in-law's pub in Margate (and by his own extensive collection of funny postcards), had one of the most complex structures of any I have ever read and the editing of so many ingredients took twice as long as normal. Of the end product, Sean Day Lewis had this to say in the *Daily Telegraph*: 'It may be unusual for a local government officer to become gripped by an obsessional desire to run a knees-up public house on the front at Margate, as the main symptom of a nervous breakdown, but the situation was turned into a major television event last night through the skills of Douglas Livingstone as writer, Alan Clarke as director and Nigel Stock as leading actor' (20 November 1970).

Livingstone's second play for the programme, *Everybody Say Cheese*, commissioned in June 1970 and screened the following June, drew on the same sources and techniques as *Willie*. It told of the fate of Henry Hunter, a seaside photographer, who is trapped into marriage by his grasping landlady. Again, Henry sees much of the action in terms of taking photographs and moving stills.

Neither of Livingstone's scripts could really have worked in any other medium. They would not have had the substance for a full-length feature film, nor could they have been done on the stage or as fiction or radio. They were truly 'televisual' creations.

A criticism that has frequently been levelled against television is that it has not produced any plays of major political, philosophical or sociological impact, Perhaps this is so, but on a more intimate level, television has undoubtedly given birth to a distinct type of satirical writing not found elsewhere.

Rhys Adrian, like Livingstone, had experience of the theatre before coming into television; he had worked as a stage manager and director and had also written short stories. A much more 'verbal' writer than Livingstone, he had started in radio with programmes being transmitted on the Third and Home Services from 1956 on. As early as 1958, Barbara Bray in radio had been passing his scripts on to Donald Wilson in the BBC script department (he wrote under many names at this time: L. R. Adrian, L. A. Reece, Jimmy McReady, among them), suggesting that they might be suitable for television. But it was commercial TV (Associated Rediffusion) which put on his first play, *The Prize Winner*, in 1959. I had first met him when one of his plays, *No Licence for Singing*, was produced on 'Armchair Theatre' in 1961. By the time I commissioned *The Drummer and the Bloke*, in August 1967, Adrian had had a considerable number of plays performed on ITV and BBC.

Both Adrian and Clive Exton seem to me the nearest we have (amongst writers I have dealt with) to genuine television satirists, who portray the state of the world and their prophecies for the future in uniquely 'televisual' terms.

Like Alun Owen, Clive Exton, who went from acting to writing, was one of television's most applauded early writers. His first play, *No Fixed Abode*, was produced by Granada, after which he formed a close association with ABC, Sydney Newman and Ted Kotcheff. Like Owen, he is one of the few television writers whose early plays have been given a second production; the BBC screened both an Owen and an Exton 'retrospective' season.

To begin with, Exton's plays were strictly realistic both in form and content. In early interviews he had this to say: 'I like writing for television because it's such an effective way of forcing action out of character. The play that shows people being forced by their natures into a conflict that they can't avoid – that's the sort of play I like to do . . . The demands of a television play make it not too hard to find material . . . You don't need a lot of plot. You tend to take one situation and look very hard at it. In *Where I Live*, all that happened was that relations came to tea and there was a flaming row over the old man.' (Article by Peter Black, *Daily Mail*, 2 April 1960.)

Questioned by another interviewer (*The Times*, 16 February 1960) as to whether he was wedded to realism, Exton said: 'In television, yes. I cannot conceive of a television play which is not realistic in style.' He also gave an interesting clue to the inspiration of his writing: 'The idea at the back of much that I write, it seems to me, looking at it after the event, is a regret for established values such as one imagines existing before 1914 – that magic number which always seems to mark the borderline between 'then' and 'now'.

The way Exton's writing developed, however, belied his early remarks about realism. He was to take a distinctly surrealistic and Swiftian turn, in order best to express his regret for past values.

In 1962 Exton's play *The Big Eat* went to the BBC because the commercial company which commissioned it, ABC, refused to screen it. The subject was an attack on advertising. It mapped the course of a promotion campaign by Ffarmyarde Ffreshe Ffoods which culminated in a ballyhoo eating contest in which one of the participants dies from the effects of overeating. At the same time, Exton's play *The Trial of Dr Fancy*, about a group of people who band together to stunt people[1] for their own profit, was held in abeyance by ABC who were frightened of the offence it might give to those not quite clever enough to grasp its satirical import. *Dr Fancy*, though recorded, was not in fact screened until 1964.

Exton's television work, perhaps because of its 'prophetic' quality, always seems to have some such controversy attached to it. His play *The Bone Yard*, screened in 1966, was also held up for two years. It concerned a mad policeman, or, at least, one who had visions, and it was considered to have too many possible affiliations with an actual inquiry going on about a real policeman, the Challenor case.

Meanwhile, Exton was drifting away from television into the more profitable world of film. (His work on screenplays includes *Isadora, 10 Rillington Place, Entertaining Mr Sloane*.) He also wrote, in 1969, a satirical stage play, *Have You Any Dirty Washing, Mother Dear?* (produced at the Hampstead Theatre Club), about the antics of a parliamentary committee meeting to empower the government to send troops to Africa to avert a racial war.

Although I had known Exton since 'Armchair Theatre' days, I did not, in fact, commission *The Rainbirds*, which went out on 'Wednesday Play' in February 1971. This was commissioned by the Head of Plays as part of an agreement with the European Broadcasting Union that every member should annually commission one play which would be separately produced and simultaneously transmitted in each country belonging to the Union, under the title *The Largest Theatre in the World*. Each year an author of a different nationality is chosen, and the names have included Pinter, François Billetdoux and Ingmar Bergman.

The script of *The Rainbirds*, on a realistic level, told the story of a middle-class young man, John Rainbird, who attempts to commit suicide by jumping out of a hotel window; he is unsuccessful and ends, instead, in a hospital bed, where he lies inanimate and unconscious until his mother agrees to an operation which brings him back to consciousness but with his mind and will reduced to that of a vegetable, a state which his possessive mother finds quite to her liking.

The realistic level, however, was the least important level of the script. If *The Rainbirds* had a fault, it was probably that it tried to do too much and cover too many areas of both psychoanalysis and satire simultaneously. While John Rainbird lies in his coma, we are

---

[1] By cutting their legs off.

shown the various pressures which led him to attempt suicide, all depicted as in his surrealistic dream images, sometimes grotesquely funny, at other times terrifying. His middle-class parents are seen as working-class, engrossed in tele-violence and trying to push their docile son, who likes working in a pet shop, into violent action in the army, to prove he is a man. His defender, the only likable character in the piece, is a grandfather who fought at Spion Kop and remembers the good old days. Meanwhile, around John's bed, the cynical doctors plan to use him for an experimental operation and enlist a hypocritical churchman to convince his mother to let them do so. John then visualizes himself as a side of meat in a slaughterhouse.

To expect a television audience to cope with such a concerted attack on the army, the media, the medical profession, the Church *and* possessive mothers, all within seventy-odd minutes, is undoubtedly too much. The director compounded the crime by over-complicated technical feats (and sexual overtones of his own, introduced whenever I was away from the filming), which undoubtedly added to the confusion. Nevertheless, for thought content, *The Rainbirds* was a unique piece of writing and, in my personal experience a play, like all of Exton's, which was remembered far longer than most. One critic (Patrick Skene in *The Spectator*, 20 February 1971) interestingly pointed out a resemblance in Exton's work to that of a writer much admired by both Exton and Rhys Adrian. Remarking on some of the satirical dialogue, Skene said, 'At times like that, *The Rainbirds* seemed like something written by Kurt Vonnegut Jr. I can think of no higher praise for a work in this genre.'

Rhys Adrian's play *The Drummer and the Bloke*, was a mini-satire depicting the buck-passing that goes on between workers and management all along the line during a strike. In *The Foxtrot*, which followed (it was screened in April 1971), he gave his satirical picture of the changing face of England as seen through the lives of a middle-aged *ménage à trois*.

Gwen and Arthur (played by Thora Hird and Michael Bates) seem to be a normal, well-suited married couple in their fifties. Then Tom, an old friend (played by Donald Pleasence), turns up from his travels abroad. Gradually, it transpires that Tom is the real husband who left years ago after finding the other two having an affair. By the end of the play, a happy *ménage à trois* has been established as the three huddle snugly together in front of the television

11 Donald Pleasence, Thora Hird and Michael Bates in *The Foxtrot*.

to watch an American comedy series which exactly reflects their own situation.

The plot of *The Foxtrot*, however, was the skeleton upon which Adrian hung his observations of urban life in England in the 1970s. Wherever the three go, they are hounded by statistics, advertising, traffic and redevelopment. Near the beginning of the play, for example, Arthur tells Gwen, over the dining table, about his experiences with a street interviewer:

ARTHUR: I was stopped in the street today and asked about my sex life.

GWEN (*smiles*): Your what?

ARTHUR: They're doing a survey connected with some product or other, the product she wasn't at liberty to reveal, and did I have false teeth. It's to do with sex and the elderly. How old, I said. Older than sixty? She wouldn't say. Under sixty, I said. That would defeat the object of the survey, she said. What is the object of the survey, I asked. I can't reveal that, she said. Do I get paid? No, she said. Can I go? No, she said. Not until you have completed the questionnaire. Who's going to stop me? No one. Thank you. Then why did you say I couldn't go until I had completed the questionnaire? Why should I reveal the intimate moments of my life to you? In this street. In this weather. Is it to make someone else richer? And me poorer?

GWEN (*mirthful*): Did you tell her about your sex life?

ARTHUR: In the end I gave in.

GWEN: What sort of questions did she ask?

ARTHUR: Did I think permissiveness was a good idea? What sort of deodorant, if any? Size of family? Did I prefer single beds to double beds? Questions like that. Nothing you could make any sense of. Then she walked off with a smirk on her face, as I knew she would. I wanted to ask her about her sex life. And was she fulfilled? And was she happy? And was she permissive? And if you're doing a survey on sex and the elderly, why pick on me? Do I look that old? To me you do, she said. I followed her down the street asking her these questions. In the end she jumped on a bus, poked out her tongue at me and made an obscene gesture in my direction.

Later, the two decide to go and visit a pub in Marylebone which was a haunt of their youth. They eventually find it, through motorways and supermarkets, only to discover it has been turned into a plastic, modernized, unrecognizable version of itself.

Gwen and Arthur's friends, Harry and Maisie, have a flat which seems to be virtually in the middle of a motorway; all night long, lights flash on and off through their bedroom window. Here is a midnight conversation between the two:

(*Harry gets up and goes to the window. He looks out into the dark night.*)

HARRY: Look at me! I'm up now! Eight hours before I should be up! What am I going to do for these eight hours! Eh? What am I going to do?

MAISIE: Read a book.

HARRY: I don't like books. (*Looks out of the window.*) Seventeen million vehicles a year up and down that road. Where are they all going? It's going to be twenty-two million vehicles a year by 1973. So they say. Official estimates. As if they knew! How do they know it's seventeen million vehicles a year now? How do they know it won't be thirty million by then? The fight to work. The fight back. It's getting worse. And for what? I wonder where the planners live? Some rural paradise? Somewhere that'll never be touched. (*Pause.*) I caught a bloke with my car the other day. Right down the side of his car. I got the soft skin off his car. Right down the side.

MAISIE: I noticed the dent in the mudguard.

HARRY: It'll cost him. It won't cost me. He'd been cutting me up. So I went for him. A big fat bloke. Then I went and reported him for dangerous driving. I said he'd swerved into me. They were very pleased. I came out of there feeling like a good citizen should. (*Pause.*) The big bloody bang, eh?

MAISIE: Not the big bang?

HARRY (*softly, dreamy*): The big bloody bang.

(*We leave him gazing through the window.*)

The elderly characters in the play find themselves gradually being turned into ticks and crosses on surveys made by a society they cannot comprehend. Their only refuge is a club for their fellow elderly where they dance the foxtrot, or the television where they sink into the plastic glossy world of the American situation comedy series.

Again, still photographs of the past life of the trio were used effectively to link the action. Peter Fiddick, of *The Guardian* (30 April 1971), described *The Foxtrot* as 'The best television play I have seen in years'. The 'class' papers were unanimous in their praise (as they were with *Little Willie*), while the popular press apologized for being so amused by a play with so nebulous a plot. Any innovation in technique inevitably receives this reception on television.

As with Exton, Adrian's writing seems to be motivated by a regret for past values and an apprehension about the future. To my mind, of any play I have ever produced, this one would give a visitor from another age the truest picture of life in urban England, 1970s style. Once more, this was a play that could not have fitted any other medium: a true television creation.

David Halliwell's play *Triple Exposure* (originally entitled *Triptych of Bathroom Users*) was also a satire, as well as the modern equivalent of a French farce, but it was less concerned with environment than with people. It is the form, rather than the content, which makes this play a particularly interesting example of television writing.

Halliwell has always been a rugged individualist. After studying art in his native Huddersfield, where he began writing on college reviews, he won a scholarship to RADA which, he told one reviewer, he found 'dull and unintelligent' (*Evening Standard*, 14 January 1967). After acting for two years in provincial rep., he wrote, in 1964, his widely publicized stage play *Little Malcolm and his Struggle against the Eunuchs*, an *exposé* of a student malcontent. This was produced two years later at the Garrick Theatre and won the *Evening Standard* award for the most promising playwright of the year in 1967.[2]

Halliwell has said of himself: 'I don't belong to any group or school, the Aldwych means nothing to me, nor does the National Theatre, nor even the Royal Court' (*Evening Standard*, 14 January 1967). As a result of this feeling of isolation, Halliwell founded his own small company, Quipu, in 1966. Later he described the policy of the theatre thus (*Evening Standard*, 12 January 1968): 'The season of Quipu plays will have a kind of organic unity – the one theme running through them will be criticism of many accepted social attitudes; another will be the line dividing pretence and reality.' For the latter, to show modern man's 'fragmentation', Halliwell decided upon using the Rashomon-like 'multiple viewpoint' technique: showing a character the way he sees himself and the way others see him; showing events as interpreted by different characters.

Halliwell has not written much for television. His first television play, *Plastic Mac in Winter*, was done by Granada in 1963. His second, *Cock, Hen and Courting Pit*, was produced by Peter Luke on 'Wednesday Play' in 1966, after Luke had unsuccessfully tried to purchase *Little Malcolm* for television. It told the story of a tempestuous young love affair as recalled by a man and a woman who meet again some years later and try to relate the individuals they now are to those they once were.

I had been asking Halliwell to write for the programme since I had come on to it, but he was always too tied up with his theatre work until, in March 1971, he accepted the commission for *Triple Exposure*, which was recorded the following February with Alan

---

[2]The play was revived on the London stage in 1998, starring Ewan McGregor, and was much acclaimed.

Cooke directing. The script was one of the best-constructed and economical pieces of writing I have ever had on my desk. It told the farcical story of a middle-class, middle-aged couple, Veronica and Percy, whose house is broken into one night by a young hippy burglar, Len. Percy catches Len but, instead of calling the police, decides to invite him back to dinner to show how magnanimous he is. Gradually Len turns cuckoo in the nest and ousts Percy, taking over house, car, money and Veronica, until Percy returns to throw him out. The story is told three times over, or at least on three parallel lines, as each character reveals his own image of himself and of the others and each shows his own motivation. For example, here is Len's description of Percy, who first apprehends him hiding in the bathroom; Len sees himself as a worm-like creature and Percy as the essence of suave man-of-the-world:

> LEN'S MEMORY VOICE: Pow! There 'e was! Mr Cool. Mr Power. Mr Control. A very attractive figger. The exact opposite of wot I felt. But I soon decided that there wasn't much future in givin' way to me admiration. I mean I 'ad er try an' keep an 'old on a bitta the old ego or I woz gonna be a gonner. So I rapidly reminded myself that I liked ter fink of meself as standin' for the dead opposite of all the fings I saw 'im as standin' for. I mean I was into the animal trip. The juices, the spontaneity, the noble savage, livin' fer the bleedin' ultimate, bein' unashamedly barbaric, oh yare.

Here, in turn, is Percy's version of the same scene. He sees *himself* as a middle-aged square and Len as the essence of youthful energy:

> PERCY'S MEMORY VOICE: The look of him! Sensual, sexual, intuitional! I hated him on sight, his youth, his beauty, his withitness, his serendipity, his air of secret means to secret knowledge.
>
> Yes, forever close to me. His dismissal of all I'd built up. I read it all in a flash. I was about to smash my fist into his sensitive face when – hold on. I wasn't scared of him. Far from it, I could see he wasn't violent. No, but hold on, that's what he expects. Violence, yes, that will only confirm his opinion of me. Why not surprise him? Make him respect me, put the hatred on one side. Show him I can excel in terms he can appreciate.

In planning rehearsals, we decided to do each point of view as a separate story and then mix them together in the editing. This was the only way the three artists, Alec McCowen, Sheila Allen and Tom Chadbon, were going to be able to keep their sanity and keep track of which version they were being at the time.

Alan Cooke, Fanny Taylor (the designer), Barbara Dyer (the costume designer) and I then had to decide how to make all the visual side of the production: sets, costumes (and make-up, of course), look sufficiently the same for the audience to know it was the same house and people and sufficiently different for them to appreciate that they were seeing everything through three different pairs of eyes. Len, of course, saw the house as rich and spacious, Veronica and Percy saw it in different degrees of ordinariness and shabbiness.

After discarding one of Fanny's suggestions to do it all in a cartoon-like style, we settled basically for a change in dimensions and set dressing. For instance, Len's sets were pushed out to be much larger than the others and were dressed much more luxuriously; a stuffed head seen above Percy's bed was, in Len's version, a lion while, in Percy's version it was a small rodent. The kitchen, in Len's eyes, was pure *House and Garden*, while in Veronica's it was pure 'kitchen sink'. By recording each character's story on three different nights, we were able to strike and rebuild and redress the sets each day; likewise the costumes and make-up were changed, each artist having a slightly different hair-do and slightly different costume (the colour and general style remaining the same) for every scene. An actor of the calibre of Alec McCowen was able to delineate sharply the 'three' Percys by giving him three different speech patterns and sets of idiosyncracies; similarly there were three Veronicas and three Lens.

When the material was edited, the story twined around itself like a snake. As a door opened or closed, we went from one viewpoint to another: from a luxurious house to a shabby one, from a powerful Percy to a cringing, timid one. This was an unusually original way of using television technique to tell a story and make a satirical comment on certain types of social pretence.

Plays that are innovatory in technique inevitably command smaller audiences than more conventional works, and must expect to be dismissed by a certain type of popular critic. It is, however, only through finding its own techniques and story-telling devices, as in the four instances described, that television can hope to develop. Too many plays still fall between the two stools of stage play (verbal and static), and feature film (too visually expansive to have real impact on a small screen). Many writers, too, have mistakenly used the increasing freedom which technical advances in television have given them to become lazy in the construction of their plays. The remarkable aspect of all the plays described in this chapter was their meticulous structure, within their complexity. They were equally as well-made, for instance, as those early Exton and Owen plays I read on arrival on 'Armchair Theatre' a decade earlier, but at the same time, they had developed a long way from being strictly representational art.

Chapter 14

Is there anybody out there watching? Audience and archives

Once a production has been completed and the necessary promotion material has gone out to the various departments which handle publicity, it passes out of the producer's hands, awaiting a transmission date which may sometimes be as much as a year away.

For the first time, on transmission night, looking at it in his own living room, away from the hothouse technical conditions of the place where it was made, the producer will see the play objectively, as a member of the audience. The change in the viewing conditions often produces startling, and sometimes horrifying, revelations in terms of pace, clarity etc., especially if a long time has gone by since the piece was made. Now, for the first time, the producer really asks himself, what will the audience think of it?

Unlike in the theatre, the television producer has, of course, no direct contact with his audience; he cannot hear their applause or boos. Nor can he, as in the cinema, count the box-office returns. How, therefore, does he get any indication of whether a play was liked or hated; whether it held or lost an audience and, in fact, whether there was anyone at all out there watching?

There are three sources of such information (apart from the highly prejudiced opinions of one's colleagues and friends): the audience research unit, correspondence and phone calls from viewers and the critics.

In England, two different methods are used to measure the size of the viewing audience. The JICTAR[1] rating system employed by ITV differs from the BBC system in that it measures the number of

---

[1]Joint Industry Committee for Television Advertising Research.

families (as opposed to individuals) viewing a programme, by attaching a meter to a certain number of multi-channel sets throughout the country, recording the times the sets were turned on and which channels were being viewed.

The BBC favours, instead, a method whereby a selection of individuals throughout the country are interviewed daily, regardless of whether they possess multi-channel sets (i.e. can receive all BBC and ITV programmes). Starting with the premise that the population of the United Kingdom is approximately 50.5 million people, audience sizes are worked out on a percentage of that figure.

A group of trained part-time interviewers (about 200 in number) are sent out daily to question a sample of 2,500 individuals simply in order to ascertain what programme they were watching the previous day – not to find out why they watched or what they thought of the programme. This is merely to estimate audience size. The people interviewed are selected by the 'stratified quota' method of sampling in order to obtain a microcosm of the population. The interviewers are distributed in different geographical areas and instructed on the kinds of people they should interview according to age, sex, social class and occupation.

Unlike the JICTAR system, which may be measuring a set that was on in an empty room or in front of a snoring audience, the BBC method tries to ensure that the individuals questioned actually saw the bulk of the programme.

The other factor measured is the audience reaction. To gauge this, a panel system is used. Over a fixed period of time, a selected panel of viewers, recruited either by public appeal or from those questioned for ratings purposes, are asked to fill in questionnaires. They are asked to answer questions only on those programmes they would, anyway, normally have watched and they are asked to tick their preferences out of paired questions like, 'Did you find this "boring" or "entertaining", a "good plot" or "poor plot"?' Their qualitative answers are then translated numerically into a quantitative estimate of audience reactions, from which one receives an audience reaction index.

The producer will, therefore, receive both an estimate of the size of the audience for his production and of its reaction index to the programme. How much can he learn from these figures? And how much will they influence his choice of material or production techniques? He can certainly gauge which programmes in his own series had bigger audiences than others; as I have pointed out elsewhere, amongst my own productions it has always been the straightforward documentary-type subject which gets the highest audiences, while the more adventurous a play is 'stylistically' the smaller its audience is likely to be. One can certainly conclude (if one did not know it already) that the majority of people favour the familiar and expected over the new and unusual – why else would *Coronation Street* and *The Archers* run successfully from here to eternity?

Viewing figures are, of course, also dependent on a number of measurable and immeasurable outside factors, such as: what was the programme on the air before; what are the alternative choices on the two other channels; what is the weather like? (Sydney Newman always used to save what he called 'the real dogs' for transmission on August Bank Holiday, the worst viewing night of the year.) Another factor which audience research has never effectively dealt with is how much effect pre-publicity has. The *Radio Times*, newspaper and magazine advertising for a programme, as well as the on-air trailers, must obviously have some influence on the number of people who watch.

So far as the composition of the viewing audience is concerned, it is, of course, partially in correspondence with the composition of the population; i.e. it is estimated that, out of a population of 50 million, 35 million will be workers, so there will inevitably always be a bigger working-class audience than 'upper' class audience. The over-thirties and over-fifties also make up 60 per cent of the UK population – only 10 per cent more than the younger age groups – but, not surprisingly, the older groups are definitely found to be in the majority as viewers. In fact, a surprising revelation about a programme which has always carried the 'hard-hitting' 'gutsy' image of 'Play for Today' is that the largest section of its audience would once more seem to be recruited from Terence Rattigan's Aunt Edna and her friends. As a whole, middle-aged ladies watch drama more, while men and teenagers prefer films on television. For example, take two very 'hard-hitting' programmes: *Cathy, Come Home* was watched by nearly 4 million males but over 6 million females, while *The Big Flame*, by Jim Allen, was watched by 2.75 million males and 4 million females.

Within the framework of his own programme, therefore, the producer can get some idea from programme research as to which plays were most watched and most liked; to compare one's own programme with other types of programmes, for example comedy or documentary or sport, is a useless occupation as it is accepted that audiences for different types of viewing will differ.

Viewers' letters and logged phone calls are so varied and so contradictory that they can tell the producer little other than that some people loved what others hated.

The television critics, as I have pointed out elsewhere, are predictably divided. A certain number, in the popular press, purport to be representatives of the people: 'Mr Joe Average' reacting; others, usually on the 'class' papers, take a more professional approach as critics of the art or craft of television-making, though few have any practical or inside knowledge of that field. Knowing that their criticism can make no difference to the audience figures for a programme, coming, as it does, after the event, some critics seek to be more columnists than critics and concentrate on their copy rather than the programme itself.

What then is the producer to do? Luckily for someone working in England, particularly at the BBC, he need not, at least, worry about the sponsor, unlike his hard-pressed American counterpart. His immediate superiors may, of course, decide that his programme isn't worth putting on but he won't have materially to alter it in order to sell more soap powder.[2]

Who, therefore, is he to make the plays for? For Aunt Edna? For the working man whom he wants to enlighten (and who is undoubtedly watching *Match of the Day* or an old war film)? For the critics who are judging the play as an avant-garde piece of modern writing or for potential employers in the film industry who may be impressed by the production values?

The answer, of course, must always be that he is making the programme for himself, or at least that he is using his own judgement in choosing material that he feels will work on the screen and will possibly appeal to, enlighten or entertain someone else out there in the audience (always bearing in mind that every producer is at some point pushed into putting on inferior material for want of anything better).

[2]'Playhouse 90' was the closest American equivalent to 'Play for Today'. In its heyday, it was estimated to go into 24 million American homes. It fostered such directors as John Frankenheimer and Bob Mulligan and such writers as Chayevsky, Rod Serling, Tad Mosel and Gore Vidal. It was taken off the air when its ratings fell, essentially through the opposition of a drama series, 'The Untouchables', because its sponsors decided to withdraw their support.

What is the fate that befalls the material once it has been screened? John Osborne is credited with having remarked on this subject, 'Millions might watch television, but on the other hand, last night's television was even deader than yesterday's newspaper because you couldn't even wrap fish and chips in it' (*Guardian*, 12 August 1971, interview with Terry Coleman). A damning indictment, indeed, of television's ephemeral nature.

A 'Play for Today' is quite frequently repeated once in England and many are sold abroad. The script, of course, remains for posterity in the files of the BBC registry. In a sense, this makes the play itself as enduring as a piece for the stage, though not as accessible. How many members of the theatre audience, for example, actually go to see a stage play more than once?

What of the production itself? A satisfactory system of keeping television archives has yet to be evolved. For printed work, of course, we have a system of 'statutory deposit'; one copy of every printed work must be donated by the publishers to the national archives at the British Museum. Some think it should be so with television programmes. As yet, no solution has been found to the enormous problems of storage and preservation that would be involved.

The BBC, of course, has its own archives; the Heads of the Production departments recommend those programmes they consider worthy of preservation to the archive department and the archive department also makes some of its own selections. All else is wiped, in the case of tape, or junked, in the case of film, when the copyright expires. Undoubtedly, much of it is not of sufficient importance or aesthetic value to warrant long-term preservation, but this is a system whereby early works of authors or artists or directors who later become famous could easily be lost for good, while certain pieces might later prove to be valuable sociological documents of our time. Moreover, the BBC archives are not available for members of the public to view.

Some years ago, a committee was set up of various notables in television, sociology, history etc. to decide which programmes would be most valuable to preserve for future generations. It is on their recommendations that the archive section of the British Film Institute requests copies of programmes from the television companies, to be kept in its own archives, which, of course, *are* available to the general public.

For ITV programmes, a fund exists in the ITCA (Independent

Television Companies Association), which covers the cost of donating such prints or tapes to the BFI. The BBC, supported by the taxpayer's money, has no such fund. The BFI, itself, has only a slender government allowance for such purchases; all it can do is send its recommended lists to the BBC in the hope that the programmes will not actually have been wiped or junked. Meanwhile, there is no guarantee that a student in 100 years' time, hoping to make a study of English television productions in the 1970s, will have sufficient material available to do so; most of these 'chronicles of our time' will have vanished into the ether, condemned, by the sheer weight of their numbers, to oblivion.

Edna

22nd September 1970

General Comments and Cuts

The script lacks dramatic progression and lacks sufficient exploration of the central character. The flashbacks are inadequate to do so for us. What is the climax? And how much does she attempt to fight back, and what possible suggestion is offered of what society should do? I think we should have her thinking every phone call may be for her as a recurring theme.

(a) She loses her initial lodging. (We don't ever know how she got money for that; begging? pension? stealing – or what?)

(b) She can't stay for any length of time in a vagrant's home.

(c) She can't collect social security without an address or an address without a job.

(d) Desperation sends her to a psychiatric home where they won't let her stay.

(e) Further despair sends her to jail.

(f) Josie constitutes a ray of hope but the hostel is closed and she is turned out into nowhere once more.

This story-line must somehow emerge dramatically and the extraneous stuff be cut away or it becomes totally boring and repetitious. Certain practicalities, like where she does get any money at all and what she eats when on the road etc., I really long to know. Also a much more subtle explanation of her background.

My cuts would eliminate:

CHARACTERS: p. 14 . . . one old woman and Jamie
(Irene and Doris amalgamate?)

Manor House lodging house . . . people in canteen and living room.
One set of social security people. Nina, and various other characters in mental hospital, apart from staff. Lodging house keeper on
p. 32. Characters in scenes 52 and 53. Bill and woman in court.
Landlady in sequence 66. Man and old woman in sequences 75
and 76. Cut down speaking parts of other inmates of Jesus Saves,
and street sequence outside it.

Edna

27 August 1970

Specific Notes

Page

9 Unclear what exactly this office is. What does 'tachy' mean? Don't understand why Edna is allowed in and then told they are closing the women's wing. Audience will want to know who runs this place and why. Later on Edna suggests to Jessie (p. 14) to go to the 'Spike' yet here she is told it is closing.

11–13 This scene is too long and digressive. Why do we need three old women? Wouldn't Jessie do alone, and couldn't all Edna's dialogue to Jamie be transferred to Jessie? This way we'd establish a bit more contact with another character and eliminate one. We get later on all the mental hospital bit and other social commentary. Don't need it here.

14 Edna, having just been told that the 'Spike' is closing its women's wing, advises Jessie to go there. Why? Also how is the audience to know what the 'Spike' is? Very confusing when we've just seen her turned out.

15 This totally didactic passage is undoable as it stands. Are we meant to think that this is a newspaper article contained in the newspaper that she is unwrapping? What is said by the commentator ought to come out in the incidents of the script. (Not sure I believe that nurses would refuse treatment to these vagrants.)

16 *Lodging House Canteen*. What kind of house is this, how run etc. What are the tokens? Could this not have been the same as the 'Spike'?

17 Absolutely no need for the four-letter words, which we can't have anyway; better to start in middle of fight.

19 *Manor House Lodging House*: Can't see any need for so many rooms. All we really need in this set-up is the dormitory and Irene smuggling Edna into it and her being found and kicked out.

Suggest cutting scenes 21 and 22 . . . canteen and living room here.

Is Irene meant to be foreign? Don't understand why we have two Lesbian type ladies one after the other: Irene and then Doris. Perhaps the two incidents should be separated or the two characters amalgamated? The Doris sequence is so short as to be almost meaningless; think it would be better to amalgamate and establish some continuity.

26 I think we should amalgamate this and later national insurance sequence and also here make the points that are made in a didactic speech voice-over . . . for example scenes 53 and 55 (p. 36). All we need to know about not being able to collect insurance without any address, etc., could be in one scene.

26 What does the social security man mean in saying go to '*the* Lodging House?' Which one does he mean?

Sequence 30. I very much question whether in any mental hospitals patients could have their own pills in their possession.

Sequence 31. Edna's sudden flipping seems unmotivated unless we previously intimate that it is a deliberate ploy to stay in the hospital. Also her drinking is never really established.

We should concentrate entirely on Edna in the mental hospital, almost as a montage, and cut nearly all the other characters. All we want to see is the treatment she gets; her attempts to stay and her getting turfed out into nothingness. The other characters only divert our attention and weaken the script.

We don't need the Nina sequence at all; better to go straight to (sequence 33) psychiatrist's office where Edna is allowed to stay longer. Nor do we need sequence 36.

I would cut completely the following sequences: 33, 34, 36, 39, 40 and also possibly 42 and 43.

30 Why is there a sudden switch from Edna talking to herself to Edna addressing the audience as a commentator? Don't like it. Also how is the audience supposed to know that the vicar's voice is the vicar? Why, in any case do we need him at all here?

32 *Sequence 48.* Don't understand this bit of lodging house at all, and which one it is meant to be. I would cut it altogether and put the important part of her always thinking that the phone is for her somewhere else (possibly even in the opening lodging house scene) and also as a recurring motif.

33 The voice-over here is making exactly the same point as is made on p. 15 and as is illustrated in the action when Edna tries to get to prison.

34–5 Again all these didactic passages are only comments on what the script, if it succeeds, should illustrate first-hand.

35 We've already seen the bit about the social security illustrated. Let's see first-hand the lodging house requirements which make Edna undesirable, instead of being told about them.

36 We've already had identical scenes to scenes 52 and 53 (Edna asking for boots, not having an address for the social security). Can't we amalgamate and strengthen without all this repetition.

39–41 We don't need these scenes at all but should go straight to sequence 60. The other characters are of no interest; we want to show Edna trying to get herself into prison. (Cut Bill and the woman in court.)

42–3 We don't need the voice-over again surely; it's all illustrated through Edna.

45 *Sequences 66 and 67*. We don't need this boarding house and landlady sequence again, surely it could be amalgamated with one of the earlier sequences where we see that she can't get social security without a room or a room without a job. What the script needs at this point is to establish a link between her coming out of prison and going to Josie and 'Jesus Saves'; to feel some possibility of her being helped. Otherwise we completely lose track of who Josie is and the connection and also lose interest in Edna. I think she should be going to Josie after prison, decide on the doorstep or something not to, be knocked over and be taken there by the nuns.

From here on in the connection between prison, the nuns and Josie is terribly confusing. The trip through London of the nuns, though a great sequence in itself, is totally unconnected with Edna.

I would cut sequences 75 and 76 (man and old woman) and put Edna's dialogue about not being a vagrant in sequence 78 elsewhere. (Could easily fit into the car sequence with James – Sequence 46.)

As I see the sequence of the script it should be: prison; Jesus Saves; drunken aberration from there; back to Jesus Saves, an illustration of Edna working there; and then the closing of it. (Her last hope.)

56 *Sequence 80*. We don't want the life histories of all the other inmates. It's Edna we want to know about. I would cut all the stuff preceding p. 58 with Teresa talking to Edna. Why can't Edna tell her life to the others instead of them to her? Besides which, the inmates are later referred to as drunken old women, and yet these seem to be nothing but unmarried mums and young potential suicides; I would have thought that some of our previous characters (like Irene and Doris, etc.) belonged here more than these, who seem to come from the script of 'Arlene'.

I would like here to see Edna doing her work (which she is referred to as doing so noisily), getting her booze from wherever she gets it, waking up the street and finally defeated by the hostel being closed. Keep in Josie's explanation of how the hostel is run and how the food is received; this is interesting and important. Josie's connection with the nuns is so vague; needs explanation.

96 on *Sequences 91, 92, 93, and 94.* We don't need at all: again a digression; only Edna's remarks about not being vermin are important and can be kept elsewhere.

73 All this stuff about the hostel and nuns is interesting and important, although it could be presented in a less didactic way.

Sequence 98. I don't understand exactly what sort of official meeting this is.

101 The flashbacks, in my opinion, should be distributed through the script, i.e. during her lonely treks on the road; during her sleeps in the dormitory and mental home . . . and could come into her conversation with various people she meets (if thought in character). They can't be done as a lump here, and are in any case somewhat oversimplified and like Victorian melodrama.

126 We've already had one wrist-slashing and I don't think we should have another. I think it is much more pathetic if she simply resumes her wandering once more, accepting it as inevitable.

Notes on Edna

16 October 1970

I still wish we had more indication of what Edna actually lives on, and where she gets the money for the meths – are we actually going to have a scene of her begging?

I thought we were going to have a telephone call at the beginning in the first scene where she gets thrown out.

Page
 26 (*Sc. 18*) The reference to 'Mr K.' is completely out of date, should it perhaps be 'Chairman Mao' instead?

26A (*following Sc. 18*) Must we add this absolutely revolting dialogue? I don't see what additional value it gives the play.

 28 (*Sc. 21*) Why is this now a kitchen and not the dormitory?

 31 (*Sc. 23A*) I don't understand where this scene shifts from the road to the car.

The psychiatrist section may need to be cut considerably for budgetary reasons. I would cut completely scenes 31, 32, 34, and possibly 35.

 57 (*Sc. 52*) There should be more connection between Edna's crime and her appearance at the Magistrates' Court, perhaps we should put Sc. 54 before Sc. 53 which would explain why she was arrested.

 58 (*Sc. 53*) I would retain Bill and cut the woman. We already have too many women in the script anyway, and Bill is a better

contrast to Edna; and what the Judge has to say does not make sense in reference to the woman.

61 (*Sc. 56*) Cut 'official voice' – also on p. 63 (Sc. 60).

74 (*Sc. 69*) We absolutely have to cut the four-letter words here and following it. All that will happen if we film them is that they will then be edited out later, which may well ruin the scene.

I am still disturbed that the following section fails to do what I asked for in my first set of notes, namely to establish a connection between the visit of Josie to the prison and Edna's coming to Jesus Saves. I thought we were going to have her getting out of prison, coming to the doorstep of Jesus Saves, losing the courage to go in, getting drunk, ending up at the Arches, and finally coming to Jesus Saves. As it stands it seems like the long arm of coincidence when she ends up at the place where Josie is.

80 (*Sc. 73*) I still think there is far too much of Teresa.

98 (*Sc. 86*) I don't understand this scene at all.

107 (*Sc. 91*) This whole scene is discussing whether the Home for women vagrants should be closed or not. The speech of Mrs Behan 'A man came in my hall' etc. would therefore seem to me totally irrelevant. Surely we should change this to 'A Woman' as presumably she is giving evidence against the women in the hostel.

111 The enormously long speech of Captain Cave and her dialogue with Council should definitely be cut.

125 (*Sc. 117*) Why does Josie refer to herself as 'a father figure' instead of a mother figure?

Scenes 117 and 118 are very awkwardly placed in relation to each other. Surely there should be something about Edna working or being happy in between the two scenes, or else Sc. 117 should come earlier before the public enquiry. How are we going to cut from Josie to Josie and make any sense?

Part two

Chapter 15

The history of
Rumpole of the Bailey

The story of *Rumpole of the Bailey* which became the very popular Thames Television series really begins at the BBC with a play by John Mortimer which I have already mentioned in Chapter 9, called *Infidelity Took Place*, which I commissioned and produced on 'Wednesday Play', and which was transmitted in May 1968, directed by Michael Hayes. In many ways, here was Mortimer's initial sketch for the subsequent character of Horace Rumpole. The play was about a deception carried out by a client on Leonard Hoskins, a divorce lawyer. John's initial description of Hoskins was 'His suede shoes are shiny, his RAF tie is threadbare, his macintosh pockets bulging with divorce petitions . . . the crumbs of the pork pie (which he has eaten in a crypt of the law courts) hang on his waistcoat.' Played by the somewhat portly John Nettleton, Hoskins was a younger, slightly thinner, mother-ridden version of the later invention, the wife-ridden Horace Rumpole.

In the mid-1970s Mortimer still seems to have been mentally germinating the same character, who was of course not without elements of himself and his father, the blind barrister so movingly commemorated in his play *Voyage Around my Father*. He initially suggested to me that he write a 'Play for Today' about a barrister which he wanted to call by the somewhat obscure title of *My Darling Prince Peter Kropotkin*; his brief synopsis described the main character, Horace Rumbold, as a liberal, with an optimistic view of life and human nature. He respects the nineteenth-century anarchists, especially the Russian, Kropotkin, author of *Memoirs of a Revolutionist*.

Later John did a more detailed background for Rumbold whose name we subsequently changed to Rumpole because, as I recall, we discovered the existence of a real barrister called Horace Rumbold.

Our imaginary Horace was born in Dulwich in 1910, the son of the Reverend Wilfred Rumpole and Alice Rumpole. Educated at Lancing and Keble College, where he acquired a lifelong antipathy to clerics, he got a poor third in law.

At the out-break of war in 1939, Horace's call-up was delayed owing to a medical problem, namely flat feet. By now he had joined chambers headed by C. H. Wystan. The delay proved beneficial to Rumpole's career. Because of lack of competition (i.e. most of the other barristers had been called up) he was given an important brief, the so-called 'Penge bungalow murder' case, and achieved an acquittal for his client. (This famous case, his one moment of glory, is constantly alluded to by him in the future.) Rumpole had already caught the eye of Hilda, daughter of C. H. Wystan. After his legal triumph, Hilda became determined to marry the barrister whom her father described as 'The best man he's ever known on bloodstains'. Rumpole married her thinking he'd be killed in the RAF, which had by now accepted him. Instead of dying a heroic death, however, he got posted to the ground staff at Dungeness.

In 1946 when he is demobbed Horace faces unaccustomed competition from the wave of returning barristers and lapses from being the star of the 'Penge bungalow murder' into the role we come to know well of 'Old Bailey hack'. Hilda is deeply disappointed in him and never lets him forget it. Some Rumpole fans may be shocked to learn that in the first synopsis John even hinted that the marriage broke down because 'it's rumoured Rumbold had a tendency to prefer young men'.

Most of the above ingredients (except the latter), as well as the propensity of Rumpole to literary quotation were to become staples of the first script and the subsequent series.

As to the title of the 'Play for Today', John subsequently suggested *Jolly old Jean Jacques Rousseau* as an only slightly less *outré* alternative to *Kropotkin*. Eventually he ceded that this was also too obscure for most of the audience and we agreed on the name of *Rumpole of the Bailey*. I asked John Gorrie to direct the piece and we set about looking for our hero and the rest of the cast.

Initially Mortimer was very keen that Michael Hordern with whom he had previously worked should play the lead but Hordern was not available for our studio dates. It was, as I recall, John Gorrie who first suggested Leo McKern as an alternative, a suggestion which was not initially greeted with much enthusiasm by Mortimer. I had never worked with McKern before but could see the potential of his rotund shape and deep, sonorous voice in the part. He would be very different from the thin, eccentric, shambling Hordern but equally as good. Mortimer eventually concurred. When rehearsals started it was immediately apparent to all of us that Leo was made for the part and, by his physical presence, added immeasurably to it.

In this first BBC *Rumpole*, Rumpole chooses against all odds to defend a young black (played by Herbert Norville) on a charge of attempted murder. As Horace ironically puts it 'If the judge turns out to be a Jamaican teenager with form we might have a chance.' 'I could win most of my cases', he says 'if it weren't for the clients . . . they will waltz into the witness box and blurt things out.' He eventually does win the case because he discovers the police confession is invalid. The accused is totally illiterate and could have neither written nor read it.

As with the series that followed, the plot of this first play was slender. It was Rumpole's character and John's satirical analysis, through him, of the law itself and those who live off it and those who break it which were the strength of the scripts. This first one began typically with Rumpole's voice-over quoting Wordsworth. 'There was a boy: ye knew him well, ye cliffs/And islands of Winander.' We hear this over a teaser in which Ossie Gladstone, the young black, is running away from the bus stop where the stabbing occurred. We then cut to Horace in his kitchen, still reciting while he prepares breakfast for his dreaded wife, Hilda. His dialogue when he presents her with her tray is typically cynical. 'They say crime doesn't pay but it's a living, you know . . . Think of it sometimes, old dear. That nice breakfast egg of yours. Probably a tiny part of the proceeds of an unlawful carnal knowledge.' In this script and most of the later ones Rumpole's obsession with and permanent vendetta against judges is also expressed. 'Judges used to scare the living daylights out of me' he says. 'Terrible old darlings who went back to their clubs and ordered double muffins after death sentences.' His melancholic self-analysis at the end of the script is also typical. 'Everyone knows me', he says to the uncomprehending and unsympathetic Hilda, 'down the Bailey. An amiable eccentric who drops ash down his waistcoat and tells the time with a gold hunter and calls them all "Old Sweetheart". Also I recite Wordsworth in the loo . . . Who *am* I exactly?'

For Hilda Rumpole, later renowned as 'She who must be obeyed', we cast Joyce Heron, a tougher and more raddled character than the subsequent feather-brained Hilda played by Peggy Thorpe Bates in the series. Although the former was a more formidable opponent, the latter, being so idiotic, gave Horace more of a chance of witty, sarcastic comment. The play went into rehearsal in January and February 1975. The designer was Fanny Taylor, the cameraman Phil Mayheux. It was largely a studio production. The only filming was at Lord's cricket ground and at a bus queue where the stabbing for which Rumpole's client is arrested takes place.

The transmission was on 16 December 1975 and a BBC audience research report estimated that 13 per cent of the UK population were watching it. The reaction index, which indicated the audience's enjoyment, was a high 66. The average for 'Play for Today' was 59. The reviews were uniformly excellent and appreciative of the humour of the piece and of Leo's performance. All three of us, Mortimer, McKern and myself, sensed that we were on to a winner. John said he had many more stories in him about the character. Leo said it was the first time he had ever played a character whom he would not mind playing again in a series.

Before I continue with this particular story, it is necessary to give a brief background of the changes going on at the BBC in general and in particular in the drama department at this time. In a nutshell, the BBC was in a state of financial crisis and was citing government orders as a reason for having to freeze staff wages. Even without this freeze, there already existed a high differential between BBC and ITV pay which had resulted in a considerable exodus of BBC staff to the other channel which still seemed to have 'a licence to print money'. While ITV wallowed in its advertising revenue, the unfortunate BBC could only cry poverty, alleging that its own revenue from the licence fee (as fixed by the government) was no longer adequate to cover its ever rising costs. Some extracts from newspapers which follow will give an idea of the situation.

'Brain drain saps morale at BBC' was the *Sunday Times* headline on 10 July 1977 for an article about Bryan Cowgill, who had been expected to become director of the BBC news and current affairs department but instead was leaving the BBC to become managing director of Thames. The article claims that his salary at

Thames will be double that at the BBC and more than the new director general of the BBC, Ian Trethowan, will make. The article quotes Cowgill himself:

> At a lower level, technicians and administrative staff are leaving the BBC in ever-increasing numbers. It's because the money is lousy that these people, who really make the BBC work, are getting out. They earn on average 30 per cent less than ITV companies pay. There is more talk within the BBC now about money than there is about programme-making and the effect on morale is corrosive.

The article quotes a joke going around the BBC. Thames was going to bring back the programme *Double Your Money* and ex-BBC men would be used as contestants.

A headline in *The Times* on 6 October 1977 read 'BBC "bleeding to death" because of meanness and cowardice, 13 broadcasting unions maintain.' The safeguards committee of the unions stated that 'Dozens of jobs and job opportunities are being lost to staff and performers. Men and women, many of whom have given or would have been prepared to give a lifetime of service to the BBC, are leaving or being driven out.' The committee said that if the BBC and the system of public service broadcasting it represented were to survive, the government must give it the money necessary to restore its programmes, maintain its lead as a programme maker and pay those it employed.

Television Today, on 18 August 1977, talks of a letter from the Chairman of the BBC, Sir Michael Swann, received by all members of BBC staff about 'the acute problems of BBC pay' and the government demand that the rise in earnings next year should not exceed 10 per cent.

Allowing for exaggerations in the press, there is no question that there was a distinct change of atmosphere in the mid-1970s at the BBC; the 'golden age' was being replaced by a long winter of discontent. In the Plays department this feeling was exacerbated by a constant chopping and changing of top personnel – new brooms sweeping clean every few years. After Sydney Newman's departure to Associated British Pictures, Saun Sutton, who succeeded him as Head of Drama, brought in a series of directors to replace Gerald Savory, who had retired as Head of Plays. Directors, in my experience, are not particularly good at administration. The talented ones miss their more directly creative role and usually want to return to directing before long. Others become absentee administrators, giving themselves plum projects to direct while still allegedly running the department.

To begin with I was a beneficiary of these changes when the director Christopher Morahan took over as Head of plays department. He sensed accurately that I was in need of a break from my long run on 'Play for Today' and asked me to look at Thomas Hardy's short stories and see if I thought they would make an anthology series of short films. I fell in love with them immediately, said 'Yes, I know they will work' and spent an idyllic year filming *Wessex Tales* on locations in the West Country. It was also Christopher who gave me the go-ahead when I asked if I could commission six more *Rumpole* scripts from John Mortimer, after the success of the first production. Unfortunately Christopher left his post shortly after this to go back to directing. It was then that the bureaucratic muddle and office politics began which eventually led to my going to Thames and taking *Rumpole* with me.

Thames had fairly recently acquired a new Head of Drama, Verity Lambert, who had been a production secretary at ABC before I arrived there and had later been turned into a producer by Sydney at the BBC. It was, according to Sydney, also he who had recommended her to Howard Thomas, managing director of ABC and later Thames, to head the drama department there. He told me, in typical half-joking Sydney fashion, that he had done so because he admired Verity's legs, her ambition and her aggressiveness.

Verity Lambert now came to me with a proposition. She was desperately looking for new up-market series ideas. As I was in touch with all the top writers would I be interested in a freelance contract to look for three such ideas? Since I was on a short-term rather than staff BBC contract, I could accept this work without conflict while still producing at the BBC and could thereby supplement my frozen BBC income. It seemed like a good idea to me and I accepted the Thames offer on 25 October 1976 of the grandiose sum of £3,500 (half on signature of contract and half on their acceptance of my work) to provide Thames with three format stage series ideas.

At the BBC, Saun Sutton had by now appointed another director, one with whom I had never worked, James Cellan Jones, to take over from Morahan as Head of Plays. Before leaving,

Morahan wrote his successor a memo on 23 March 1976 with a copy to me, telling him that he had put in hand a new two-year contract for me to include the completion of an anthology series I had been producing about extrasensory perception, called 'The Mind Beyond' (which included stories by Daphne du Maurier, William Trevor and David Halliwell, and was subsequently published by Penguin Books in 1976). Other projects in hand were a trilogy by William Trevor for 'Playhouse', several possible 'Plays for Today', and a series of half-hour films which had been started by Innes LLoyd called 'Young Film Makers' which Chris wanted me to take over. About 'Rumpole' he told Cellan Jones that he had suggested to Saun Sutton that 'these might be better done in Series or Serials Department, though with Irene as Producer. You will need to follow this up.' Logically, of course, it could be argued that *Rumpole* no longer belonged in plays department according to those distinctions which ironically had been introduced by Sydney Newman when he first reorganized the drama department. *Rumpole* had running characters who recurred in more than one episode; it therefore now belonged in series. Cellan Jones, who was not keen on it, preferred that I should start producing 'Young Film Makers'. (Many years later I was surprised to see Cellan Jones's name as a director on an episode of *Rumpole*.)

On 19 October 1976 I wrote to Saun Sutton asking whether, since Cellan Jones had said it was dubious that *Rumpole* would be accepted as a plays department offer, it could instead be submitted as a series or serial at the next offers meeting where the Programme Controllers decided which programmes they wanted to make in the following year. Saun answered that after discussions with the Heads of Series and Serials he could see no way that it could be fitted into the schedules for at least two years. This was disappointing but, since I was so busy with the other projects, the delay was not a real problem. When I mentioned to John Mortimer that it was possible *Rumpole* might not be done in the immediate future, however, he fell into a decline. I was surprised by this unexpected behaviour from one who presented such an outwardly jolly personality to the world and was such a success story both as a barrister and as a writer. Later I was told by someone close to him that the jolly exterior was deceptive; John got deeply depressed if he wasn't either published or mentioned in at least one of the Sunday papers every week. Although he was still only half-way through the scripts he kept asking if I could not do something about getting the series put on sooner.

There was one other possible route to take, although it was one which made me slightly uneasy. I had mentioned the situation of the delays on *Rumpole* to Verity Lambert who had seen and liked the BBC play. 'Bring the series to Thames', she said, promising more money and wonderful working conditions. My format development contract could be converted into a story-editing fee, she said, and would be paid in full separately from the producer's fee Thames would offer me. I had been trying for years to get my BBC establishment officer who dealt with contracts to recognize financially that by not using a story editor, like most producers did, I was doing two jobs for the price of one. The only reply I ever got from him was that it was my own choice to do the story editing, the BBC wouldn't pay me more for that but if I wanted one (which I didn't) they *would* give me a story editor.

When I told John Mortimer of Verity's offer, to my surprise he perked up immediately and said that he would rather do the series at Thames than at the BBC anyway; they would pay more money and it would be more fun working for ITV. On 23 November 1976 Anthony Jones, John's agent, wrote to Saun Sutton saying that unless the BBC could provide firm dates by the start of December for when *Rumpole* would be produced he wanted to buy the project back and take it elsewhere. Without any argument, Saun agreed to let him do so and I, with many qualms about leaving the protective womb of the BBC after fourteen years, turned down the renewal of my contract and signed up with Thames for a year.

With hindsight what I obviously should have done for my own protection at this point was suggest to John and Leo that we form a company together to supply Thames with the productions. This was the direction in which television was later to go. In the 1970s, however, the concept of independent producers and productions on the networks was almost unheard of. The BBC had not yet had a quota system imposed upon it by the government whereby it was bound to use a certain number of independents. Channel 4, which functions as a commissioning editor, rather than as a producer, did not exist until 1982. Almost everything was done 'in house' with the companies paying the salaries of the creative staff and owning the rights to their work. Producers like myself working in the drama departments of the existing companies were expected to think up ideas, take full artistic control of their programmes and stay as much as possible within their agreed annual budgets. That was the end of it. Financially they took no personal risks; equally they made no personal gains outside their salaries; even residuals for producers on repeats did not exist until 1976. Few if any had an equity in their own programmes. If you needed to buy the rights in a book or commission a certain author, you simply phoned copyright department and asked them to do so. From then on the company owned the property. It is dubious whether Thames would have accepted to engage us as a company which owned the rights in the property. John and Leo both had high-powered agents capable of getting them good individual deals. I, having been at the BBC for so many years, had not needed an agent. In my naivety, I was unworried about the situation. I was, after all, going back to the company where I had spent the happiest years of my television career when it had been called ABC and I was going to work for someone I considered a friend who had made me generous promises, albeit not all of them on paper.

Chapter 16

Rumpole at Thames:
setting up the series

In setting up a series the producer is facing a different challenge from that of the single play. You are in fact making a set of prototypes which once created will carry on for many weeks or years. In the case of *Rumpole* they were to continue over forty-two episodes. Once the prototypes have been impressed upon an audience's mind and they become hooked on them probably a computer or a trained chimpanzee could keep reproducing the ingredients in a way that would satisfy them. One often feels this about long-running series which are kept going past their sell-by date, as indeed *Rumpole* was.

The kicking-off point, of course, in determining the style, is the script. In *Wessex Tales* for instance I sought to convey Hardy's fatalistic attitude to human existence by always starting with the characters as tiny figures dwarfed by a vast landscape, coming nearer and nearer on the screen, enacting their stories and then dis-appearing into the landscape again. In *Rumpole* John's satirical approach and witty lines were the starting point. In addition, however, one already had the great advantage of having cast a larger-than-life lead, Leo McKern, whose looks and voice were uniquely memorable. To me, when I first saw him in his wig and gown, he seemed to have stepped out of a nineteenth-century satirical cartoon about the law. He could have been drawn by George Cruikshank, the nineteenth-century caricaturist and illus-trator of Dickens, or by Spy. As to his wonderful deep voice, it went back further. I was sure that the equally portly Dr Johnson must have sounded like that. The first job therefore was to try to get these ingredients into the opening titles and music, which would set the style and mood of the series. The second job would be to surround Rumpole with an equally cartoon-like cast.

When I first went to the graphics department at Thames I realized how spoiled I had become at the BBC. The young man assigned to me, Rob Page, was bemused when I mentioned Cruikshank and Spy; he had never heard of either of them and seemed uncomprehending of what I had in mind for graphics. At the BBC, so geared to doing classic serials and with a vast back-up of reference material and knowledge, this would have been unthinkable. There was no library, either, on the spot to find illustrations of the works I had in mind. Ultimately, however, having done some research, Rob Page did extremely well with his cartoon-like pictures of Leo in wig and gown, sometimes brandishing his umbrella while hugging the statue of Justice atop the Old Bailey.

For the music I chose a classical composer, Joseph Horovitz, who had composed the music for *Wessex Tales*. At our first meeting about *Rumpole* at his house one afternoon in May 1977 I gave him the first script and brought some stills from the BBC production as he had never seen Leo McKern. I told him about Leo's portly figure and wonderfully sonorous voice and he immediately suggested using a bassoon and played on the piano the sort of effect he would try to get. When we finally recorded the music at Teddington on 4 August 1977 it was with a most unusual combination of instruments; two first-rate bassoonists and one contra-bassoonist were accompanied by a cello, played by Steven Gabbaro. Joe later told me he had not only thought of the legal cartoons I had mentioned as inspiration but also of the clerk of the court in Gilbert and Sullivan's *Trial by Jury*. I was delighted with the result which absolutely realized the kind of heavy and humorous sound I had hoped for. There is no question but that Horovitz's opening and end credits music and commercial break stingers over Rob Page's graphics added immeasurably to setting the style of the series.

Two Thames designers, David Marshall and Mike Hall, working in tandem, designed and had built permanent studio sets of the Old Bailey, the chambers where Rumpole worked and the interior of Rumpole's flat. There was not much filming in the early *Rumpoles* which I produced. Mainly it showed Rumpole around the Temple, where John Mortimer had chambers, the Old Bailey and Brixton Prison.

The first six *Rumpole* episodes, which were transmitted between 3 April and 15 May 1978, contained all the ingredients as before. Rumpole has chambers in the Temple and is often at the Old Bailey. He quotes Wordsworth fluently and frequently and refers to

12

13

188

14

12–14 Opening graphics from *Rumpole of the Bailey*.

his wife, Hilda (Peggy Thorpe-Bates) as 'She who must be obeyed'.
In court Rumpole's thoughts, expressed by voice-over, are full or
irreverent reflections on the hidden motivations of the judge and
the other legal figures. In addition Rumpole is now surrounded by
a permanent repertory company of fellow barristers and clerks. The
casting of most of these was done later, when all the scripts were
in and I had engaged Herbert Wise and Graham Evans to direct
three of the six episodes each. We did the casting together with the
help of a new phenomenon to me, a casting director. At that time
at the BBC no such animal existed. Directors and producers did
their own casting and then asked bookings department to contract
them. At Thames, where everyone I encountered, from the music
fixer to the Head of Drama, was desperately anxious to stake their
territorial rights and impress one with their importance, my previous training was to cause me much grief. Whatever one had been
used to doing oneself naturally, like finding an actor in a small
fringe theatre (this is how I found and cast a then more or less
unknown actress, Patricia Hodge, as Phyllida Trant, the first
woman in chambers), was interpreted as overstepping one's mark

on to someone else's territory. When I asked the casting director to double-check the availability of an actor she said was not available, I received a memo of reprimand from the Head of Drama for daring to want a double check. I replied that when I had first wanted Pat Hayes for *Edna, the Inebriate Woman* I had been told she was not available; only further persistence gained her release and subsequent award-winning performance.

The regulars in the cast chosen by myself and the directors were to be Peter Bowles as Guthrie Featherstone, QC, the suave, ambitious Labour MP who ends up beating Rumpole to it as head of chambers; Julian Curry as the pernickety Erskine-Brown who resents both Rumpole's slovenliness and the disreputable clients he brings to chambers; Moray Watson as George Frobisher, a quiet bachelor who admires and fears Rumpole's flamboyant approach to the law, Patricia Hodge as Phyllida Trant, and Derek Benfield and Jonathan Coy as the two clerks, Albert and Henry, who vie with each other for seniority. The prototypes to whom the audience become addicted and most of whom were to be seen until the end of the series had thus been set.

In undertaking the job of writing the entire series himself John, who was still a full-time practising barrister, had set himself a pretty formidable task. He seemed to be not only a workaholic but also a playaholic who got up to write at 5:30 a.m., went to the Old Bailey, lunched somewhere fashionable and ended the day at some 'in' party or first night, usually well reported in the newspaper gossip columns.

My first visit to the Old Bailey with John when he was defending a case was typical. We lunched extremely well at a nearby restaurant where John, replete with good food and wine, drew out his brief and skimmed through it some ten minutes before the proceedings were due to start. Whether this was a revision or the first time he had ever read it, I don't know. He seemed remarkably unworried and casual about the whole thing. His client, who published a magazine devoted to bottom-smacking, smackers and smackees, was on trial for obscenity. The very respectable-looking members of the jury each had a copy of the bottom-smacking magazine in front of them and were several times solemnly referred by the judge to various pictures of bottoms which they equally solemnly examined. It was an instant *Rumpole* in the making.

My most memorable lunch with John was some time before that when I was still at the BBC where a rule prevailed that if the lunch bill looked like exceeding a certain limit one had to check with the head of the department about whether it would or would not be allowed on expenses. John had suggested I meet him at the White Elephant club in Curzon Street, then the favourite watering hole of the fashionable show-biz set. When I arrived at the appointed time, I found him already ensconced with a good-looking Israeli girl and a large bottle of champagne. He said he was sure I wouldn't mind if she was included in our conversation about his play, nor would I mind that he had already ordered some drink. Half-way through the very long lunch, during which I was mainly preoccupied with mental calculations about the final bill, I excused myself to phone Gerald Savory and apprise him of the uncontrollable situation before my week's wages vanished down the throat of John's uninvited guest.

John's own dialogue was often remarkably like that in *Rumpole*. On one occasion when telling me about a murder trial he had defended in which his client was a dwarf he kept referring to the latter as 'Dwarfikins'. I often wondered if he took any of the legal procedure at all seriously or whether it was all a form of entertainment to him, which also paid his bills. Being happily tucked away at home writing, John was luckily oblivious of the day-to-day experiences of working at Thames as opposed to the BBC. Not so Leo from whom I once received the following letter which described better than I can the attitude that seemed to prevail at Thames to outside creative people.

The letter is dated 20 October 1977 and refers to an occasion when Leo arrived to do a voice-over recording at Thames's Euston Road studios and was refused the right to park there. I can do no better than quote the letter in full. His reference to 'wining and dining afloat' refers to the hospitality boat which Thames kept on the river at the back of the studios.

Dear Irene,

As an explanation (not an excuse) of my suddenly blowing my top today at The Big Place at Euston I would like to tell you a little story that is pretty hard to beat for the Cynical Statement of the Year Award.

The shivering actors were sheltering under an outside staircase at Teddington some years ago, waiting for the set-up for night location shooting for a then top Thames series.

A group of top brass replete from wining and dining afloat drifted on the scene.

1st Man. (Sponsor? Pub. Rel.?) 'I say, what's all the lights?'

2nd Man. (Studio Rep.?) 'Oh, they're doing some night shots for *Callan*.'

1st Man. '*Callan*? . . . Oh yes . . . That's one of the fillers, isn't it?'

(*Long pause.*)

1st Actor (through dropped jaw) 'We're in the wrong business'.

The scene above really occurred. I pass it on to you because I hope that perhaps through you, Somebody Up There might become aware that maybe the 'Filler' attitude is beginning to inflitrate the structure to an alarming Trade Unionistic degree. This is a pity because what we all see on the screens at home are people who actually *do* it all; but of course that also includes people like yourself.

In fact all concerned, except that there seems a puzzling gap between these and the ones behind desks. Today I felt for a mad moment that I had gone in the wrong door to Rank Xerox. Their ignorance of magic words like '*Rumpole of the Bailey*', 'Herbert Wise', 'Recording Session' and (alas) 'Leo McKern' would have been acceptable.

It would be nice to be able to squeeze the car in beside the boilerman's, and in other small ways to feel that maybe after all people may begin slowly to accept that the teeth of my small cog really do mesh in the wonderful machinery that turns out those interesting pictures we all stare at.

Yours sincerely,
HORACE RUMPOLE
(Failed Silk)

I knew exactly how Leo felt but was powerless to do anything about it. My own situation was absolutely similar. Having been promised a car park space I found myself driving twenty miles every morning only to be refused entry to the studios by a bolshie attendant whose preference was always for the boilerman. Having been promised a permanent secretary of my own (at the BBC, when very busy, I had sometimes had two) I had to beg for letters to be typed for me.

Thames Television, born out of the merger of Associated Redif-fusion and ABC when the ITV franchises had come up for renewal, bore no resemblance to ABC Television where I had first started my TV career and spent some of the happiest days of my life on 'Armchair Theatre'. I soon came to appreciate what Thomas Wolfe, the American novelist, meant by the title of his novel, *You Can't Go Home Again*. Only Teddington Lock looked the same as it had done when I was there before; there the resemblance ended. Thames's drama department bore no trace of the happy, creative atmosphere it had once had during the time of Sydney Newman. After only a short time I realised I had made a great mistake in thinking it could still be the same without the personalities who had made it such an exciting and vibrant place in which to work; all of them were gone. Democracy had been replaced by dictatorship. During my time there Thames was riven with numerous industrial disputes and strikes; in the drama department there were several instances of less than honourable dealings over contracts and credits. The most notorious of these cases was that of the series *Rock Follies* which came to court in 1982 and was widely reported, as will be seen in the following extracts from the newspapers.

The *Daily Express*, on 15 June 1982, described how 'Three actresses formed the Rock Bottom pop group and hoped for stardom with their idea for a TV series about a singing trio just like themselves trying to make the big-time.' 'Thames Head of drama, Verity Lambert', said the *Daily Mail* on 21 October 1982, 'paid the group £500 for an option on their services in 1974 amd a further £250 when it was extended until 1975.' According to the *Daily Express* article, however, Thames copied the idea and did not use them as actresses as they had been promised. Annabel Leventon, Gaye Brown and Diane Langton, along with their composer manager Donald Fraser, were suing Thames and scriptwriter Howard Schumann and producer Andrew Brown for damages for breach of contract and breach of confidence. (The defence denied that the show was based on the group's idea.)

On page 3 of *The Times*, 21 October 1982, a headline read 'Band robbed of "Rock Follies" idea, judge says.' The article that followed told how Thames was ordered to pay £100,000 costs as well as the sum paid to the girls. *The Times Law Report* two days later quotes the judge, Mr Justice Hirst, as saying 'there was no reason in principle why an oral idea should not qualify for protection under the law of confidence provided certain criteria were complied with . . . On the facts of the case, the defendant had used the plaintiff's idea and had been in breach of confidence in so doing.'

The *Daily Mirror* on 4 July 1983 ran an article headlined '"Ditched" girls win damages fortune'. It says that the girls won a £500,000 payment. They had already won an earlier hearing against Thames for breaching their contract. Gaye Brown was quoted as saying 'When we went with our idea to Thames we thought we would be doing the series. It was devastating to our careers when three other actresses took our parts.' The *Daily Express* report on the same day adds that the girls were gagged from speaking about the case with a 'no publicity' clause.

Had I the talent of Paddy Chayefsky, the famous American scriptwriter, and were the English libel laws more like the American ones, I might have been able to pour my own unhappy experiences of this period at Thames into an English version of *Network*. Suffice it to say that the latter brilliant film, which came out in 1976, directed by Sidney Lumet with Peter Finch, Faye Dunaway and William Holden in the leads, should be prescribed viewing for any media studies student or aspirant to a job in television who wants to know what it is really like working in the medium and how one should behave to survive. It may be thought by some to be an exaggeration. Unfortunately it isn't.

Chapter 17

'A verbal agreement is not worth the paper it is written on' – Sam Goldwyn (attributed)

The first six episodes of *Rumpole* at Thames went out to uniformly enthusiastic reviews, many of them castigating the BBC for having let the series go to Thames. 'Destined to be one of the great winners is *Rumpole*' said the *Times* preview on 3 April 1978. 'Not to be missed. Leo McKern is superb as the wild and wily barrister Rumpole. . . . The series is a spin-off from one BBC play with the same character, which Thames TV were clever enough to snap up. I wish it well' said the *Sunday Mirror* the day before. 'I wouldn't say the BBC has thrown away a pearl richer than all its tribe,' said Nancy Banks-Smith in *The Guardian* on 4 April, 'but it has mislaid a tasty box of kippers.' 'Mr Mortimer, Mr McKern, and their producer, Irene Shubik, and director, Herbert Wise, may be on a winner,' said Stanley Reynolds in his review in *The Times* on the same day, 'one of those series which grows on one after the oddity of its particular world becomes a bit more familiar.' The reviews continued in this vein throughout the first run of the series.

As the ratings were also good, half-way through transmission Jeremy Isaacs, then the director of programmes at Thames, asked for more episodes to be commissioned for a second series, which I immediately put into motion with Mortimer and his agent. Thames may have had an ulterior motive for promoting this untypically 'up-market' series, a fact which was remarked upon by Stanley Reynolds, in his review above. Here is what he had to say:

A great character actor like Leo McKern looking like an over-laden Spanish galleon, spouting great chunks of Wordsworth and snatches of Shakespeare in a drama which was full of the minutiae of the legal profession is hardly the stuff that popular independent television stories are made of. But the viewer should remember that franchise time is coming round again and the commercial companies will be wearing a pious look.

Shaun Usher in his review in the *Daily Mail* on the same day echoed Stanley Reynolds in observing that this was a departure from the ITV norm. 'One wonders – and I'm not being patronising – what the majority audience for ITV drama, accustomed to car chases, big bosoms and loud explosions in anything to do with crime, will make of it', he wrote. It was always before franchise renewal time that the companies sought to prove their respectability.

Here is a brief indication of the subject matter and flavour of the first series. The first episode, *Rumpole and the Younger Generation*, begins very much like the BBC *Rumpole* with a teaser showing boys robbing two butchers. Other familiar ingredients follow. Rumpole is first seen at breakfast, reciting Wordsworth's 'Trailing clouds of glory'. He refers to Hilda as 'master of the blue horizons'. Once more he goes to court to defend a teenager, this time Jim Timson, who is accused of robbery with violence. Although the boy is probably innocent on this occasion, Rumpole realises sadly that he is destined for a life of crime because he comes from a well known family of traditional East End villains. Picking up on this theme, Nancy Banks Smith, in the *Guardian* review mentioned above, remarked that this episode 'was about the ineluctable process whereby lawyers beget lawyers and crooks for ever. The continuity of crime. Looking at the judge on the bench and the boy in the dock, Rumpole ruminates, "his father was Lord Chancellor about the time Jim's grandfather was doing the Co-op".' Rumpole's opponent in court is none other than the smarmy Guthrie Featherstone who is prosecuting. Of the latter's obsequious behaviour to the judge, Mr Justice Everglades ('known to his friends as Florie'), Rumpole asks (voice-over) 'Why don't you crawl up on the bench with him, Featherstone old darling, and black his boots for him?' The script ends with Featherstone being appointed head of Chambers instead of Rumpole. It seems that smarminess and obsequiousness pay off.

Calling the series a 'juridicial soap-opera', *Punch*, 12 April 1978, noted 'Mortimer's ambivalent attitude towards his first profession, half snobbish admiration, half derisive contempt.' Of the plot it said 'the dénouement, which depended on the production in court of a concert poster much as George Brent used to save Bette Davis from the electric chair by suddenly producing Claude Rains from his briefcase, was feeble stuff'. There was much praise, however, for the performance of Leo McKern.

The second tranmission, *Rumpole and the Alternative Society*, gave the audience a change of scene from the Old Bailey. In this script Rumpole goes out of town to a dismal seaside resort, Coldsands, to defend a damsel in distress (played by Jane Asher) on a drug-peddling charge. Here he stays at a pub called 'The Crooked Billet' run by one of his old RAF friends, Pilot Officer 'Three-fingers' Sam Dogherty (the 'three-fingers' nickname refers to whisky consumption not heroic loss of digits). For the first time we get some insight into his wartime days, when he was apparently in love with Bobbie Dogherty, Sam's blowsy wife. (Sam and Bobbie were played by Peter Jeffrey and Liz Fraser.) Then Rumpole, surely the most unlikely romantic hero since Woody Allen, visits his client at her hippy commune in a house called 'Nirvana', 34 Balaclava Road (a typical Mortimer address), where he is sorely tempted to drop out. His client, Kathy Trelawny, who is accused of possession of a suitcase of cannabis, turns out to be a beautiful teacher of poetry and wins Rumpole's heart not only with her looks but also with her ability to complete his Wordsworth quotations for him. After a dinner with the hippies Rumpole declares 'I would rather live at 34 Balaclava Road than at flat 386 Earls Court Avenue with "She who must be Obeyed". I would rather lie on your Indian scatter cushions and listen to flute music from the Andes than drag myself down to the Old Bailey on a wet Monday morning to defend some over-excited Pakistani accused of raping his social worker.' Later, however, he returns to London disillusioned when the girl confesses that she did indeed have the drugs and they were not planted on her by the police as he had suspected.

In episode three, *Rumpole and the Honourable Member*, Rumpole defends a henpecked Labour MP (Anton Rodgers) charged with the rape of a worker in his own party. The henpecked state is one with which Rumpole can fully empathise but he now has to fight on another front as well: his son has brought home as a fiancée an ardent and humourless American Women's Libber who does not find Rumpole's attitude to women funny, especially as exhibited in court.

In episode four, *Rumpole and the Married Lady*, our hero descends to divorce, a type of case he normally abhors. Rather like the lawyer in *Infidelity took Place* he is much taken with his client, Mrs Thripp (played by Phyllida Law), whose husband hasn't spoken to her for three years but communicates via sarcastic notes. So much so that Hilda suspects from a phone call at home that he is having an affair and threatens to leave him. When it turns out to be Norman, Mrs Thripp's obnoxious child, who is typing the vicious notes in order to separate his parents and gain the maximum attention from each of them, the couple make up their differences while Rumpole quotes the following description of marriage. 'With one single friend, perhaps a deadly foe/The longest and the deadliest journey go.'

In episodes five and six, *Rumpole and the learned Friends* and *Rumpole and the Heavy Brigade*, Horace returns to his favourite territory defending East End crooks, one a safe-breaker, the other accused of murder. In the first case he so incenses the ferocious Judge Bullingham (played by Bill Fraser, who made a marvellous opponent for McKern) that he is sent for a disciplinary hearing which could cost him his profession. In the latter case, the judge seems more concerned with Rumpole's rumpled appearance than his defence.

The natural assumption would be that, when a series is as great a success as *Rumpole* was, those responsible for its creation are the beneficiaries. It was certainly so for Leo McKern who told a reporter at the end of the first series that he had been offered more work in the last two weeks than in the last two years. I have not retained the figures for Leo's fees but know that his agent negotiated a considerable and well deserved increase from Thames for the second series and undoubtedly for those that followed. For the second series of scripts which I commissioned John Mortimer was given by Thames an increase of £700 per script, raising his fee from £1,800 to £2,500 per script.

When it came to the renewal of my own contract, however, I was in for a shock. Not only was there no recognition of my part in the success of the series; instead I was painfully to learn the validity of various famous Hollywood adages. The first, usually attributed to Sam Goldwyn, is 'a verbal agreement is not worth the paper it is written on'. Difficult though it may be to understand, I was offered a new contract by the Head of Drama, whereby I would be paid less, not more, to produce and story-edit the second series than I had been for the first. I shall not go into details here; suffice it to say that this all hinged on the verbal agreement I had made with

Verity Lambert that the fee originally offered to me by Thames to find three series ideas should be converted into a story-editing fee for *Rumpole* and that it should be added to my producer's fee. For book-keeping purposes only the second half of the fee was listed as applying to the series. It was only now, when it was too late, that I realized I needed an agent to handle the situation for me. I asked an excellent agent, Robin Dalton, to approach Ms Lambert on my behalf. The latter denied the existence of the verbal agreement and told Robin Dalton it only existed in my mind. I was not as lucky as the actresses in the *Rock Follies* case who had negotiated their contract with a shrewd manager who was willing to fight in the courts for it.

Why had this happened? There is another old Hollywood adage, 'It's not enough that I'm a success; my best friend has to be a failure.' In office politics, I was to learn too late, it is always best to keep a low profile. When I brought *Rumpole* to Thames, the press had made much of the BBC's mistake in letting 'one of its best producers' go; when Rumpole proved such a success, the story was reiterated. In the *Daily Mail* on 25 March 1978 Martin Jackson wrote:

> The Beeb will, I fancy, be kicking itself on Monday week when *Rumpole of the Bailey* picks up critical acclaim and a discerning audience for Thames TV. This was, of course, originally a much-praised BBC play starring Leo McKern, and a series was then commissioned. But the BBC mysteriously pulled out. McKern and producer Irene Shubik – the woman behind many of the *Play for Today* triumphs – took it to Thames. So the Beeb not only lost a TV series but also one of their very best TV drama producers. Sad.

Shaun Usher, the *Daily Mail* television critic remarked in his review of the first Thames transmission on 4 April 1978, 'I hope that *Rumpole* catches on. Not only because producer Irene Shubik has put her heart into getting it screened, but because it is so well written and performed all round.'

These favourable mentions in the press were probably the worst thing that could have happened to me. When I asked the Head of Drama if she was not pleased with the success of the series I was told that it was my success, not hers. I realised I had put myself in an invidious position for which undoubtedly my own naivety was to blame. I had by now presented Thames with the writer, the scripts (three for the new series had already been discussed with Mortimer and were well under way) and the star for the series. I had set the prototypes. Of the whole package I was now the most disposable element. *Rumpole* had endeared itself to the audience. It could now become a self-perpetuating money-spinner. The new contract offer was undoubtedly a clever way of freezing me out.

'Do you want to accept or tell them to jump in the lake?' my new agent asked in a letter on 9 February 1978 when Ms Lambert had made it clear that she would not shift an inch on her offer. It was a good question and one I was to debate with friends, family and most of all myself on many a sleepless night that followed. I loved the series. I had given up the security of a long career at the BBC in order to get *Rumpole* on the air instead of leaving it on the shelf for years to come. I had loved working with Leo and John, the directors and the rest of the cast. This was also the first time that I had a stake in something that looked set to become a long-running commercial success. For the first time I would get producer's residuals on all the overseas sales and repeats.

Before I made up my mind about leaving or staying, another shock awaited me. I told John Mortimer of my situation. Since we were such old friends and I had left the BBC in order to get the series done, I was certain he would be my strongest supporter in negotiating with Thames. He was a man who carried considerable weight, and not just physically. One would not have guessed this by his reaction. 'Poor John' were the first words that came from his lips. 'What do you mean?' I asked. In mournful tones he said that now Thames wouldn't do the series which he had been counting on to keep him and his family in his old age. No amount of pointing out that Thames was not going to drop such a successful series and that he had a contract for more scripts would convince him. He spoke not like a highly paid, influential barrister and eminently successful playright but like a man who had never had a script on before and would never earn any money again.

It was only later that I learned that after this John had agreed to accompany Verity Lambert, at her behest, to Manchester, where Leo McKern was acting on the stage in *Crime and Punishment*, so that they could talk Leo into doing the series even if I ended up not producing it.

For me the negative side of continuing at Thames was considerable. Only at rehearsals or working with John or my immediate production staff had I felt the usual pleasure in the work. Compared with the democratic regimes I had lived under at the BBC, it had been like working in an Iron Curtain dictatorship where my artistic freedom and my self-confidence were being eroded daily. Later the famous temper tantrums of the Head of Drama, who had by this time established for herself a personal identification with *Rumpole*, were several times described in the press. On 7 February 1984 a headline in the *Daily Telegraph* read ' "Rumpole" producer finds herself in the dock.' 'Verity Lambert, the television executive behind the series *Rumpole of the Bailey* found herself on the wrong side of the law at Horseferry Road Court yesterday', it said. Referring to her arrest as a suspected drink-driver, it continued, ' "She became extremely aggressive and abusive", P.C. Mark Horsley told the court. "She was objectionable and had been striking out at a WPC assisting to search her." ' The article reported that she was subsequently fined and banned from driving for a year. Another article in *The Mail on Sunday* on 8 April 1984 described Ms Lambert's 'high-tension lifestyle, which often sent her into ferocious tempers'.

I finally decided that traumatic as it would be to leave *Rumpole* there was no way I could continue at Thames with the conditions offered. Before I left I went to see Jeremy Isaacs about the possibility of retaining a credit on the forthcoming series in recognition of the fact that I had set it up. Jeremy later told a mutual friend, then head of Israeli Television, that Ms Lambert had threatened to resign if I were given such a credit. Only Howard Thomas, who had been Chairman of ABC and was still Chairman of Thames, was sympathetic. In a letter to me on 8 September 1978 he said:

> my personal view was that although you had been fully remunerated for your work on the production, the company might feel that once you had ceased to be directly associated with it, the company could consider the possibility of some modest payment in appreciation of your bringing the proposition into Thames. This is something with which I cannot be directly associated but which your agent might like to take up with the Managing Director, Mr Cowgill.

The latter replied in the negative both to the financial and the credit side.

Sean Day-Lewis, the *Daily Telegraph* critic, on 28 May 1979, writing on the eve of the transmission of the second *Rumpole* series, called it 'quite simply the most classy situation comedy now extant.

Horace's exploits never assault the emotions, they cleverly under-
line acceptable truths and the only possible response to them is a
contented purr.' He went on, as often happens with journalists, to
tell half the story of my departure:

> The first series started going out a year ago and was received
> with general acclamation, not least due to the excellent Shubik
> casting of the continuing characters around Rumpole . . . alas,
> behind the scenes the Shubik–Lambert friendship was turning
> sour . . . There was certainly the proverbial 'clash of personali-
> ties' resulting in Shubik's withdrawal. . . . John Mortimer QC
> considers it a 'tragedy' that Shubik has not stayed as producer.
> Irene Shubik has reasonably asked for a credit on the second
> series as the person who set the style and the main casting. Verity
> Lambert has refused this request on the grounds that you cannot
> credit a producer who chooses not to produce.

The Stage and Television Today on 3 May 1979 came nearer to the
truth:

> What particularly irks Irene Shubik is that if she had bought the
> rights in *Rumpole of the Bailey* before taking the project to
> Verity Lambert, she would have been sitting pretty now and
> would not have had to experience what she calls the 'we own
> the rights so get lost' attitude with which Thames answered her
> request for a screen credit. This was refused because it would
> 'create a precedent'. . . . 'Verity Lambert, speaking to *Television
> Today* this week, said that Irene Shubik was invited to produce
> the second series of *Rumpole* but eventually decided that she did
> not wish to. Although obviously some of the cast of the first
> series continued into the second, there were no scripts when Irene
> Shubik left and she had not set up the second series.

The latter statement was quite extraordinary. Not only did I
already have by the time I left Thames three of the six scripts commissioned from Mortimer, *Rumpole and the Man of God*, about a
vicar accused of shoplifting, *Rumpole and the Show Folk*, about
the alleged murder of her co-star by an actress, Maggie Grimble,
during a production of *Private Lives* at a provincial theatre, and
Rumpole and the Fascist Beast, I also had copious correspondence
with John about them. Most tellingly, I also had a letter from
Anthony Jones, John's agent, informing me that Verity had asked
him 'to let her have such copies as were in my possession for pro-

duction purposes'. She must therefore have been sent copies of the scripts herself.

The *Stage* article ends with the following paragraph, which is particularly relevant to the general picture of the Thames Drama department of the time:

> Irene Shubik is not the only drama producer to have left Thames recently. June Roberts, who produced the first series of *Hazell*, left before the second got under way . . . Barry Hanson, who produced *Out* for Thames's subsidiary Euston Films, is not doing a second series – certainly there was talk of a follow-up, but Thames categorically denies that it was ever intended to make one. Barry has now gone to ATV's Black Lion Films.

Gradually, so far as *Rumpole* is concerned, I become an Orwellian unperson. As the saying goes, 'Success has many parents, failure is an orphan.' There was no shortage of contenders to claim a share in the parentage of *Rumpole* after my departure.

Chapter 18

The Jewel in the Crown: how it all started

As I have mentioned in Chapter 3, I originally came to the BBC in 1963 to set up (as story editor) the first play series to be screened on the new channel, BBC-2. Called 'Story Parade,' the programme was based on adaptations of contemporary fiction. Not long after my arrival, I had my first encounter with Paul Scott, future author of the Raj Quartet.

One of the books which I purchased for 'Story Parade' was Scott's autobiographical novel *The Bender*, published in 1963. Explaining the meaning of the title in a letter to his Swedish translator, Scott, himself a frequent participant in benders, wrote 'to go on a bender has almost come to mean, in English, to go on the kind of drinking spree that will strip the drinker down to his inner nakedness'.[1]

I commissioned Jeremy Paul to do the adaptation, which was transmitted on 31 July 1964 with an excellent performance by Paul Rogers, who bore a marked physical resemblance to the author. I only met Scott once briefly at that time. Unfortunately, it was to be our only meeting. Nor did I encounter his work again until 1978 when my agent Robin Dalton recommended to me as a good read his Raj Quartet. She added the words 'Why don't you and Waris film it?' She was referring to one of her clients, Waris Hussein, a director who was an old BBC acquaintance of mine.

Scott, after *The Bender*, had given up the small, domestic novel and expanded his horizons to India. As he put it, he felt that he had been twice born . . . first in London in the ordinary way, and a second time twenty-three years later when he was shipped out as

[1] Hilary Spurling, *Paul Scott: A Life* (Pimlico edition), 1991, p. 245, letter by Paul Scott to Magnus Lindberg, 25 March 1963.

a soldier to India in the Second World War. When he returned to his roots in suburban London he 'saw images of India everywhere . . . the maidan, the club, the cantonment, the governor's residence. Only the names were different.'[2] In India he had found the metaphors he needed as a writer.

After my conversation with Robin Dalton, I took the four paperbacks of the Raj Quartet away with me on holiday. They were a fascinating, if demanding, read. Unlike so many contemporary British novels, which concentrated solely on the minutiae of their characters' sex lives or psychological problems, they were about something important: the end of the Raj in India and the traumas of partition. The idea of filming an epic with such historical significance and such a colourful background was both thrilling and also extremely daunting because of its sheer scale. I asked myself if there would be an audience of any appreciable size for it. The books were so convoluted in style that they could only appeal to a minority taste. More important, would any television company be daring enough to foot the bill for such a way-out project?

My answer to the first question was 'Yes, there would be an audience if one could simplify the story-telling enough.' The subsequent wide appeal of the screen dramatizations of both *Staying On* and *The Jewel in the Crown* were to prove me right. I believe this can partly be explained by their metaphorical nature. Although exotic, they had ingredients which were very familiar to a Western audience. As Scott realized, the social structure of the Raj was a clear metaphor for the class system in England. Women could certainly identify with the problems of the numerous transplanted female characters; men would be interested in the military and historical ingredients.

As to the second question, it was a foregone conclusion that the project was likely to be rejected by most companies. The filming requirements were far more ambitious and costly than any English television company had ever undertaken. The most obvious starting point, because of the non-commercial subject matter, was the BBC, which also still observed a certain moral code about not appropriating other people's ideas. When I approached Graeme McDonald, then controller of BBC-2, however, he told me that the

[2]Spurling, *Paul Scott*, quote from interview with Scott by Caroline Moorhead in *The Times*, 20 October 1975.

BBC had already considered the books and deemed it impossible to adapt four such vast and complicated volumes for the screen. They had also baulked at the cost and the notorious difficulties of filming in India.

Having in my mind the dreadful example of what had happened to me on *Rumpole* when I had no rights in the project, I had managed with Robin Dalton's help to persuade Paul Scott's agent John Rush of David Higham's (the agency where Scott himself had worked) to give Waris and myself a short option on the books during which time we had to try to find finance for a series. To begin with John Rush promised only that he would not dispose of the rights elsewhere for one month; he later extended the time to three months. He did not want to actually sell an option but promised that, if we failed to raise the cash during the time allowed, he would mention Waris and myself to a TV company which had also enquired about the rights so that perhaps we could get together. He would not divulge which company it was. Rush told us that he would not sell the rights for less than a guaranteed £13,000 against £26,000, representing a guarantee of thirteen hours' TV time at £2,000 per hour. This was for one showing on British television; the normal Guild repeats and residuals were additional.

Both Waris and I were, of course, absolute novices at raising money, having grown up in the protected world of the BBC where it was all done for you. I did, however, come close to success from an unexpected source, an American soft drinks company. Through one of my brothers I had met the vice-president of Royal Crown Cola, who were hoping to open up a plant in India and were interested in the possibility of using their frozen rupees there via an investment in our filming. My application for development money was reviewed favourably by their legal department but unfortunatly their plans were delayed by negotiations with the Indian government and they finally declined. Our option had run out and we had no other bites. Nowadays, of course, there would be the European Script Fund, the Lottery Film Fund, Channel 4 and many other places one could try but none of these existed then. As two freelances Waris and I could not possibly afford the investment for both rights and scripts without some backing.

By now Robin Dalton had ascertained that the interested TV company mentioned by John Rush was Granada, where Sir Denis Forman, the chairman, who, like Scott, had been in the army in India during World War II, apparently shared our enthusiasm for the books. Robin therefore approached Granada with the suggestion that Waris and I should respectively direct and produce the Raj Quartet for them. Waris, an upper-class Indian brought up in England and educated at Eton and Cambridge, was himself a close approximation in background of Hari Kumar in the books. Luckily he had not shared Hari's unhappy fate but had become a successful television and film director. Knowing India and England as he did, he was ideal for the subject matter.

Sir Denis Forman, the large, imposing man whom Waris and I went to see at his London office in Golden Square to discuss the project, was welcoming and very complimentary to us. His company, he said, had in fact been considering the books (following Granada's success with *Brideshead Revisited*). They had not, however, been able to see a way of adapting them to make a manageable project for TV. Having examined our credentials and met Waris and myself, he flatteringly expressed the opinion that he had now found a producer and director who were capable of bringing the books to the screen. We left his office in a euphoric state.

We had barely closed the door to Sir Denis's office when he, as I learned the next day from David Higham's, had picked up the phone to instruct Granada rights department to snap up the books immediately; unlike Waris and myself, he had the money and the power to do so. This time around, however, one was less worried than before. Sir Denis seemed a highly civilized and charming man and Granada had a good reputation for doing quality work and treating people well. Once more, however, as things were to turn out, none of the prime movers on *The Jewel in the Crown* project were to prove beneficiaries. Tragically, Paul Scott died of cancer before the project began. Only his family, agent and publishers were to benefit from the immense success of the television productions and the boost they gave to the book's sales. Waris did not end up directing either *The Jewel in the Crown* or *Staying On*, to which I shall come later, and I, although I set up the entire project and was named its 'deviser' on the screen, did not eventually produce *The Jewel in the Crown* but *Staying On* instead. But that is a story yet to come.

Chapter 19

The breakdown

Immediately after our meeting with Sir Denis Forman I was contracted by Granada TV as producer of the Raj Quartet. Later Sir Denis and I decided to make the title of the first of Scott's four volumes, *The Jewel in the Crown*, that of the television series.

The daunting task I now had was that of finding a way to break down Scott's four densely written volumes into a story-line which, while being manageable and affordable in terms of filming, would at the same time be comprehensible to a mass audience. Anyone who has read the books will appreciate the complexity of Scott's multi-viewpoint style. The story is told over and over again from different perspectives. Only an art house film like *Last Year at Marienbad* or *Rashoman* could approximate this style on the screen. We, however, were not addressing an art house audience. We needed to engage the lasting attention of the average fickle television viewer.

As a producer, I realized that in this case I could not simply hand the books to a tried and trusted adapter and leave it to him or her to come up with the scripts. Important decisions had to be made before one could do that. I would have to weed out of the books those episodes which I considered vital to the story-line from those which I thought could be sacrificed. An overall style of story-telling would have to be arrived at which while remaining true to Scott's intentions would suit television. Above all one had to go through the books with costs in mind. Essential production decisions had to be made from the start regarding numbers – how many speaking parts, locations, sets etc. could we afford and still do justice to the epic quality of the Raj Quartet? Only after all this had been decided could one safely hand over to an adapter.

A lot of hard, even boring, labour was now involved. There was more perspiration than inspiration to start with. The only feasible method was to sit down and make a detailed, page-by-page breakdown of each volume in terms of dialogue, action and historical background. After that one could match up particular episodes as described in each of the four volumes, decide which characters were dispensable or indispensable and which point of view would best carry on the narrative. A computer would have been invaluable at this stage but at the time I had none. It was like unravelling the threads of a complex and fascinating piece of literary knitting and reusing them to knit a more workaday garment. I was aware that it was perhaps a form of philistinism but it seemed the only way to bring the quartet popular accessibility.

Scott, apparently worried that few people would buy all four volumes and that many readers would not, therefore, understand the whole story, repeated himself many times over. The plus side of this is that we know in great detail what all the central characters think about each other and about certain events, such as the Hari Kumar episode and the meaning of the Raj. I charted and cross-referenced the location of all these thoughts in my breakdown. Scott's dialogue was unusually copious and so speakable that it was ready to leap off the page into the mouths of actors. One of my first requests to the adapters was to use as much of it verbatim as possible, which they did. Most of what the characters say comes straight from the original author.

At the same time as I was doing the breakdown, several other people were put to work. Sir Denis Forman and I agreed that a potted history of India in this period would be invaluable to the adapters and production crew who were unlikely to know much about it. In covering such major historical events as World War II, the end of British rule in India, and the period of partition, it was essential that we got our facts and our atmosphere right.

Granada, in those days, struck me as a curiously old-fashioned company. One was aware of a patriarchal control emanating from above like that in an Arnold Bennett novel. The control, as I was to discover later, gave the illusion of being benevolent but only if you complied with the patriarch's wishes. It could prove punitive if you were thought to have strayed. There was an air of earnest intellectuality about certain departments, like that of a turn-of-the century redbrick university. It was different from anywhere I had ever worked before. Within the vast framework of the BBC one had taken for granted an established, though impersonal, back-up of research and resources, physical and intellectual. Thames Television on the other hand was a crassly philistine and commercial company. Granada, by comparison, had the cosy atmosphere of a cottage industry.

When Forman suggested that Duncan Crow, an old Granada documentary hand, be commissioned to provide the Indian history, it was almost as though the headmaster were setting a school essay. At the same time I asked Peter Yapp (who filled in as a researcher when not acting) to make lists of all the locations, exterior and interior, in the books, which he did in painstaking detail, complete with maps. He also did family trees for the characters and listed all European characters and Indian ones separately, accompanied by all the descriptions of them found in the books.

A list of all those characters who had been selected as necessary to the action then went to Barbara Muxworthy, a Granada researcher, who checked their names, especially the army ones, with places like the India Office to make sure they were not real people and we would not be open to libel suits, especially, for instance, from a real-life Ronald Merrick, the villain of the series. John Leech, in graphics, meanwhile instituted a search for the definitive *Jewel in the Crown* picture, as described in the books. The work had begun too of looking for co-producers and facilities people in India like Ismail Merchant, Shashi Kapoor and Film City in Bombay, where I entertained the thought of using the studios.

By the end of March 1979 I was beginning to see the light of day. The essential characters and locations had been weeded out. A manageable and comprehensible story-line for the TV series was emerging. The time had therefore come to discuss this with Sir Denis Forman and to suggest to him my choice of adapters to write the scripts. At that time, Granada was eager to go into production as rapidly as possible. We therefore needed the scripts as fast as we could get them. It would obviously take too long to wait for one writer to complete them. There would have to be at least two adapters.

On Tuesday and Wednesday 27 and 28 March I arrived at Sir Denis's office armed with my detailed breakdowns of the four books, an estimate of the production problems involved so far as numbers of locations and characters were concerned, and, most important, my vision of the narrative line. I had decided, for instance, that the series should start *in medias res* with Sister

Ludmilla, out searching in the dark for dead bodies and finding our hero, Hari Kumar, lying drunk, instead of with the incident concerning the attack on the old English missionary, Miss Crane, as in the book, which, though important, is basically a side issue. Sir Denis had had the walls of his office pasted with large sheets of paper on which we could chart the episodes and characters involved in them; it was something, he said, he had learned from the director Claude Whatham. (It was, of course, also a system used by most production managers when working out such matters as when actors are required for filming and which scenes take place in the same locations.) During those two days of meetings we agreed details of a skeletal outline for thirteen episodes, a story-line which I would then develop with the adapters.

I was surprised, a few days later, to receive from Sir Denis's office a typed version of the story-line as recorded on the charts, accompanied by a long philosophical essay justifying in ten points what had been done, both of which bore the name of the chairman and myself. I was perplexed at the time as to the purpose of the essay or for whom it was intended. The answer only came many years later, after the series was transmitted, when real life began to imitate the multi-viewpoint texture of Scott's novels.

On 3 April 1979, after our March meeting, I received the following memo from Sir Denis Forman about the work I had done in devising the series and my request for a credit for it. It was not a usual part of a producer's job to produce a blueprint for such a complicated project.

I have given some thought to the matter you raised last week about some form of participation or royalty payment for your work for Granada on 'The Raj Quartet'. There is no legal, moral or financial objection in my mind to the recognition of creative work in senior people by some form of participation. But – and here is the rub – if it happens for one it must happen for all . . . so the answer I give you to your question must be the same as when you raised it at one of our first meetings. It is impossible to make an exception of one person, even though I rate very highly that person's ability to produce a truly big and difficult series.

He ended by asking if I wished to continue on the series despite this 'unsatisfactory answer'. A dreadful feeling of *déja vu* began to creep into my mind but, as I patently did wish to continue on a series which had by now become an obsession, I had no alternative but to cut my losses and progress to the next stage of commissioning the scripts. Besides, Sir Denis gave the impression of being such a civilized and benevolent figure, it seemed paranoid to have any suspicions of him. On 27 April 1979 I wrote to Joyce Wooller in the contracts department at Granada saying that I would like to commission six or possibly seven scripts for *The Jewel in the Crown* from Ken Taylor and to commission one script with an option for another five from Michael Robson. Both were to deliver their first scripts in June.

I had worked with Ken Taylor on a number of occasions before and knew that he had a strong sense of structure, would remain true to the original material, and was reliable about deliveries. In addition, since he had served in the army in India during World War II, he had the virtue of first-hand knowledge of the country and the period. I had not worked with Michael Robson before but had read his recent film script of John Buchan's *The Thirty-nine Steps*, a well structured adaptation. He too knew India, having filmed there. He had written a number of radio plays set there and had a wide knowledge of its military and social background. Although it would have been better to have only one adapter, pressure of time made that impossible. Since the blueprint for the series had been drawn up by myself, and most of the dialogue could be taken directly from Scott, I felt it safe to assume that there would not be too much discrepancy between the styles of the two adapters. At the back of my mind I knew I could ask Ken to do rewrites on the later scripts if it was necessary to make the style more uniform.

To both writers I gave master-scene synopses of all the action, containing blow-by-blow descriptions of each move. As they got to work problems arose and changes were necessary. After numerous discussions both returned amended synopses. Both were given the detailed breakdowns of the books saying where various events were covered in all four, and where various dialogues and descriptions of characters occurred. They were also given the lists of locations and characters and asked to keep these down for the sake of costs; they were given too the potted history of India.

One central dramatic problem was that of the physical disappearance of both hero (Hari Kumar) and heroine (Daphne Manners) very early in the action. When Ken Taylor delivered his amended outline of episode three on 14 May 1979, he expressed his concern that Kumar's last major appearance came in this episode. He felt, rightly, that we must use him as 'a ghost whose presence haunts us and Merrick throughout the serial, but is scarcely seen again'. A recurring image of Hari had to be found for the other episodes in which we shifted to other heroes, like Guy Perron, and heroines, like Sarah Layton.

While all this initial planning for *The Jewel in The Crown* was taking place, events took an unexpected turn. Before we came to Granada with the Raj Quartet, Waris Hussein had been contracted by Anglia Television to direct Scott's Booker Prize-winning short novel *Staying On*. Waris and the eminent actress, Dame Wendy Hiller, had suggested the book to the company as a vehicle in which Dame Wendy would play Lucy Smalley, the elderly Englishwoman left in an Indian hill station after the departure of the Raj. Anglia had decided against going to film in India and had instead commissioned a script written in such a way that most of the action could be shot in the studio and the rest filmed somewhere like Wales. Waris was unhappy about this. India with all its eccentricities was a quintessential part of the story, almost like another character with whom the two protagonists, Tusker and Lucy, were interacting.

The suggestion was made by Waris and myself to Sir Denis Forman that Granada should purchase the rights of *Staying On* from Anglia and that we should film it as a pilot for *The Jewel in the Crown*. Not only was the book well worth making in its own right but it would also give us an indication of the problems of filming the much more ambitious and expensive series in India. Sir Denis agreed and the rights were duly purchased. Waris was to direct and a new script was needed to allow for filming in India.

Chapter 20

Staying On

In switching my attention from *The Jewel in the Crown* to *Staying On* I was to discover a new aspect of Paul Scott's writing. In this short novel, written as a postscript to his vast epic, he emerges as a miniaturist with a wonderfully humane sense of humour.

In many ways the Raj Quartet and *Staying On* are opposites. In the former, the characters, especially when portrayed on screen, tend to be one-dimensional or symbolic, prototypes silhouetted against the vast, historic landscape of India before and during partition. Apart from Guy Perron's occasional cynical remarks and the 'gay' banter of Corporal 'Sophie' Dixon, the medical orderly at Pankot hospital, there is barely a touch of humour in either the books or the television series. In *Staying On*, however, Scott, with Chekhovian humour and compassion, portrays the comic minutiae of his characters' everyday existence as the last relics of the Raj stranded in an Indian hill station when everyone else has gone home. His depiction of their human foibles and of the problems of old age and death are funny, deeply moving and universally recognizable. When I read the book for the first time, I could immediately picture it on the screen. The images and dialogue were all there. I laughed out loud at many of the lines, like those of the servant Ibrahim, explaining to Joseph, the new gardener, certain expressions in the English language, like 'bugger off'. 'It is a very old English phrase meaning "jeldi jao". Likewise "piss off". These are sacred phrases, Joseph, never to be used by you or me when speaking to Sahib-log but I will teach you some of them.'[1]

After the tortuous adaptation problems of the Raj Quartet con-

---

[1] Paul Scott, *Staying On* (London, Heinemann), 1977, p. 52.

cerning selection and style, *Staying On* was like a rest cure. One could almost have filmed it straight off the page. My choice of Julian Mitchell (best known at that time for his stage play and film *Another Country* and later for his *Inspector Morse* scripts) as adapter was guided by two considerations, his quintessential old-fashioned Englishness and his somewhat sardonic sense of humour, which suited the style of the characters and the book. Waris Hussein was also keen to use Julian.

In Julian's economically constructed script the dialogue is taken almost verbatim from Paul Scott. Only the structure differs slightly from that of the book in which Tusker Smalley dies at the very beginning. We decided to start instead on the night when a very drunk Tusker is brought home from a mess dinner and begins to manifest the symptoms of the heart condition which will eventually kill him. This would give a glimpse of Tusker, in full regalia, as he once had been in better days and would then introduce the fatalistic theme of the story, that he is a doomed man and that the destiny of his wife Lucy is to be left alone in India, the thing that

15 The film crew of *Staying On*.

she fears the most. Largely for budgetary reasons (so that we should not have to film in England as well as India), but also for stylistic reasons, we decided to dispense with flashbacks to the past. Lucy mentally telling her story to her future visitor, Mr Turner, in voice-over and Lucy dancing to her old gramophone records would better reveal what we needed to know. Tusker's past and his philosophy of life would come out in his conversations with his Indian landlord, Mr Bhoolabhoy (alias 'Billy Boy') on their Friday night drinking sessions together. Other than these changes, the film exactly follows the book.

Having handed the adaptation over to Julian, it was now the moment for me to test the water in India for the first time. Until now my knowledge of the place had all been theoretical.

When the mature Paul Scott returned to India in February 1964, to research the quartet, he found that it was not the same country that he had known before. He noticed things that he had not done when there in the army as a young man. He recorded in his 'Indian spiral notebook' his great shock at the sight of the shanty towns outside Bombay airport with labourers squatting in the fields, heat rising even at dawn, and kite hawks scavenging and screaming overhead.[2] My own culture shock on arriving at Bombay on that first recce in January 1979 was considerable. Later, on the perilous drive to Simla, I began to realise, accurately as was later proved, that culture shock was likely to be a major psychological problem for some of the crew, even the more cynical ones, when they arrived from Manchester.

When I walked around Simla, which, by a process of elimination, we finally decided would be our best bet for a hill station location, because it was both beautiful and had enough acceptable accommodation to house a large film crew, I began to appreciate the accuracy with which Scott's book had portrayed a place half caught in a time warp and half in the process of being swallowed up by modern India. There was evidence of the departed Raj everywhere. Most of the houses looked like those in the English counties; there was a proliferation of funny, fading English signs, like one ironically located on the road where the Nepalese and Tibetan road gangs were slaving away, saying 'Rest-a-While' and one on an English birdhouse in a restaurant garden which said 'We protect birds too. Simla Police.' The faded teashop signs would not have

[2]Spurling, *Paul Scott*, p. 270.

looked out of place in any English village. In the centre of town there was an old English post office, which must have been there in Kipling's time. The famous Gaiety theatre was now mainly used as a club by retired Indian Indian Army officers who, with their walrus moustaches, their tweed suits and their pipes were exact replicas of their English predecessors. There were of course the viceregal residence, the old barracks, the cemetery full of English tombstones.

I was with a production manager whom I had never met before but whom Granada, with Sir Denis's approval, had assigned to me. He was a kind and competent man when sober but no one at Granada had bothered to tell me about his drink problem. He came to the recce fresh from a drying-out clinic which I was to discover all too soon had not done its job terribly well. On the plane, a worried-looking hostess stood by his side for most of the journey monitoring the lighted cigarettes that he was constantly dropping on the floor as the whisky overcame him. On our arrival in India, at four o'clock in the morning, he was promptly arrested for not filling in his customs and immigration forms properly and for staggering around the airport. I had to use the full autocratic Memsahib technique to demand his immediate release, showing the officials various pieces of important-looking but meaningless correspondence about our trip, trying to prove that we were VIPs and knew other VIPs in India who might get them into trouble. The technique (which I had been primed about by a director friend who had filmed in India) worked successfully but I did not thank Granada for landing me with this extra problem.

Our main contacts in India were to be the son, Valmik Thapar, the daughter and son-in-law, Mala and Teshbir Singh, of one of Sir Denis Forman's close Indian friends, Romesh Thapar. They had a small documentary company called Nigaar Workshop and although they were totally unversed in the feature film business they had good social connections and Sir Denis was keen to give them work. Usually at this stage the director, producer, production manager and designer go on the recce together. As Waris was busy filming in England, however, he and I agreed that I would do this preliminary testing of the water, search for locations and line up Indian actors. He would come out on the next occasion, probably with the cameraman, designer etc. We needed to find a Smith's Hotel, (the small hotel owned by the villainous Mrs Bhoolabhoy) complete with a bungalow annexe housing Tusker and Lucy, overlooked if possible by a modern Shiraz Hotel with a mountain-view dining room. We needed a Rose Cottage (for the garden party given by the posh Col. Menektara at which Tusker collapses), a graveyard and an English church as well as other minor locations.

Smith's Hotel, at least its management structure, was, according to Scott's biographer, largely based on a hotel in England which Scott visited as a child, Laughton's Pavilion Hotel in Scarborough, which, curiously enough, was run by Charles Laughton's aunt and uncle, friends of Paul's father.[3] Here, the child Scott saw the formidable proprietress terrorizing her compliant husband as later in *Staying On* the enormous bully, Mrs Bhoolabhoy, known as 'ownership', terrorizes her poor little husband, Frankie, known as 'management'.

Another hotel, Green Hotel in Belgaum, which Scott had known in its heyday during the war, was the physical inspiration for Smith's Hotel. When Scott revisited it in the late 1960s and early 1970s he found it sadly decayed, smelling of ancient damp and stagnant water and being run by a belligerent Mrs Ranji. Here, in the hotel annexe, without modern sanitation, an elderly Englishman, a friend of Paul's, Peter Goodbody, was unhappily eking out his last days with his Eurasian wife, having suffered the indignity of a heart attack, from which he subsequently died, while sitting on the 'thunder-box'. Here was the inspiration for *Staying On*.[4]

In the end, when we came to film, we decided to make our own Smith's Hotel at Mashobra, just outside Simla, converting Teshbir Singh's large family house for the purpose. From the windows of the room which we turned into Mr Bhoolabhoy's office one could see the wonderful little English church left over from the days of the Raj. It was abandoned when we found it and had to be cleaned up. The church was approached by what looked like an English country lane. The English churchyard at Sanjoli in which we filmed Mr Bhoolabhoy finding the new 'mali' Joseph was deeply moving with its gravestones commemorating so many early deaths, probably from tropical diseases. It was a true corner of a foreign field that was for ever England. For Tusker and Lucy's run-down hotel annexe we found a colonial bungalow, precariously perched on the edge of Strawberry Hills in East Simla with a magnificent panoramic view of the foothills of the Himalayas.

[3]Spurling, *Paul Scott*, p. 58.
[4]*Ibid.*, p. 379.

We were not able to find an old hotel next to a new hotel, so that we could pan from the Shiraz to Smith's, showing, as described in the book, how the encroachment of modern India on the last relics of the old India was eventually going to finish off the Smalleys. In fact, there was no really modern hotel in Simla, nor, according to everyone we spoke to, were there any in other hill stations. Eventually we turned the local medical school building, the only modern building we could find, into the exterior of the Shiraz.

We did, however, find a perfect mountain-view dining room for Lucy and Tusker to lunch in, in another hotel, Clark's Oberoi, where, as I noted to Julian Mitchell with great joy on my return, we found a three-piece orchestra. Normally they played Western-style pop music but the manager promised us that if we brought the music with us, they would play what we wanted. I wanted it to be one of Lucy's old-time palm court favourites. I suggested to Julian that Mrs Bhoolabhoy and her party of sinister business associates should walk across the dining room in the scene, thereby ruining Tusker and Lucy's outing, and disappear behind a screen to a private dining section which I had noted in the hotel.

Many of our locations, like Rose Cottage, the church etc., were to reappear on the screen in the Pankot scenes in *The Jewel in the Crown*. For instance in *The Jewel in the Crown*, set nearly thirty years earlier than *Staying On*, Rose Cottage belongs to Mabel Layton. Then, after her pathetic companion, Barbie Batchelor, has been cruelly evicted from it on Mabel's death, it is taken over by the acid-tongued Mildred Layton and her daughters, Susan and Sarah. When they have gone home, the Smalleys, Lucy and Tusker, move in. In *Staying On*, set in the post-Raj 1970s, Rose Cottage has reverted to Indian occupation. The elegant Col. Menektara and his socialite wife Coocoo live there.

'Chapslee', the freezing cold but beautifully furnished house, turned hotel, belonging to a charming minor maharajah called Reggie Singh, where we stayed on that first trip to Simla, was to give me the inspiration for the wardrobe that both Tusker and Lucy Smalley wear in the film. The maharajah had an elderly English housekeeper. She walked around wearing woollen half-mittens, baggy pants, several baggy sweaters and an old Jaeger dressing gown. She was one of only three English people left over in Simla and her pathetic wardrobe dated back to her last visit to England at the end of the 1940s. When we did return to film, Trevor

16 Trevor Howard in *Staying On*.

Howard, who had ignored my warning that Simla could still be very cold in March, and who had come without any warm clothes of his own, spent many of his days wrapped in the old moth-eaten Jaeger dressing-gown which had been hired for the filming.

Time prevented me from tracking down, on that recce, the other two English people who had 'stayed on'. One was Mr Goldstein, the retired headmaster of one of the numerous English-style public schools in Simla, son of a Viennese musician who had come to India to arrange music for the viceroys. By the time I returned he was dead.

Meanwhile the one piece of major casting which I needed to do in Simla on that first visit was to find a Bloxsaw. He was the dog whom Tusker took for 'walkies' throughout the film and whose cries alerted Mrs Bhoolabhoy to the fact that Tusker was dead. His name was an Indianization of 'Blackshaw', the surname of his previous owners who had left him with the Smalleys when they went back to England. Pet dogs were in short supply in Simla. After many enquiries, however, a perfect, ancient and hideous bulldog was found and immediately contracted. In a prophetic note to Sir Denis, enclosing Bloxsaw's picture, when I got back to England, I expressed the hope that he would last until we started filming . . . alas, because of unexpected delays, which I will come to soon, he didn't.

Waris and I had already agreed on the part of Tusker; no other name was ever discussed than that of Trevor Howard. We had already talked about the two main Indian male parts and about Sayeed Jaffrey for Mr Bhoolabhoy and Zia Moyheddin for Ibrahim, the servant. I had worked with the latter years before when he took the lead in a Simenon story I had produced, *The Lodger*. I had never forgotten his brilliant performance then as a murderer hiding from the police, nor his stage performance in *Passage to India*. Ibrahim is one of the best drawn, most complex characters in *Staying On*. He treats his elderly master and mistress like children, humouring them, occasionally cheating them but always protecting and loving them in a deeply moving way. He also has many of the funniest lines in the book and film.

Zia Moyheddin, when interviewed by an Indian journalist, Tariq Ahmed, while we were filming, said that he based his performance on a similar character he had met in Rawalpindi years before.

> Ibrahim is not an easy character to play. He is not just another servant. Indeed, he considers himself the last true representative of a generation that served the British, and is proud of it. He is intensely loyal to his employers though they are down and out, and he is as sad about the passing away of the Raj as the Smalleys. The similarity between him and a person I met in Mrs Davies's Guest House in Pindi years ago is striking, and helps me enormously.

In the same article Sayeed Jaffrey described his role as Frank Bhoolabhoy, downtrodden, henpecked husband of 'Ownership', secret lecher and drinking companion of Tusker, as 'lovingly overblown'. Of his performance he said 'I am trying to tone down the exaggerated bits so that he evokes sympathy and understanding rather than pity or laughter.' A goal which I believe he admirably achieved.

The only part of the equation which was missing at this point in the casting was Mrs Bhoolabhoy, described in the book as weighing sixteen stone and favouring pink saris. I was destined to find her in Bombay at a party given by Uma da Cunha, who was acting as a talent scout for us and who had told me that only one actress in India was right for the part, Pearl Padamsee, a Parsee lady of considerable girth, who spoke perfect English and ran her own English-language theatre group in Bombay.

When we were introduced at Uma's party, the first word of greeting from Pearl was in Hebrew. 'Shalom, Irene', she said. It turned out she was not a Parsee at all but had been married to one. As the product of a Punjabi father and a Turkish-Jewish mother she considered herself Jewish. She had grown up largely in Australia where her father had been Indian High Commissioner. In real life Pearl was cultured and meditative but her larger-than-life appearance and extrovert personality made her an ideal Mrs Bhoolabhoy. It is she, a scheming businesswoman, planning the removal of the Smalleys from their annexe because they stand in the way of her deal with the Shiraz hotel consortium, who represents modern, commercial India. She holds the Smalleys, two helpless, impotent remnants of the Raj, in low regard and has no pity to spare for them. 'When they ruled the roost they did not concern themselves with us' she tells her soft-hearted husband. 'It's tit for tat.'

The day after the party I boarded the plane at Bombay airport. By the time it had reached England my voice had vanished completely. I remained totally dumb for ten inconvenient days, unable to convey the results of my recce to Sir Denis. Whether the condition was due to pollution or shock at the sights of Bombay, I don't know to this day. At Uma's party I had started to cough and been taken into the garden to get more air. In the dusk, one could just make out the silhouette of rats the size of small cats, running around on the paths.

Chapter 21

Unexpected changes

A different kind of shock awaited me in England. I was going to be without a director. From the time the project had started at Anglia, Waris Hussein had wanted for *Staying On* a particular freelance cameraman with whom he was used to working. Knowing how important the relationship between cameraman and director is on a film, I had tried to prevail upon Granada to let Waris have his choice. The camera department, however, wanted the job to go to a staff man, who, they loyally considered, was due for the treat of working overseas. Since I was a newcomer to the company and not versed in their ways, as I had been with those of the BBC, I was not in a strong negotiating position, especially as their recommended cameraman had a high reputation. An impasse was reached. Waris was adamant that he wanted his own man. Granada, who had the upper hand and the union power, were equally adamant in their refusal. Waris, who had received an alternative and more lucrative work offer in America, where he was living most of the time, decided to pull out. Ironically, when *Staying On* was eventually made, it was in fact shot by a freelance cameraman.

I was now in a strange situation. I was about to produce *Staying On* though I had come to Granada to produce *The Jewel in the Crown*. The director with whom I was supposed to work on both projects, Waris Hussein, was no longer with me. The only remaining element of the original equation was the leading lady, Dame Wendy Hiller. I, of course, had had nothing to do with casting her. She had preceded me on the project, having originally brought *Staying On* to Anglia, as a vehicle in which she would star. I had always greatly admired Wendy Hiller, yet when I first read *Staying*

On a different actress had immediately come into my mind for the part of Lucy Smalley. Only Celia Johnson had that grown-up schoolgirl quality, that vulnerability, that wrinkled English-rose look which Lucy needed. Wendy Hiller's personality, though equally British, was very different. She was a strong and stalwart type of woman who, one felt, would be capable of conquering Everest. I could not visualize Tusker telling her off for talking like a child of seven although she was a woman of seventy. She would be wonderful for a role like that of Mabel Layton or Lady Manners in *The Jewel in the Crown* rather than for silly, frightened Lucy.

The magic chemistry between Celia Johnson and Trevor Howard had been famously demonstrated thirty-three years earlier in *Brief Encounter* in which one of the best-known love stories in British cinema had been born on a dingy station platform when Trevor Howard removed a piece of grit from Celia Johnson's eye. How wonderful, I thought, it would have been to reunite these two for the first time since then, had the part not been cast already.

Dame Wendy, although always charming and gracious, was understandably disturbed by all the chopping and changing that had by now occurred. She had lost Anglia, she had lost her director, and she had quibbles about the new script by Julian Mitchell. Her main objection was to the structural change from the book. She preferred Tusker to die at the beginning, as he had in the novel and in the previous Anglia script by Alan Seymour. In her words, in an undated letter to me, 'By putting the audience in possession of a fact unknown to Lucy, the death of Tusker, he (Scott) raises the novel far above the story-line and lifts it to the level of real tragedy.' She also objected that in the new script too much comic business was being given to the Bhoolabhoys and that there was too much made of minor characters like Susie, the Anglo-Indian hairdresser who is doing Lucy's hair while Tusker dies, and Father Sebastian, the 'black as your hat' clergyman. In a word she wanted more concentration on Tusker and, above all, Lucy. However, despite these reservations, she still wanted very much to do the part and already had clear ideas about the wigs and wardrobe she wanted to wear.

Once word had got out of a vacancy there was no shortage of candidates to take over in the director's seat on *Staying On*. David Hare, the writer, then still fairly inexperienced as a film director, was among those who expressed themselves keen to do so. Sir Denis thought of his friend Karel Reisz, who seemed to be put out by the fact that, by force of circumstances, much of the casting had already been decided. He told Sir Denis that he would only direct if he could also produce. Eventually Sir Denis and I agreed on Claude Whatham, whom we both knew. He had worked in the past for Granada. His credits were distinguished and included the original stage and TV versions of *Voyage Round my Father*, as well as *Cider with Rosie*. I had known, though not worked with him, in BBC days.

There was also the important question of future director, or directors, for *The Jewel in the Crown* now that Waris was gone. At the end of April 1979 I wrote to Christopher Morahan who was then at the National Theatre. The main purpose of my letter was to find out if there were any Indian actors working at the National who might be suitable for the series, especially for the part of Hari Kumar, who would need to speak perfect upper-class English. I told Christopher that I was planning a 'mammoth epic for Granada' and enquired whether he was intending to return to TV at all and if so when. He replied immediately that, by coincidence, he was reading the Raj Quartet at that moment. He loved it and would welcome the chance of directing it as soon as he was free of other committments.

In describing Morahan later to Sir Denis I pointed out that I had found him to be extremely efficient and well organized, two qualities which would be essential in a director for such a complicated and enormous project. I had last employed Morahan as a director on a very successful Peter Nicholls play, *Hearts and Flowers*, when I was producing 'Play for Today'. Later we reversed roles when Chris became Head of Plays at the BBC and hence my boss. His well earned reputation as a strong, even dictatorial, character who did not suffer fools or inefficiency gladly, could be of distinct advantage on such a demanding project. A weak or vacillating director would be disastrous.

As with adapters, *Staying On* and *The Jewel in the Crown* required entirely different types of directors. Apart from its complicated logistics, the latter was far more of an extrovert and action piece than the introverted story of two old leftovers of the Raj in the twilight of their lives. I also made inquiries about John MacKenzie with whom I had worked at the BBC and who had directed the gangster film *The Long Good Friday*. As with adapters, one was going to need more than one director on such a vast project.

By 4 March 1980, before I went filming in India, I had sent Chris Ken Taylor's first four scripts. He liked them very much and said he would be available to work with me on the planning of the series for a preliminary period of three months beginning in August and then would be fully available as of January 1981 when he was leaving the National Theatre.

While all the changes of personnel and plans had been going on with *Staying On*, the scripting of *The Jewel in the Crown* was progressing. The problem all along, as Ken Taylor and I agreed, was that of simplification. He wrote to me that he was making a rule of simplifying so long as it did not lead to a gross distortion of Paul Scott's original.

In November 1979 Ken, Michael Robson and I met to discuss the middle section of the series where their work converged. We realized at this point that it was impossible to squeeze all the action called for in the outline into the originally envisaged thirteen episodes and decided that Ken should write an extra episode (then called episode 8A) to cover the missing scenes. When I informed Sir Denis Forman of the problem, he agreed to a fourteenth hour on air, although the standard number of episodes for a series to run on the ITV network at that time was normally thirteen weeks, or a quarter of the year.[1]

The saga of *Staying On* was meanwhile to take yet another unexpected turn. Claude Whatham and I went off to India for another recce in June 1979, accompanied this time, on Sir Denis's instructions, by a semi-retired Granada business manager who was addicted to sea-food though it always seemed to make him ill. Like many of the Granada employees whom I had encountered in my brief time with the company, he was also quite partial to the whisky

---

[1] In his introduction to the Granada coffee table book about the series, *The Making of the Jewel in the Crown* (London, Granada Publishing), 1983, p. 8, Sir Denis wrote that the scripts were delivered 'after Irene Shubik left Granada'. In fact they had all been completed long before I left. There are memos recording the fact that Sir Denis himself was distributing copies of them to various departments suggesting, among other things, that Granada might make a documentary to go with the series. His confusion may have arisen from the fact that when Christopher Morahan took over as producer, he asked Ken Taylor to re-script some of the later episodes originally written by Michael Robson, to preserve the continuity of style. When Morahan in fact courteously phoned me to inform me that he was going to do this, I agreed with the idea and told him that only the pressure of time when we started the series and intended to film it much earlier had initially made me commission two adapters instead of one.

226

bottle, an expensive habit to maintain in India but one which he claimed was necessary for medicinal purposes. We saw more cast and locations and arrived back in London only to find that the offices of Granada Television were now out of bounds. The ACTT, the Association of Cinematographic and Television Technicians, had called an all-out ITV strike. Since Claude and I were both members of the union we were not allowed to work or enter the company buildings. I next saw Sir Denis Forman when he was going into his office at Golden Square and I had been ordered by the union to stand on a picket line on the street outside.

Although frustrated by our numerous delays, I was reasonably happy to have the time to confer on *The Jewel in the Crown* scripts with the two writers. I was able to work surreptitiously as a story editor, though not actively as a producer, and to devote myself to the logistics of the future series, contacting people like Mike Satow, who was in charge of the Delhi railway museum, about the type of railway carriages we would need and matters like that. By 13 November 1979 I already had seven of the fourteen scripts completed and in hand.

Not everyone on the project, however, was equally contented, as still more time went by. The delay due to the strike was to cause *Staying On* two more serious casualties. Dame Wendy Hiller was the first. She had been offered a film part which her agent strongly advised her to take. She wrote to me with great regret to explain that she could no longer wait and was withdrawing from the part of Lucy, a decision which I knew was very painful for her.

As there was a limited season in which the weather would be suitable, we had to reschedule the filming, once the strike was settled, for March and April 1980. Claude Whatham's agent suggested to Granada that Claude, who was freelance, should be paid a retainer until then. The reply came back that Granada never paid retainers. When an offer came up to direct a film in Australia, with much regret Claude, who had been hanging around unpaid, opted out of *Staying On* and accepted it.

If there is anything predictable about filming, it is that it is unpredictable. By the time I did actually return to Simla for filming in 1980, with a third change of production staff and director from those I had begun with, there had been two more casualties. The dog booked to play Bloxsaw was dead as I had feared he might be and Mrs Bhoolabhoy no longer looked like a woman who weighed sixteen stone. Pearl Padamsee, having been ordered by her doctor

17 Irene Shubik, Trevor Howard and Silvio Narizzano in *Staying On*.

to go on a strenuous diet because of her diabetes, had shed an amazing five stone. She was going to require a great deal of padding.

My third recce to India was to be in the company of a third director and the production designer and new production manager. The three, who in the event did actually remain to make the film, were Silvio Narizzano, Eugene Ferguson and Lars McFarlane. The latter two, who did an excellent job, were Granada staff members, which, so far as I was concerned, was reassuring because they would not need retainers if something untoward delayed us yet again. Also, unlike myself, they were well versed in the idiosyncracies of Granada. I did not realize just how idiosyncratic the company was until Lars, in an unguarded moment after the filming finished, confessed to me that he had been set to spy and report on me by Sir Denis Forman. They had agreed on certain code words for myself and Silvio which he could telex back to base, letting Sir Denis know how things were going. As I recall, the messages were something like 'the wind blows south', 'there's a storm brewing in the north'. I was incredulous. It all sounded like a mixture of Orwell's *1984* and *Boy's Own Annual*.

It had not been easy getting our script passed by the Indian

Ministry of Information, without whose permission we could not film. The scripts of both *Staying On* and the early part of *The Jewel in the Crown* had been sent from England months before but had lain around without response. I had counted on the fact that, since Scott was so sympathetic to the Indian characters in his books and was, therefore, well regarded in India, we would not have any trouble. 'It would not be the same', an actor in Bombay told me, 'if you were filming a book by V. S. Naipaul.'

On this particular recce the production designer, Eugene Ferguson, and I had an appointment at the Ministry of Information in Delhi, a Kafkaesque experience which will always remain in my mind. As we waited endlessly in the Minister's office, where dust lay inches thick on every surface and the telephone wires were bare of insulation, an endearing old man, bent double with age and disease, came in, bearing two cups of tea in which floated large globules of buffalo milk fat. With his pathetically gnarled hands, tipped by filthy finger nails, he presented us with crude lumps of sugar wrapped up in newspaper, to accompany the tea. As soon as he had left Eugene flung the tea into one of the Minister's flower pots. Eventually, after several fruitless hours, we gave up waiting.

Later, after the script had finally been passed, we were told that a censor, whose food and accommodation we would have to pay for, would be assigned to us while we were filming in Simla. In the event I can only remember this innocuous-looking little man, who accompanied us everywhere, ever objecting to one thing. When we showed porters carrying baskets of fruit in the market, he complained that the fruit looked rotten and it would give the impression that India was a poor country.

Silvio Narizzano, director No. 3, was a Canadian who had come to England in the 1950s, on a wave of Canadian *émigré* directors which included Ted Kotcheff, Al Rakoff and others. His most successful work to date had been the 'swinging sixties' film *Georgie Girl*. He had also directed a film of Joe Orton's *Loot*. Silvio, himself, had the reputation of being something of an anarchic, Ortonesque character. Wherever he went, unexpected things happened. After his wife's tragically early death he had 'come out' as a homosexual.

I had known Silvio, though not well, for some years and had always considered him extremely talented. There was something highly original about his work at its best, especially when the subjects were humorous. Sometimes he went over the top but in general he got good performances out of actors. I had last worked with him at the BBC when he directed an Isaac Bashevis Singer story, *The Cafeteria*, for me, starring Donald Pleasence, Oscar Homolka and Sara Kestelman. I was very pleased with the result, as was the Nobel Prize-winning author. Silvio and I had been in perfect agreement about the casting, the production style and the editing. He had been pleasant and stimulating to work with.

Working with a director on a show which like *The Cafeteria*, and many other productions at that time, was shot entirely on video cameras in a television studio, is a very controllable situation from the producer's point of view. In the studio gallery you have in front of your eyes everything that is on camera. You can give your notes to and have your discussions or arguments with the director, designer, costume and make-up people etc. there and then. If emergencies, either technical or temperamental, arise, trusted technicians and managerial back-up are near at hand. At the end of the day you and the director part company to go back to your own particular life-styles without worrying about what the other is doing.

Filming on location is, of course, the opposite case, especially when the location is somewhere as remote as the foothills of the Himalayas where *Staying On* was shot. The situation is always far more volatile. Disparate life-styles and personal problems inevitably impinge upon each other and on the work when people are thrown together at such close quarters for such a length of time, as Francois Truffaut so effectively demonstrated in *Day for Night*. From the producer's point of view overall control is far more difficult to keep. Managerial back-up is far away and, especially if you have to depend upon the Indian telephone system, almost impossible to reach. Gossip, backstabbing, union disputes, jockeying for status, drink, drugs and offbeat sexual activities may seriously affect punctuality and the committing of scenes to celluloid.

Several other producers gave me warnings about using such an unpredictable director in such uncertain circumstances as a remote Indian location. Foolishly, I did not listen to them. I was relying on the fact that Silvio and I had worked together so well before. I was sure it would happen again. He had always struck me as an innocent 'little boy lost' who probably got into scrapes by accident rather than design. His offbeat sense of humour was dead right for this particular subject. If producers went only for safe directors there would hardly be a great film made in Hollywood. Besides, by now I was desperate to start filming and running out of alternatives. The ITV strike had caused a backlog of work to pile up. Most directors were already employed. Sir Denis had vetoed a number of my other suggestions, like Michael Tuchner and John Gorrie with whom I had worked happily at the BBC. They had not worked at Granada and were therefore unknown to him. He was, however, happy with the choice of Narizzano whom he had known far longer than I had, since much of the latter's early television work had been for Granada.

At last, after all the changes and delays, it looked as though we were actually going to go to India and make a film.

Chapter 22

The filming of *Staying On*

The filming of *Staying On* started on 20 March 1980 and finished on schedule and, miraculously, under budget on 2 May. It was the most fraught production in which I have ever been involved, illustrating the problems one can encounter in filming in exotic locations and the heavy cost one can incur by making an error of judgement about a key member of the team. I shall, however, always be grateful for the opportunity it gave me of working with two of the greatest, most professional and nicest artists I have ever known, the stars of one of my favourite classic English films, *Brief Encounter*, Trevor Howard and Celia Johnson.

The moment Dame Wendy Hiller had opted out of *Staying On* I had checked on Celia Johnson's availability to play Lucy Smalley. To my joy I found that she was free for our filming dates, although hesitant about coming to such a remote location and being away for so long from her beloved grandchildren and her comfortable domestic situation. To reassure her, I promised to schedule all her scenes to be shot first so that she could be released early, a plan which, as usual with filming, went awry due to an accident. Apart from an early release, the most important considerations to her were whether she would be able to get the BBC World Service on the radio in Simla and whether she would be able to find some bridge partners there. Here I am afraid I misled her somewhat. It was possible to *get* the World Service; whether you could actually hear it was another matter. As for the bridge, she was welcomed with open arms by the retired Indian Army officers and their wives at the bridge club in the Gaiety theatre.

When I first met Celia, who was seventy-two at the time of our filming, my reaction was the same as that of an American interviewer who was struck by her 'thoroughly British, Miniveresque tea-coziness'. She did indeed belong more to the era of Mrs Miniver than to the 1980s. She was quintessentially sensible, a no-nonsense British type. There was nothing either *grande dame* or 'luvvie' about her, although by marriage and by family connections she was anything but ordinary. Her late husband, Peter Fleming, brother of spy-novelist and James Bond creator, Ian Fleming, had been a writer and explorer of note who had once, amongst other adventures, walked from Peking to India. As a young actress and wife Celia had regularly dined at such places as Clivedon, the country home of Nancy Astor. She also had royal connections, as I was to discover on our return to England when she invited me to lunch at her country house and a car bearing a crest decanted another lunch guest who was dressed from head to foot in powder blue. It was the Queen Mother, an old friend of Celia's.

We had arranged to accommodate most of the cast and other key people on the film, including myself, in 'Woodville' guest house, which, like 'Chapslee', was the private home of a maharajah, Kanwar Uday Singh of Jubbal, who kept one wing for himself and ran the rest as a hotel. In appearance it was exactly like a large English country house, surrounded by a lovely garden. In keeping with its English style it was freezing in the winter (I had slept in my sheepskin coat on our first visit) but was wonderfully pleasant when we returned in springtime. The monkeys which scurried up and down the house, appearing unexpectedly at the windows from the roof, were scared off every so often by shots from a gun wielded by the houseboy, Beli Ram. It was he who rescued me when I left my window open one night and returned to find a virtual ceiling of writhing moths in my room. He dealt too with the flying squirrel which had tried to get in through the window and which I had inadvertently trapped by its tiny, uncannily human-looking, hand. Every morning, Beli Ram, who looked about sixteen, knocked on my bed-room door with a cup of tea and the inquiry, 'Are you happy, madam?' Later he was to throw himself at my mercy and beg me to take him back to England as my servant, falsely imagining that, since I was the producer, I must live in the grandest house of all the crew. By that time Trevor Howard had discovered him to be a married man with a child. He had spotted him in the market accompanied by offspring and spouse.

I had chosen the pleasantest suite of rooms on the ground floor of the house for Celia so that she should not have to climb stairs.

Usually, after filming, she was to be found sitting on the floor, laying out a game of patience for relaxation. She also proved to be surprisingly skilled at snooker, playing regularly on the maharajah's private snooker table. Although I had checked out her room myself, I could not have foreseen that Celia would slip on the bathroom floor on the first day of shooting and crack her head on the soapdish which jutted out from the wall, giving herself a very nasty black eye. Celia, needless to say, was uncomplaining but subsequent filming had to be rescheduled around the state of the eye and how well it was healing. She could not go home as early as planned. Many of the shots in the film focus on the uninjured side of her face.

It was at 'Woodville' that the two famous lovers of *Brief Encounter* had their first reunion after thirty-three years. In actuality they were very different types of people. Although they got on well, they appeared to have little, apart from their profession, in common. On seeing them together, one appreciated all the more the acting prowess which had so magically brought to life on the screen such a heartbreaking and totally convincing doomed romance. It would probably never have happened in real life. Trevor Howard, who was some years younger than Celia, had a reputation as a tearaway. He was renowned for his hard drinking and, in his earlier career, brawling. In Simla, however, he proved to be a model of professionalism. If he did drink during our filming, it must have been in secret, although I was told that he had needed assistance in getting off the plane on arrival. He was very much at home in India as he had been born and brought up in Ceylon, now Sri Lanka, where his father was an insurance man. His first childhood memory, he told one reporter, was of an elephant parade there.

The problems of filming in India, which we had come to discover for the future of *The Jewel in the Crown*, were to manifest themselves immediately. As it turned out, the most pressing ones were not to do with the country but with the Granada unions and the attitude of some members of the crew to working there.

If I was lucky in the cast, I was equally fortunate in my choice of lighting cameraman, Wolfgang Suschitzky, and in the camera operator whom he brought with him, Gerry Anstiss. On this occasion, the Granada union allowed me to choose a freelance cameraman because, thanks to the strike, the backlog of work was more than the staff people could handle. Suschitzky, who had been born in Vienna and fled from the Nazis, belonged to the same generation as Celia and Trevor. He had shot such films as *Get Carter* and *Entertaining Mr Sloane* and is still a superb stills photographer. The look of *Staying On*, in which the snow-capped foothills of the Himalayas are ever present as a symbol of Lucy and Tusker's isolation in a foreign land, owes everything to him and Gerry. It was a look which was hard for them to achieve due to circumstances beyond their control.

Back in Manchester, the Granada unions had decreed that our filming day should start at 9:00 a.m. Wolfgang was rightly unhappy about this. He pointed out to the chief electrician, who was also the union representative in India, that the light in Simla was at its best in the early morning. Later in the day it cast shadows on faces. Since the quality of the scenery in the early morning mists was absolutely magical, it was also a tragedy not to be able to capture it on film. We asked our man to request Manchester to authorize an earlier start. He replied that the matter could only be decided if the Manchester shop steward came out and saw conditions for himself. That trip, of course, would have to be paid for out of our budget. Everyone back home seemed keen on a pretext for a free trip to Simla.

One morning, in a desperate bid to get some atmospheric establishing shots of Simla to use under the front titles, Wolfgang and Gerry crept out secretly at 6:30 a.m. When they got back to the Oberoi Cecil Hotel where most of the crew were staying, the shop steward saw them and demanded to know where they had been with their camera equipment. He agreed to let them keep the shots only if he logged the time sheets for the entire crew for a 6:30 a.m. start. They were paid accordingly. Most of the crew's creative energy went into these time sheets on which 'golden hours', for which they were paid double time, and fictitious working hours had a prominent place.

Shortly after our arrival, various members of the crew, who it seems had never before looked at a map or realized that the Himalayas were mountains, complained about being expected to work at such heights. In compensation, they demanded extra 'oxygen deprivation' money. Previously they had absolutely vetoed the idea of our using any Indian labour. Everyone, including carpenters and painters, had been flown out from Manchester although good local Indian workmen were available at a fraction of the price. Eventually, however, the crew consented to allow Kashmiri porters, most of whom were half starved and half their size, to carry their heavy equipment up hills for a few rupees. This happened after the shop steward had persuaded Granada to raise their daily allowance from £25 to £30, thus establishing the subsequent allowance given on *The Jewel in the Crown*, a substantial addition to its budget.

Culture shock, which affected most people, had many variations. One 'grip' disappeared for days on end to join the hippies whom we later filmed in a scene with Trevor, sitting on the ground outside the post office. Marijuana in Simla, I was told later, cost something like two rupees for a pound. At the opposite extreme, a young 'chippie' (carpenter), who had never left Manchester before, was so frightened and shocked by the sights of India that he refused to go out and stayed in bed in the hotel until he was eventually sent back home. By contrast, people like Gerry Anstiss, who already knew India from filming there on *North West Frontier*, made themselves extremely comfortable. He tipped one of the boys at the Oberoi Cecil Hotel most of his daily allowance with which the boy furnished his suite for him so well that it became the club-room for the crew. At Gerry's behest, the boy also went to Chandigar every week to bring back booze.

Whether it was culture shock or some other cause, Silvio seemed to undergo the most extreme character change of everyone. From the start he adamantly declined to stay with the cast and myself within the conventional confines of 'Woodville', where we would have been able to discuss production and acting problems together in the evenings. He chose instead to lead an independent life far away at the Oberoi Hotel with the crew, who told me that he had installed a companion he had brought with him from Bombay, a young Indian boy who was only glimpsed occasionally at mealtimes by the others, rather like Suleiman, Ronald Merrick's mysterious Pathan servant in *The Jewel in the Crown*. I never in fact saw the boy myself.

As producer, I found myself held personally responsible by the locals for the moral behaviour of the crew. One of my most embarrassing encounters was when the maharajah at Woodville asked to speak to me privately and demanded that I do something about 'the two fat people', members of our team whose illicit sexual activity and creaking bed-springs were bringing shame to his respectable house. To make matters worse, one miscreant was Indian and the other white. The servants were obviously reporting all their goings-on. An even more excruciating situation arose when

Silvio's permanent partner, whose dyed hair and bizarre appearance were more suited to *Cage aux Folles* than an Indian hill station, turned up unexpectedly from England and became publicly hysterical when he found a rival in his place. The maharajah, catching a glimpse of him, made it crystal clear that it was my responsibility to keep all parties concerned away from his premises. Not an easy job and one which aroused much hostility. Before we left England a memo had gone out, as I understood, to all the crew about the scarcity of accommodation in Simla. It requested everyone not to bring extra people on the filming. It had been the idea, I believe, of the production manager and was partly based on the accommodation problem and partly a ruse to avoid such scenes as we were now witnessing. I was told many years later by Wolfgang Suschitzky that this may have been the root cause of Narizzano's animosity. He had questioned Wolfgang as to whether he had received such a memo. When Wolfgang answered in the negative, Silvio assumed it was directed only at him.

The relationship between the producer and director on any film is always a delicate balance. From the producer's point of view, when he (or she) engages a director it is an act of faith, expressing belief in the director's talent and taste by entrusting him with a most precious possession, often a project which the producer has nurtured for many months or years. The producer expects differences of interpretation and opinion during the course of the production; no two people ever see things precisely alike. In return for his act of faith, however, the least he expects is that the director will observe the normal disciplines of filming and the normal lines of communication with the producer and cast.

I had only been in Simla a short time when I began to realize that the director to whom I had entrusted *Staying On* seemed more interested in going native than in planning the film. Every night, often in his absence, the production staff, mainly Les Davis (who in Granada parlance was called the floor manager but was virtually the first assistant), and Gerry Anstiss would do a breakdown of what was going to be shot the next day. In the morning Silvio, once Les had managed to get him out of bed, would usually ask 'What are we going to shoot today?' In the car, on the way to the location, he would discuss the shooting for the first time with Wolfgang. On arrival at location, he would usually do his yoga exercises and was frequently to be seen standing on his head while Gerry and Wolfgang waited to shoot and Trevor and Celia watched in wonderment. I could hardly believe he was the same director with whom I had worked so happily in the studio, where he was well planned and totally in control. I began seriously to wonder if he was a man on the verge of a nervous breakdown. 'Continuity is an old-fashioned concept and out of date' was one of his cries when I and others pointed out the lack of it in a shot which would obviously not cut together with the rest of the scene. It was rapidly becoming clear to me that I should have heeded the warnings I had been given in England. The cast were becoming understandably disgruntled. 'The chap's mad as a hatter', Trevor Howard kept repeating to me. 'Can't you fire him, darling?' Similar requests came from other leading actors who felt they were getting no direction. It was not an easy option. To replace a director in the middle of a production, on a remote foothill of the Himalayas, was a daunting prospect. I still prayed Silvio would revert to his former self. I could see no way out but to carry on, regardless, and try to hold the whole thing together. Besides, what none of the cast realized was that I had no back-up from Granada management to do what they asked.

Fortunately the main cast were so thoroughly professional, and had established such firm interpretations of their roles, that their performances were not badly affected. On rare good days, Silvio would become his old self. His considerable talent, originality and humour would return and add a special dimension to the scenes. The comic scenes between Mr and Mrs Bhoolabhoy were what he seemed most interested in and where he re-emerged best. Trevor and Celia, largely left alone, were able to create their own rapport with my help and that of the camera crew. Things came to a tragicomic climax on one particularly bad day when we were shooting the scene in the church where Tusker and Lucy sing a hymn and the English words turn into Hindi. Silvio, whose unhappy and voluble partner from England was now present at most of the filming, began shouting four-letter words at me in front of the highly respectable Anglo-Indian congregation who had been hired as extras. Les Davis, who could stand no more, took him outside and threatened to sort him out with his fists.

To add to our troubles, we were shooting almost blind. Another union problem had precluded our seeing rushes on our remote location. If we wanted a 16 mm projector with which to screen them, we were told we would have to fly not one but two projectionists out from Manchester. Apart from the hefty addition this would

238

have made to our budget, the transport problems of getting the film back and forth from the labs in Bombay, whose technical standards were questionable, made us decide against the risk. In the event none of us saw a foot of film until we got back to England. Our only reassurance came from Sir Denis Forman, who had undertaken to look at rushes. He sent back glowing reports from Golden Square. Unfortunately he was apparently unaware of various sound and other technical faults.

Simla, which had seemed at first sight like a Shangri-La removed from all normal everyday realities, proved to be full of unexpected problems. Transport had always been a concern. Most of the roads around the town were in an appalling state and hazardous to drive on. Since my last recce an added complication had arisen. There was a serious shortage of diesel oil. In order to get a ration of the scarce fuel, it was necessary to obtain a daily permit from the office of the governor of the province of Himachal Pradesh. Garishly decorated trucks and other vehicles started lining up for their permits, sometimes starting at midnight the night before they needed them. The resultant road blocks meant that it could take up to four hours to get to locations only twenty miles away which we had specifically chosen on our recces for their ready accessibility. It also meant that we had to use persuasion, on occasions amounting to plain bribery, to obtain enough fuel to keep our own generators and trucks going. The demand to me from one official for 'a nice Pentax camera' was quite open and unashamed.

Also on the practical level, the fees originally agreed for the use of locations on our first visit had undergone an amazing inflation by the time we needed to use them. Telephones all around the hill station must have been abuzz in the intervening period with people comparing notes and prices and deciding on their strategy. We were rapidly to learn that the well worn phrase 'no problem' inevitably indicated the opposite. There was always a reason why the price we had fixed in our original contracts should not be the price. On the actual day of filming it would frequently go up, with the alternative of our having no location.

The complaints of some of the crew continued throughout the filming, although, after the first bouts of stomach upsets and culture shock, they all looked in rude health from the mountain air. The shopkeepers of Simla were doing a roaring trade, selling them trinkets and making dozens of custom-made shirts for them. Location catering, as usual, was one of the grievances. Even when the maharajah's personal cook provided a buffet on the lawn fit for a viceregal occasion, there were objections that they were not getting the number of choices of dishes decreed in the ACTT regulations. At one point they took over the kitchens of the Oberoi Cecil to cook Lancashire hotpot for themselves.

Some also complained to Michael Farthing, the young doctor whom I had convinced Granada to let us take with us, that they were suffering from woman deprivation. Those who had not formed alliances with female members of the crew were hard pressed for female company since the local Indian women would have nothing to do with them. Eventually some of the Tibetan refugee women who sold shawls and scarves in the street, and were less prudish than the Indians, were coaxed to come to a dance. The sight of them partnering a group of ruddy-faced and beer-bellied Manchester technicians is indelibly ingrained in my memory.

At last, against all odds and mainly thanks to the utter unflappability and punctiliousness of the camera crew, the production staff and the set designer, we finished principal photography ahead of schedule and under budget. At the end of filming, the maharajah invited us to a grand dinner and told me that as a reward he intended to give the servants a meal with meat after we had left. Our departure from 'Woodville' was a scene straight out of *Upstairs Downstairs*, with the servants, including a woebegone Beli Ram, the houseboy, lined up on the doorsteps to bid us farewell.

Now it remained to see what the material we had shot, under particularly strained circumstances, actually looked like and whether it would cut together.

Chapter 23

Homecoming

At our first reunion after my return from India, I was welcomed back with a smile and a hug by Sir Denis Forman. This was encouraging. I was going to need all the back-up he could give me to finish the production successfully. Since we had come in on time and under budget despite all the difficulties, I even dared to hope for his congratulations. I was in fact to get the opposite.

Had I been returning to a meeting with Sydney Newman, I could have been sure that once I had given him a full and frank picture of our filming problems, I would have received sound advice and total back-up in solving them. As Sydney was a consummate producer himself, he would have understood implicitly. He would have berated me for having made a bad choice of director, then told me to finish the show as I saw fit, recognizing that, without the power to make his or her own decisions, the producer's role becomes meaningless and that to have one's decisions countermanded by management is like working with an albatross tied around one's neck. As Head of Drama at the BBC his greatest characteristics were his ability to delegate responsibility and his subsequent loyalty to those to whom he had delegated. Sir Denis and I, unfortunately, had a far more formal and recent acquaintanceship than that of Sydney and myself. Nor did he understand the problems at first hand. From his executive boardroom in Golden Square, Sir Denis, not having 'borne the heat and dust of the day', had no concept whatsoever of what it might be like to find oneself in a remote location, attempting to film with a director who was behaving like a hippie on his first trip to India while a distinguished cast begged for his removal. Silvio had been a Granada director in his good old days; the company, I was told, had shown him great loyalty some years before when he was involved in a much publicized court case. I was still a newcomer who apparently could not expect the same loyalty. The large number of successful programmes I had already produced elsewhere counted for nothing so far as Granada was concerned as they had not been Granada productions. My credibility within the company was still unproven. For the first time in my career, I began to suspect too that the attitude I was encountering had something to do with being a woman. Whenever journalists had asked me in interviews in the past if I was aware of sexual discrimination in my work, I had always answered truthfully that I never had been. Now I was not so sure. I suspected that Sir Denis's attitude would have been quite different had I been a man.

At that first meeting in Golden Square, I noticed several times while I spoke that Sir Denis was blushing, his whole face becoming suffused with a deep red glow. His is the type of pale British complexion on which blushes cannot be disguised. By this time I knew him well enough to realize that the blushes indicated that something mysterious was going on behind the scenes. As Bill Grundy, the late television journalist, once said of Sir Denis 'he is so diplomatic as to be downright devious'.[1] His blushes, however, gave him away. As I continued, I began to feel uneasy, like one of Stalin's generals, fresh from a victorious battle, who is about to be rewarded for his service to the country not with medals but with the firing squad or exile to a gulag. The truth about events in Simla was either being misrepresented by other sources or deliberately misconstrued by Sir Denis. I was surprised to find that those who had clamoured most loudly for the removal of the director while on location had become strangely silent, developed amnesia or simply vanished into the woodwork once back home. Probably, when faced with the daunting prospect of speaking frankly to the chairman of the company, they were frightened of jeopardizing their own future careers. Even Lars, the production manager, who had suggested to me that he take over the direction himself and whose coded messages on our filming sent to Sir Denis had recorded stormy weather all the way, had apparently not clarified to him the whys and wherefors of the storms. Much later I was to realize that Sir Denis already had a hidden agenda of his own which

[1] Profile of Sir Denis Forman, entitled 'The Crown Prince of ITV', *The Observer*, 8 April 1984.

had nothing to do with *Staying On* but everything to do with *The Jewel in the Crown*.

Ironically, too late to be of help, shortly after my return to England I was sent by a Canadian journalist friend an article from a Canadian magazine about a film called *Final Assignment* on which Silvio (unbeknown to me) had been involved shortly before he came on the recce for *Staying On*. The article, dated 1 October 1979, from *Cinemag* began as follows: 'One week into the shoot of *Final Assignment* word spread quickly through the Montreal film community: Silvio Narizzano was being replaced as the director of the film. Two days later, on Sept 13, word was out that Paul Almond had picked up the reins with only 24 hours' notice.'

The article then quotes from a frank interview with Sydney Kaufman, President of Performance Guarantees Canada Inc, the completion guarantor of the film:

> From the beginning, 'There were problems with Narizzano', he commented, saying that the director had had the script since the spring and was not, in Kaufman's opinion, adequately prepared when shooting began. 'He was not acquainted with the film or with the characters.'

Describing the first week of the shoot, Kaufman related that 'every day ran into overtime', that the script was not ready and that Narizzano was 'going to cost the production dearly in terms of overages.'[2]

A subsequent telephone conversation I had with Larry Hertzog one of the film's producers on 22 May 1996, long after the event, revealed his experience to have been almost identical to my own. He had amicably made a previous Canadian film with Silvio, called *Why Shoot the Teacher*, which was shot in a small town in Canada under very controllable conditions. On the strength of that production he had hired Narizzano for *Final Assignment* but immediately the production started Hertzog detected a character change. This was no longer the lovable Silvio he remembered. Hertzog, the executive producers and distributor felt that they had no alternative but to replace the director.

My situation, unfortunately, was not so simple. Soon after that first meeting after my return from India, I received a memo from

[2]Artiele on 'Final Assignment', *Cinemag, 1 October 1979.*

243

Sir Denis Forman, whose approach was somewhat different from that of Sydney Newman or Hertzog and his team. In it he set out instructions on how the respective roles of the producer and director should be carried out. The memo was couched in military terms. The director, he said, should be treated like the producer's first lieutenant or chief officer through whom the producer must work. He neglected to mention what army rank the producer held or to define the grounds for holding a court martial.

Meanwhile the editing and completion of *Staying On* had to be dealt with urgently. A viewing of rushes revealed plenty of technical problems which had not been reported to us from England accurately enough for us to do something about them, like re-shooting while we were still in India. From Sir Denis's viewings we had received only praise for the performances. He seemed unaware that some scenes would not cut together properly, that, for instance, there were scenes of Celia in the car on the way to the cinema, shot with the camera fixed to the car, which were so shaky as to be unusable and which should have been re-shot. We were not told that in one scene Pearl had been hitting Sayeed's microphone when she jabbed him in the chest and that this and the rustle of her sari had made her dialogue unusable. (In the end I had to re-voice this scene with another actress.) One had assumed that the technical departments at Granada would immediately report to us on the rushes from their points of view. It was evident that only the rock-solid central performances of the main actors could save the day. Only very skilled editing could give the erratically directed film some semblance of a shape. Many a silk purse has been made that way out of a sow's ear in the cutting room. The question was who was going to make that silk purse?

Again ironically, in view of what happened later, Silvio had warned me when he first joined the production that I might have to edit it myself. He might have the possibility of another film soon after we finished shooting, he said, but anyway editing always bored him. My telephone conversation with Larry Hertzog testified to this. On *Why Shoot the Teacher* Narizzano, according to Hertzog, 'had lost interest in the film once shooting was over and was only interested in finding his next job'. Hertzog had paid him off, called in a script doctor and totally recut the film, giving it a structure it lacked. It was very well received, with much praise going to Silvio. Silvio was the only director I had ever met who was not interested in doing his own editing. Most would fight tooth and nail to keep editorial control. Usually the director works with the film editor, receiving critical feed-in from the producer along the route. But the post-production on *Staying On* was not a usual situation. I had no confidence that this would work in our case. Eventually, however, it was agreed between the three of us that Silvio should start on the first rough cut with the editor.

Sir Denis at this point assumed his favourite role of diplomat. He decided to try to smooth things out, to effect a reconciliation between Silvio and myself by means of a lunch at the Ritz Hotel, so that we would finish the production amicably together. Things could not have been so serious in Simla, he felt, that a convivial meal in a posh restaurant would not resolve the problems. The lunch was indeed memorable. Much of it was eaten in stony silence. At last, Silvio, attired extremely casually in conscious defiance of the bourgeois surroundings of the elaborate Ritz dining room, brought the meal to a dramatic climax. I do not recall what the trigger mechanism was which caused him suddenly to run across the elegant dining room as fast as his jogging legs would carry him and to disappear from the hotel. The sight of his abruptly departing figure will always remain in my mind. Sir Denis at last had a first-hand sample of the behaviour that had been going on in Simla. Even he could no longer demand that I work through my 'chief officer'. He needed a finished film and a good one to prove to the board of Granada that the future production of *The Jewel in the Crown* and the large expenditure of their money on it was justified. The result of the first rough cut made by Silvio was extremely disappointing and in parts almost incomprehensible. Both Gerry Anstiss and Wolfgang were deeply unhappy when they viewed it with Sir Denis.

Soon after the memorable lunch at the Ritz and after Sir Denis's viewing of the rough cut, Silvio left for North America. I was not party to the last meeting between him and Sir Denis Forman and to this day have no idea of what actually took place between them. I only know that it resulted in a dramatic reversal on the part of the chairman, who was now politely begging me to finish the editing on my own. It also resulted in a reversal of Silvio's behaviour. His last words to me were that we should unite against out mutual enemy, Sir Denis, and make sure the edited show came out our way. He seemed almost relieved to see me take over the editing. It struck me, for the first time, that he wanted to get away from the pressures of production.

On 19 June 1980, after telling me he did not think we would be seeing Silvio again, Sir Denis wrote me a memo saying: 'It is now up to you to deliver a fine cut as soon as possible but not to hurry unreasonably. Please let me know by what date you could show me your show cut of the picture.'

He was becoming anxious, as I was for different reasons. In the next few weeks I put all thoughts of *The Jewel in the Crown* and my future on it out of my mind and sat down with Jack Dardis, the excellent editor, and with Carl Davis, the composer, to pick up the pieces. The music, as so often happens in film, was a major contributory factor to the success of *Staying On*. Carl Davis came up trumps with his score, using a group of young musicians who specialized in Indian instruments, mixing them with conventional Western music appropriate to the Anglo-Indian subject matter.

In my eyes, the basic structure of the story had always been that of the spider and the fly, or in this case flies. The venomous Mrs Bhoolabhoy, like a black widow spider, lies constantly in wait, spying through her binoculars on the impotent, vulnerable Smalleys. We know that eventually she will achieve her evil end; we wait, apprehensively, for her to pounce and destroy her two victims and their home by selling out to the Shiraz hotel group. There is also a fatalistic leitmotif running through the story. It is a foregone conclusion that Tusker is doomed to die and Lucy to be left alone, as she so greatly fears. The editing was built around this structure and this motif. It was fortified by Carl's themes: a theme for the evil spider, a theme for the unsuspecting flies and a beautiful, recurring melancholic theme for the ever present snow-capped majestic mountains, who watch impassively, cold and alien, over the tragicomic demise of these two remaining specks of the Raj. The mountain shots, largely those taken surreptitiously by Gerry and Wolfgang, were used over and over again with different light grading. In general there was a shortage of coverage of establishing shots, and problems, as predicted, with lack of continuity, which Silvio had scorned as an old-fashioned concept. Silvio's Ortonesque sense of humour, however, showed itself best in the over-the-top, comic Bhoolabhoy scenes. Trevor and Celia's impeccable performances emerged as profoundly touching, Celia's voice-over car scenes would never come absolutely right. Joseph, the gardener, whose gravestone scene had been removed by Silvio – mainly, I suspect, because the young actor Ajit Saldanha had accused Silvio of making him look like 'a grinning idiot' – was reinstated. Even the traumatically shot church scene where the hymn-singing melts from English into Hindi eventually came right.

Staying On was first screened in England on 28 December 1980. The reviews both in England and in North America, where it was shown some months later, were uniformly rapturous and particularly gratifying to me in their recognition that the film had perfectly realized the intentions of Scott's book and conveyed the universality of his themes.

The *Sunday Times* previewer, on the day of its screening, wrote, 'When Celia Johnson, tipsy, looks at her dying husband Tusker (Trevor Howard) and sobs in sorrow and anger "Alone for ever and ever. And I can't bear it", the idea of unendurable and eternal solitude lies in the brain and shudders the heart. There are moments of comedy and satire, and throughout a close love, unapproachable by words. A must.'

Herbert Kretzmer, in his *Daily Mail* review on 29 December wrote that:

> The major event of the weekend was a bitter-sweet tale about post-imperial India and its ruinous effect on a lonely ageing English couple who stayed on after the eclipse of the Raj. What a performance by Celia Johnson. A secret tippler, dancing, ecstatic and unseen, to old records, abstractedly reminiscing about the dear, dead days of British India to an imaginary visitor . . . a proud old memsahib living out the twilight of a spurned friendless life.

The *New York Magazine*, reviewing it on 8 May after its first American transmission, said:

> The film is really about loneliness and tight-lipped British reserve; the Colonel, idle and feeling useless in his retirement, becomes a metaphor for the theme of resignation that comes with age, and the impotence of a once powerful ruling class whose influence has come to a permanent and disorienting end. . . . Although the drama richly evokes the cultural diversity of modern India, its theme – the isolation and vulnerability of old age – transcends all geographical boundaries.

Auberon Waugh (quoted by Sylvia Clayton in the *Daily Telegraph*, 17 March 1980), called it an 'authentic, sad, slightly absurd accent of our times, the true voice of a country whose past dignity and vigour survive only in the memory of a few kindly old buffers, long past playing any active role.'

The film received three BAFTA nominations for Best Single Play, Best Actress and Best Actor and two nominations in the Broadcasting Press Guild's radio and television awards. It won the Best Foreign Film award in New York and the Critics' Circle award in England. By that time I had left Granada, becoming yet another casualty in the long list connected with this project. After the misunderstandings on *Staying On*, it was obvious that Sir Denis and I would never agree on my future role on *The Jewel in the Crown*. With a blush he confessed that he wanted more 'creative' involvement in the series than he had had heretofore. Although well known and respected as chairman of Granada and a shrewd businessman it appears that he wished to be remembered as more than just an enabler of other people's talents. He was nearing retirement and wanted posterity to recognize him as a hands-on creator with the words 'executive producer' on the *The Jewel in the Crown* marking his artistic swan song.

Before I left Granada, I went in confidence to Manchester to see David Plowright, then managing director of the company, who knew the history of my coming to Granada. From him I received an immediate assurance, followed by a contract, that when the series was screened I would get a screen credit as its deviser and an appropriate residual. I do not know what Sir Denis made of this. It was only after *The Jewel in the Crown* was screened and the revisionist history of its origins started to appear in the press and in Granada's own book about the series that I began to understand past events more clearly. As the Chinese say 'There cannot be two suns in one sky.' Nor, apparently, can there be two devisers of a series.

Real life, at this stage, began to imitate the multi-viewpoint texture of Paul Scott's novels. Sir Denis's own recollection of our meetings in his office in March 1979 about the format of the series were put out by Granada Publishing in 1983 in *The Making of the Jewel in the Crown*. In his introduction to the book, Sir Denis paints a wonderfully romantic self-portrait of the chairman of Granada TV in creative mode. He describes how a roll of wallpaper was pinned around his office while (apparently alone) he strolled around it, 'touching, retouching, shifting and deliberating' until the story-line for the series magically emerged. He appears not to remember that someone else (armed with months of work) was in the room with him, though he does concede in an aside that 'Irene Shubik had reached her own conclusions.'[3]

Bamber Gascoigne (a former Granada employee and friend of Sir Denis), who had been commissioned to write the book, repeats Sir Denis's revisionist version later on in the text, declaring that the chairman had personally reorganized the scenes from Scott's complex fictional technique of multiple view and flashback into a chronological sequence more appropriate to television, and had made his own draft of the content of the fourteen separate programmes.[4] Gascoigne had made no effort to contact me.

When the series went on the air, most of the press reiterated this story, which they had received in the Granada press releases or, as in the case of the *Observer* profile, which called him 'the only begetter' of the series, from Sir Denis himself. Only Frank Delaney, writing in *The Listener* on 19 April 1984, when *Staying On* was repeated after the first screening of *The Jewel in the Crown*, picked up on the connection between the two programmes:

> This exquisite television production by Irene Shubik was the one which started it all, and from which – and from her further ideas – Granada were able to unwind the entire series, *The Jewel in the Crown*. Ms Shubik did, I notice, receive a credit (of sorts) in the roll-call at the end of each episode. When *Staying On* was first transmitted some years ago, it was rightly acclaimed. For how many people, I wonder, will the India of the Raj be now for ever epitomised by Celia Johnson dancing alone to the Ink-spots – a scene which was worth 1000 elephants?

In the autobiography of the great Japanese director Akira Kurosawa I found a passage concerning his most famous film, *Rashomon*, which described my own feelings about this final chapter of *The Jewel in the Crown* better than I could.

> Through *Rashomon* I was compelled to discover yet another unfortunate aspect of the human personality. This occurred when *Rashomon* was shown on television for the first time . . . The broadcast was accompanied by an interview with the president of Daiei. I couldn't believe my ears. This man . . . after complaining that the finished film was 'incomprehensible' and after

[3]*The Making of the Jewel in the Crown*, pp. 7–8.
[4]*Ibid.*, p. 15.

demoting the company executive and the producer who had facilitated its making, was now proudly taking full and exclusive credit for its success! He boasted about how for the first time in cinema history the camera had been boldly pointed directly at the sun. Never in his entire discourse did he mention my name or the name of the cinematographer whose achievement this was, Miyagawa Kazuo.[5]

I sent a copy of the passage to Sir Denis Forman but unsurprisingly received no reply.

Much of the vital work of setting up *The Jewel in the Crown* had already been done. The scripts had been written under my supervision. At my request Christopher Morahan had been offered a contract by Granada to be its principal director. He and Sir Denis had met during my absence and apparently got on well. *Staying On* had more than served its purpose as a pilot film for the series, revealing many of the potential production problems of filming in India and providing some of the locations for *The Jewel in the Crown*. The stage was perfectly set for a take-over.

An embarrassed Christopher Morahan telephoned me shortly before I left Granada to say that he had just been asked to take over the line producing as well as the directing of *The Jewel in the Crown*, with Sir Denis as the executive producer. He was embarrassed because it was I, he said, who had brought him to the project in the first place. He hoped I realized that it was too good an opportunity to turn down. I did, indeed, realize. Chris was and is a very forceful man who, having himself been on the management side as Head of Plays at the BBC, and not having had my long emotional involvement with the series, would undoubtedly fit well into Sir Denis's scheme of things. He knew a great deal more about how to handle office politics and how to deal with the men in suits than I did. I wished him luck.

[5]Akira Kurosawa, *Something Like an Autobiography* (New York, Alfred A. Knopf), 1982, p. 188.

Epilogue

One day in autumn 1983, five years after Waris Hussein and I had come to Granada to discuss the Raj Quartet with Sir Denis Forman, I received a telephone call from Christopher Morahan. The filming of *The Jewel in the Crown* had been completed, he said. He asked if I would come and have lunch with him and then see his rough cut of the first episodes, on which he would like my opinion.

It was a courtesy I could not refuse, although my feelings were mixed. I was about to meet a child who, through force of circumstances, had been given away for adoption and was now grown up. Would I still recognize the child? Would there be on the screen anything that I had originally visualized? Would the pain of no longer being recognized as the true parent be too great to bear? My pain was somewhat mitigated by the fact that I currently had a lucrative contract with Columbia Pictures in Hollywood to script and then produce a film based on a book by Richard Adams which I had taken to them.

What I did or did not think of the finished product is irrelevant. No two producers would ever come up with an identical end product. The series, or more accurately serial, was a tremendous success not only in England but all over the world, won a number of awards, including the BAFTA Best Serial one, and was widely praised by the critics. There were, of course, some dissenting voices, notably and predictably that of Salman Rushdie. Strangely, after there being nothing on either the large or small screens about India, *Staying On*, transmitted in 1980, had marked the beginning of what Rushdie in an article in *The Observer*, 1 April 1984, called the 'Raj Revival'. 'Anyone who has switched on the television set, been to the cinema or entered a bookshop in the past few months will be aware', he wrote, 'that the British Raj, after three and a half decades in retirement, has been making a sort of comeback.' Citing Richard Attenborough's film *Gandhi* and the television serial *The Far Pavilions*, which he called a 'blackface minstrel show', 'the grotesquely overpraised *The Jewel in the Crown*' and David Lean's forthcoming film of *A Passage to India*, he was scathing about all of them for the false portrait he claimed they presented of India. His ultimate criticism was 'The overall effect is rather like a literary version of Mulligatawny soup. It tries to taste Indian, but ends up being ultra parochially British, only with too much pepper.'

Unintentionally Rushdie had hit on the basis of the great popularity of *The Jewel in the Crown* on the screen. I had known from the start that by doing away with Scott's complex multi-viewpoint style one was gaining an audience but losing a dimension. It was, however, only when I viewed the Granada serial that I realized for the first time that the books when thus pared down and cast to type could come across like a superior, thinking man's soap opera rather than as a realistic portrait of the English in India, as I had originally envisaged. Like *Gandhi* the serial had a didactic undercurrent, giving the audience the illusion of being educated in the history of India while they sat back enjoying the trials and tribulations of a rather stereotypical set of characters or, in Rushdie's words, 'a galaxy of chinless wonders, regimental grandes dames, lushes, empty-headed blondes, silly-asses, plucky young things, good sorts, bad eggs and Russian counts with eye-patches', or as what one letter to the *Evening Standard* described as 'not quite *Mrs Dale's Diary* on the North West Frontier'. What Rushdie did not recognize is that most television audiences enjoy clear-cut villains and heroes about whom they are not required to make subtle intellectual judgements.

Daniel Farson in *The Mail on Sunday*, 8 April 1984, approaching it from the opposite point of view to Rushdie, asked:

What was the point of it all? Presumably, that we, the British, are guilty. . . . The moral came with Sarah Layton's outburst: 'After 300 years of India, we've made this whole bloody mess!' Which was hard to take after the massacre of Indian by Indian as our rule came to an end . . . At no point did the series concede the good, the trust and responsibility of the British. One day the exemplary dedication of our empire builders might be honoured, but our film-makers find that unfashionable now.

Perhaps the time is almost ripe for that sort of portrait of the Raj. Meanwhile we have had *My Beautiful Launderette*, *The Buddha of Suburbia* and *Bhaji on the Beach*. The young English-born Indians have taken their revenge on the Raj by their counter-colonization of the film and television industry.

As for *The Jewel in the Crown*, it stood as a memorial not only to the Raj but also to the end of a particular era in British television. This was almost certainly the last time that a British television company, especially a commercial one, would foot the entire bill for such an expensive and ultimately non-commercial project. (The series was only shown in America on PBS and cable, never on a major network where the big money is to be had.) Since then co-production, with all its attendant com-promises, its unsuitable star casting and its bevies of decision makers with disparate ideas and tastes, has become the name of the game, resulting in such dreadful examples as the BBC's *Rhodes* and *Nostromo*.

Undoubtedly the writers who would previously have been showing their original work on 'Play for Today' are now writing serials, like Jimmy McGovern, or contributing scripts to such series as *Inspector Morse*. Series and serials are always easier and more profitable to sell around the world than single plays. Con-versely there is a better market now than there ever has been for the small British film, *The Full Monty* and *Four Weddings and a Funeral* being prime examples of productions which would previ-ously have fitted easily into the 'Play for Today' slot, and probably would have been done there, but would not have had the interna-tional exposure they got as feature films. I like to think too that the new crop of 'indie-prods' is infinitely more street-wise and versed in the art of self-defence in the market place than those who, like myself, were reared in the rarified atmosphere of the old 'Auntie' BBC.

I am told that a new school of thought in media studies is now attacking the era of the single play as elitist. The present market-led era where soap opera, fly-on-the-wall docu-drama and inter-changeable crime and hospital series reign supreme is, they say, more democratic and more what the audience wants. I make no comment other than to hope they are wrong and that there will always be a place for an original voice and a quality production on the ever-changing television screen.

Index

264